TIANANMEN SQUARE

Scott Simmie and Bob Nixon

University of Washington Press
Seattle

AJE 9687 - 8/4

90 91 92 93   5 4 3 2

University of Washington Press
P.O. Box 50096
Seattle, Washington 98145-5096

Published simultaneously in Canada by
Douglas & McIntyre Ltd.
1615 Venables Street
Vancouver, British Columbia V5L 2H1

Cataloguing in Publication Data

Simmie, Scott.
  Tiananmen Square

  ISBN 0-295-96950-4

  1. Student movements - China. 2 Students -
China - Political activity. 3. China - Politics
and government - 1976-   I. Nixon, Bob.
II. Title.
951.05'8

Edited by Brian Scrivener
Design by Alexandra Hass
Maps by Gabriele Proctor
Calligraphy by Yim Tse
Typeset by The Typeworks
Printed and bound in Canada by Imprimerie Gagné Ltée.

Contents

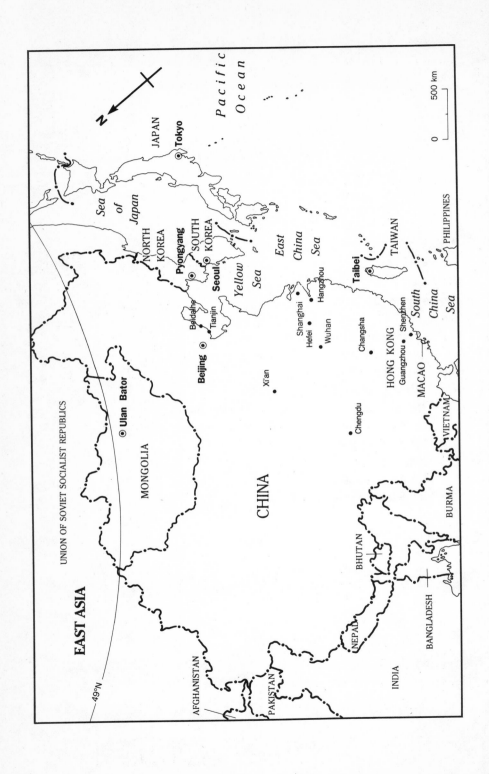

EAST ASIA

UNION OF SOVIET SOCIALIST REPUBLICS

49°N

MONGOLIA

⊙ Ulan Bator

CHINA

AFGHANISTAN

PAKISTAN

INDIA

NEPAL

BHUTAN

BANGLADESH

BURMA

VIETNAM

Beijing ⊙

Xi'an

Chengdu

Beidaihe

Tianjin

Hefei

Wuhan

Shanghai

Hangzhou

Changsha

Guangzhou

Shenzhen

HONG KONG

MACAO

NORTH KOREA

Pyongyang ⊙

SOUTH KOREA

Seoul ⊙

Yellow Sea

East China Sea

South China Sea

Taibei

TAIWAN

PHILIPPINES

Sea of Japan

JAPAN

Tokyo ⊙

Pacific Ocean

500 km

0

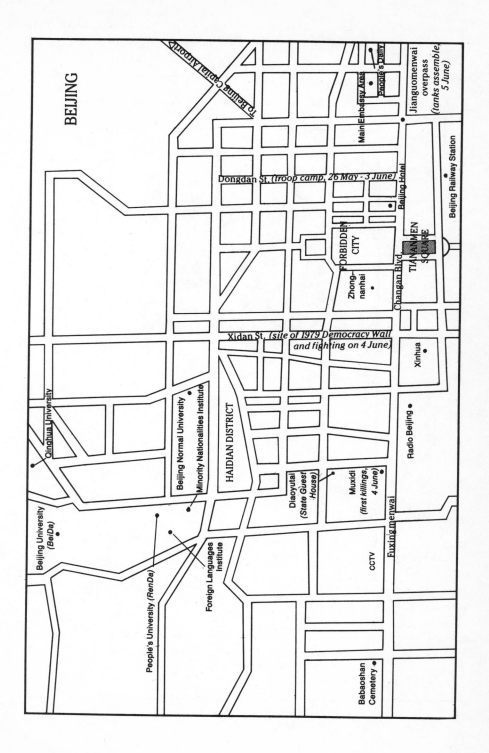

BEIJING

To Beijing Capital Airport

People's Daily

Main Embassy Area

Jianguomenwai
overpass
(tanks assemble,
5 June)

Dongdan St. (troop camp, 26 May - 3 June)

Beijing Hotel

Beijing Railway Station

FORBIDDEN
CITY

Zhong-
nanhai

Changan Blvd.

TIANANMEN
SQUARE

Xidan St. (site of 1979 Democracy Wall
and fighting on 4 June)

Xinhua

Qinghua University

Beijing Normal University

Minority Nationalities Institute

HAIDIAN DISTRICT

Radio Beijing

Diaoyutai
(State Guest
House)

Muxidi
(first killings,
4 June)

Fuxingmenwai

Beijing University
(BeiDa)

Foreign Languages
Institute

People's University (RenDa)

CCTV

Babaoshan
Cemetery

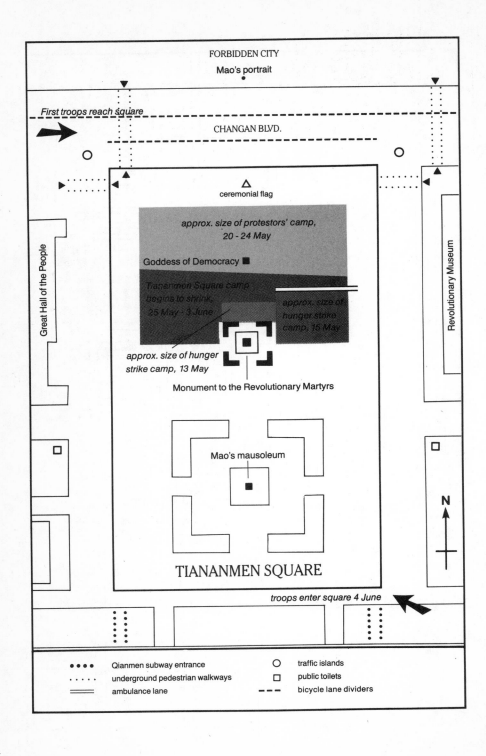

FORBIDDEN CITY

Mao's portrait

First troops reach square

CHANGAN BLVD.

ceremonial flag

approx. size of protestors' camp,
20 - 24 May

Goddess of Democracy ■

Tiananmen Square camp
begins to shrink,
25 May - 3 June

approx. size of
hunger strike
camp, 15 May

approx. size of hunger
strike camp, 13 May

Monument to the Revolutionary Martyrs

Great Hall of the People

Revolutionary Museum

Mao's mausoleum

N

TIANANMEN SQUARE

troops enter square 4 June

●●●● Qianmen subway entrance   ○ traffic islands
· · · · · underground pedestrian walkways   □ public toilets
———— ambulance lane   - - - bicycle lane dividers

Chronology

15 April 1989, 7:35 A.M.:   Hu Yaobang, Politburo member and former general secretary of the Communist Party of China dies of a heart attack at age 73.

18 April, 2:00 A.M.:   Four thousand Beijing and People's University students march to Tiananmen Square to place banner calling Hu the "Soul of China" on Monument to the Revolutionary Martyrs.

22 April, 8:30 A.M.:   Fifty thousand students defy government order and stay overnight in Tiananmen Square for Hu's state funeral.

24 April: Tens of thousands of students in Beijing begin class boycott to press home demands for talks with government.

25 April and 26 April: Chinese Television, then the *People's Daily*, label unrest as conspiracy to negate Communist Party leadership.

27 April: 150,000 students march through streets of Beijing in protest against editorials. Half a million people line the streets to cheer them on. The government agrees to talks.

4 May: After a week of inconclusive discussions, students hold another big demonstration to mark anniversary of 4 May Movement of 1919. Communist Party Boss Zhao Ziyang says government is willing to meet with all sectors of society.

10 May: More than one-thousand journalists demand talks to discuss press freedom. Students protest against censorship.

13 May, 5:20 P.M.:   Several hundred students begin hunger strike in

Tiananmen Square to demand televised talks with government and retraction of *People's Daily* editorial.

15 May, noon: Soviet leader Mikhail Gorbachev arrives in Beijing for first Sino-Soviet summit in thirty years. Hunger strikers refuse to clear Tiananmen Square. Numbers grow to three thousand.

17 May: A million people march through Beijing in support of hunger strike. Disturbances throughout rest of country.

18 May, noon: Premier Li Peng meets with student leaders to demand they end strike. They tell him they cannot control situation.

19 May, 4:30 A.M.:   Zhao and Li meet hunger strikers in square, but students stay put. Later that day, a riot occurs in remote city of Urumqi.

20 May, midnight: Li calls in army to end chaos. Students end hunger strike but vow to hold Tiananmen. Troops stopped by unarmed civilians   10:00 A.M.:   Li declares martial law over parts of Beijing.

23 May: A million people march to demand Li resign and martial law be withdrawn. Most soldiers return to bases on outskirts of city.

2 June: Mostly unarmed troops begin to move on Tiananmen Square again. People block them again.

3 June, 2:00 P.M.:   Demonstrators clash with soldiers near Tiananmen Square. Troop convoys begin moving into city. Most blocked.   11:00 P.M.:   Soldiers begin firing on people at Muxidi in west Beijing.

4 June, 2:00 A.M.:   After hours of bloody fighting, soldiers reach Tiananmen Square.   4:00 A.M.:   Students agree to leave, army retakes square. Killing continues for next few days.

Preface

This is not the book we intended to write when we began conducting interviews with Chinese citizens during the spring of 1988. Our purpose then was to understand the experiences of China's artists and intellectuals, to learn how the various upheavals and purges which occurred during the country's forty years of communist rule had affected their lives and shaped their thinking. The people we interviewed, without exception, saw a brighter future for a nation that seemed to be unshackling itself from the bonds of Maoist dogma. They told of a past that had been more bloody, more vicious and more crazy than we had expected them to tell. But it was all in the past, they said. Lessons had been learned. China was moving, albeit slowly, towards a more tolerant, a more democratic society. These men and women were mostly older people whose experiences had taught them to be cautious and patient. They expected that China's path towards democracy would also be slow, but steady.

The student movement changed all that.

It lasted just fifty days, and ended in a murderous ten hours that shook the world. Young people were not so cautious, they were not so patient, but they captured millions of hearts with their innocent optimism about China's future. People shed their reticence like unwanted clothing, pushing hard for that bright new era. Then, as quickly as it had come, it was over. China's future was suddenly its past. The book we had wanted to write was, sadly, no longer the book we were able to write.

As journalists who had both been employed by the Chinese government, we were able to learn something of the inner workings of the communist system and its media. We were given the privilege of working alongside a remarkable assortment of Chinese; people who were as eager to explain their country to us as we were to learn about it. Our fascination with the country—and our jobs as reporters—brought us both to Tiananmen Square during the spring of 1989. Between us, we tracked the Democracy Movement from its first daring march to its final and bloody conclusion.

As we witnessed those events, each day bringing wondrous surprises, we felt that the Chinese were somehow challenging their own history, and the conditions that had ruled their lives for decades. For the first time since the 1949 Revolution, it seemed as if the people of China were finding their voice. And what a marvelous voice it was. People from literally all walks of life sang, chanted and shouted their way right to the heart of communist power.

We spoke with hundreds of such people during the Movement, reporting each day's events to a world entranced by this unprecedented upheaval. For seven weeks it continued, with an apparent life of its own. The government had not cracked down, and it seemed, for a time, that the demonstrations would lead to a shining new age of tolerance. The vision died on 4 June.

When it did, we found that we could not explain what had taken place without recalling the stories we had been told of China's past. For that reason, many of those stories appear in this book.

Readers might notice that most of the students and citizens we quote are not identified directly. We would have liked to put names to their brave words, but—given how this story ended—we decided that their safety was more important. Only one person, a student who contacted us regularly, was given a pseudonym. We decided against giving even false names to the others for fear the government might seek out and punish people whose names matched those we had invented.

Student leaders and others whom we do identify are well known, certainly to the government that pursues them, and we felt that mentioning them here would not further damage their positions. Nor have we refrained from naming those who were quoted in the Chinese media during the days of the Movement. We also mention by name those artists and intellectuals we had interviewed earlier, since their tales in the main do not directly touch upon the unrest.

We are not sinologists, and the book you are about to read is by no means the definitive story of that remarkable time. But we hope we have made a modest contribution. Our aim was to capture the feel of Tiananmen Square and Beijing during those days, and to bring to life once more many of the voices of those who were there. One old man we interviewed told us "only those who have almost been suffocated can know the value of air." The Chinese people breathed very deeply, exultantly in 1989. They will do so again.

Scott Simmie
Bob Nixon
15 August 1989

Acknowledgements

We owe this book first and foremost to those many Chinese friends who assisted us throughout our time in Beijing, and after we left. Two in particular deserve special thanks. Once again, we refrain from mentioning them by name, and even the ways in which they helped us. But we are confident, as we hope they are, that a day will soon arrive when the need for such fears will no longer exist.

Among non-Chinese, we wish to thank Jonathan Annells, who gave us invaluable assistance in recording and compiling material for this book. Sheri Lecker, another China hand, also aided our efforts, as did Peg Herbst, our comrade at China Central Television. We also are grateful to several people from the Canadian Broadcasting Corporation: David Bazay, for his support of this project; Tom Cherry, for his technical assistance; cameraman Scott Troyer; and all those who worked in the Beijing bureau during those hectic weeks. Stephen Wormington helped out from Beijing; in Hong Kong, we had the assistance of Joan Thornberry. Derek Sidenius and Catherine Bauknight also provided us with photographs.

Thanks to our editor, Brian Scrivener, who began this process as a stranger but finished it as a friend. We would also like to extend great thanks to Jan Walls of Simon Fraser University, our China expert, who provided valuable insights during the writing of this book. Finally, we thank our parents for their patience, humour and love.

For our Chinese friends

1

Newborn Calves Do Not Fear the Tiger

It began softly, quietly, cautiously. Muted knocks on dormitory doors. Whispered messages in hallways. Furtive glances out windows. Under cover of darkness, students at Beijing University roused their comrades. Some were frightened. A curfew was in effect at the institute, and graduation was not far off. Defying that curfew could bring repercussions—a job assignment in one of China's more backward regions, perhaps even expulsion. And it was clear the university was taking its directive seriously. The doors of many dormitories had been locked to firmly dissuade those who might disobey regulations. Those who remembered the demonstrations in 1986 and 1987 thought of other consequences; of the network of police and its video cameras, of humiliating self-criticisms at political study sessions. They also reflected on the downfall and recent death of Hu Yaobang, the Communist Party leader who was disgraced and fired in the wake of those protests.

More pervasive, though, was the nervous excitement that grew as more and more students abandoned their dormitories—in some cases knocking down the locked doors. What started as a small group swelled to hundreds, then thousands. A few banners, hastily unfurled, flapped in the cool breeze. Scores of young men and women unlocked their bicycles and pedalled onto the quiet streets, heading southeast towards Tiananmen Square. With this advance guard on the lookout for police, the rest of the students began to march the fifteen-kilometre route. It was just after midnight, 18 April, and three days since the death of Hu.

Residents of Beijing did not awaken to angry chanting or defiant slogans. Instead—if they were disturbed at all—they heard the soft strains of "The Internationale," one of several songs which the students would eventually adopt as anthems of democracy.

1

Arise ye prisoners of starvation!
Arise ye wretched of the earth!
For justice thunders condemnation,
A better world is in birth.

The refrain was heard over and over as the students pushed their way south towards Renmin Daxue, the People's University. RenDa, as it's known in Beijing, is located along the route from BeiDa (Beijing University) to Tiananmen Square. For the students of BeiDa, it was a human refuelling point. By 2:00 A.M., the march had grown to include an estimated four thousand people.

A few red flags identifying the universities were completely overshadowed by a single huge white banner. Held proudly and protectively by twenty-four students in the centre of the procession, it elevated the status of Hu Yaobang to the "Soul of China."

The marchers, now apparently less nervous, continued their pilgrimage to Tiananmen Square. By singing a song with such patriotic overtones, they hoped the authorities would not interfere. After all, they also had the Chinese constitution, which permits ceremonies of mourning, on their side. Instead of barricading the route, police waited calmly for the protestors to arrive, then stopped traffic while the students marched through intersections. About fifty officers in several vans leapfrogged ahead of the marchers. At each major intersection, the vehicles would stop and wait as the police tracked the group's progress.

Although the demonstration was still far from Tiananmen Square, many of the students on bicycles felt confident the procession would not be stopped. The job of spotting police no longer seemed necessary, so they rode ahead to await their comrades. By the middle of the night, about five hundred people had gathered at the base of the Monument to the Revolutionary Martyrs. The protestors, meanwhile, were marching past the Foreign Languages Press—a government-run publishing house midway between BeiDa and Tiananmen Square. Groups of demonstrators began squabbling about the best route to take. Roughly half of them, arms linked in solidarity, suddenly turned east. The remainder of the group continued southward. After some confusion, those heading south backtracked and rejoined the others. Even in the early stages, it seemed the student movement was unsure of where it was going or how it would get there.

About a hundred foreigners were walking alongside the marchers at this point, mostly students of Chinese. One Western television crew was on hand, but there appeared to be few other reporters. That was in sharp contrast to the scene on the square itself, where many journalists, photographers and television cameras awaited the students' arrival.

Shortly after 5:00 A.M., the demonstrators reached their goal. They swarmed up the steps bordering all four sides of the Monument to the Revolutionary Martyrs, packing the two public terraces which surround the granite monolith. Several students, apparently organizers, tried unsuccessfully to mount the first tier of the obelisk itself. This was no easy task, as the ledge they were trying to reach was between three and four metres off the ground. After several attempts, using students who had volunteered their bodies as ladders, an agile young man stepped forward. Displaying insect-like prowess, he used the relief carvings of the men and women who fought in the 1949 Revolution as footholds. Those watching applauded and laughed as he scaled the stone.

Once there, he helped a few fellow students up. The huge white banner bearing Hu's name was passed to them, and they began trying to affix it to the symbol of Communist China. The weather did not cooperate, however, and the tribute to the former Party leader became a cloth dragon, whipping and snapping in the wind.

After limited debate and considerably more patience, the students finally opted to drape the banner from the ledge, allowing its full ten metres to cascade down into the public area. They led a few patriotic chants, most of which exalted Hu, then called on their comrades to observe a few minutes of silence in his memory. After that, they simply climbed down.

Although the protestors had succeeded unchallenged, the low-key atmosphere which had characterized the march itself did not change. There was neither triumphant cheering nor boisterous chants. Rather, as the students again sang the Internationale, the mood seemed oddly sombre.

This solemnity did not spring solely from mourning for Hu (or from the fact that it was 6:00 A.M. and they still faced a long walk back to their campuses). Another, less tangible, factor seemed to be one of awe. The students had accomplished more in one night—at least symbolically—than others had achieved in years. As the banner fluttered softly in the morning wind, an almost telepathic message moved through the crowd. They were no longer simply a collection of young people. And while there was no document to prove it, no autonomous students' union, in that night they had become a force.

The death of Hu Yaobang, although it was used skillfully by the students to their advantage, was not the underlying cause of that night's demonstration. Nor was it behind the big character posters (*dazibao*), which started appearing on the campus of Beijing Univer-

3

sity the day after he died. Hu's death was merely the catalyst, the spark. What the students would say in the coming days and weeks had been repressed for years. The night of 18 April allowed the venting of some steam; soon, the volcano of intellectual energy would erupt.

When Deng Xiaoping implemented the "Open Door" policy in 1979, he charted a course which would earn praise from most Chinese and ultimately seduce much of the West. The madness of the Cultural Revolution was behind them, the government stable, and the country appeared eager to join the twentieth century. Westerners were just as eager to embrace the Middle Kingdom. Foreign investment trickled, then flooded in over the next ten years. Teachers, technicians and doctors from around the world welcomed the chance to work in China and help the country modernize. Foreign governments, too, saw the advantages of stronger economic and political ties with the Chinese. Aid programs and trade increased to the point where the United States and Britain were selling advanced military hardware and other high-technology goods. In late 1988, then U.S. Secretary of Defence Frank Carlucci emerged from talks in Beijing to hint that American satellites would soon be lifted into space aboard Chinese rockets.

Inside the country, there were similarly dramatic changes. Peasants, suddenly able to sell excess produce on newly revitalized free markets, saw their incomes jump. Workers benefited as the Chinese authorities implemented a bonus system which rewarded productivity. The "responsibility system" allowed managers of many state factories to get on with the business of making money without the meddling of local Party officials. And with the famous phrase "To get rich is glorious," Deng gave a generation of entrepreneurs a raison d'être.

To foreign observers, China was becoming a much less threatening, less xenophobic part of the world. There were still conflicting signals, as the leadership struggled between the opposing goals of a more market-oriented economy and central control. And there was also dissatisfaction in some of the country's lesser-developed areas, which felt they were being exploited for the benefit of the newly established special economic zones (coastal regions offering incentives for foreign investment). But the overall results were less confusing. China was moving ahead at an astounding pace, evolving into a unique, if slightly muddled, hybrid of Chinese, Soviet and selected Western characteristics.

The country's intellectuals, however, were rarely the beneficiaries of this great leap forward. In fact, as China pushed ahead economically the Middle Kingdom's best and brightest were left in a financial backwater.

In an odd paradox of priorities, those who had the skills and knowledge to help China achieve its modernization goals received little encouragement. Academics, teachers and doctors continued to receive meagre salaries, which at best barely kept up with inflation. Many cab drivers, vendors and factory workers, meanwhile, earned enough money to purchase luxury items like videotape recorders, colour televisions and Japanese refrigerators. As of early 1989, the average full professor at any given university in Beijing was making about $39.50 U.S. per month—the same amount of money as a starting waitress at a foreign-owned hotel. In 1987, one professor in the Chinese capital staged a bitter protest against the injustice by polishing shoes on campus to supplement his income.

China's two million university students had little to cheer about. Their teachers were often inadequately trained, their classrooms dilapidated. Six, sometimes seven students shared cramped dormitories, with books and personal belongings stacked on bunkbeds. At mealtimes, they waited in perpetual lineups for what was often dreadful food. Privacy was, and is, virtually nonexistent.

At a meeting of the National People's Congress (China's parliament) in the early spring of 1989, the country's education system came under intense criticism. Premier Li Peng, who, as head of the State Education Commission from 1985 to 1988 bore some responsibility for the neglect of the students, responded by setting up a special committee to examine the problem, and pledged to increase spending. He also echoed the words of senior leader Deng Xiaoping, who had said "Our biggest mistake in the past ten years has been that education has not developed sufficiently." The Minister of Education, Li Tieying, was even more direct. "Our education," he said, "is backward, our people's attainments fall short, and our low level of education has become a major constraint on our country's modernization and reform."

China's schools lack proper buildings and books. The average adult has received only five years of education, and one out of five is illiterate. China's leaders were not deliberately trying to keep the masses in darkness. Rather, the government seemed preoccupied with economic reform as a means of gaining much-needed hard currency and transforming China into an industrial nation. It would have been unrealistic to expect China's leaders to repair overnight the damage inflicted on the country's education system during the Cultural Revolution. But it was the apparent complacency of the government which dismayed academics. Up until the spring meeting of the National People's Congress, the leadership had seemed satisfied

5

with merely restoring education to the level it had attained prior to the Cultural Revolution. A few of the more remote areas of China still had no schools at all, and it sometimes seemed that they only got such facilities when affluent entrepreneurs donated the money to build them. The state-run media frequently trumpeted these cases, as if to suggest that the nation's problems could be solved by charitable businessmen, a profound irony in a Marxist state. The philanthropists, it was emphasized, had invariably attained their wealth as a result of the economic reforms.

Although the students had lots to grumble about, they had also seen some benefits of the open door policy. Thousands of them were going abroad to study at the best universities in the world. State-approved Western literature was placed on reading lists. North American and European movies which passed the censor were used as learning tools for students of English and other languages. And while contacts with foreigners were still regarded with some suspicion, it became relatively acceptable to have Western friends—even to entertain them at home.

These and other changes had a pronounced effect on many of China's young people. The once-austere clothing of the Mao era, when everyone wore identical blue, green or grey, gave way to more colourful and individual fashions. In 1987, some teenagers even briefly donned garb more common to the streets of Harlem, when the American movie "Breakdance U.S.A." played to packed houses across the nation. People became obsessed with the film. One young woman admitted having seen the movie seven times and eventually obtained a videotape copy which she claimed to watch every day.

Even such innocuous effects of the open door policy seemed to disturb the leadership. At the height of the movie's popularity, the *China Daily* (an English-language newspaper accountable to the Communist Party) published an article which warned of the dark dangers of dance. The publication imparted the sorry tale of one young boy who repeatedly stole money from his parents to pay for admission to the local dance hall. And, in an equally disturbing case, a 16-year-old girl was portrayed as so consumed with the craze that she no longer attended school. Her education and future had been tragically abandoned, it seemed, for the greater glory of spinning on her head.

This wide-eyed fascination with all things Western was, for many young Chinese, less innocent and less fleeting. In recent years, students of language, journalism and political science devoured almost any foreign news publication they could obtain. Invariably, they turned first to the Asian sections where they read reports on China. More often than not, they found accounts which differed sharply from those of the official media. Shortwave radios also became increas-

6

ingly popular in the 1980s, and the broadcasts of the BBC and the Voice of America became not only a link with the outside world but also a means to discover what was going on inside China's borders. During Tibetan unrest in 1987 and 1988, and when martial law was imposed on the capital of Lhasa in 1989, many Beijing journalists who monitored shortwave transmissions confided that they did not believe the version of events being provided by the New China News Agency (Xinhua).

Growing numbers of young Chinese also began to display openly an insatiable desire for knowledge about foreign countries—a thirst which extended well beyond historical and geographical facts and into the realms of economics and politics. Questions about income and cost of living were often followed by more probing queries: How does democracy work in your country? Are people really free to say what they want? Does everyone vote?

Any foreigner who has lived in China and made close contact with Chinese will find those questions familiar. Depending upon the level of trust which has been established, the outsider might also have been privy to something few will openly admit: "I want to leave here." Few admit it, perhaps, because few actually mean it. The vast majority of Chinese students do not want to abandon their homeland. Certainly, they want the opportunity to study abroad, to see something of the world, but most say they would return to China and use their new skills to help its modernization drive. Many of those now holding green cards in the United States, however, said the same thing before they left.

As new ideals and possibilities crept inexorably into China, the roots of anomie found fertile ground on the nation's campuses. Young men and women who had learned about dynamic political systems felt trapped in a mammoth cocoon with no prospect of metamorphosis. Upon graduation, many found that they were powerless to decide their own future; bland technocrats simply assigned them to jobs where it was perceived that their skills were needed. At many institutes, including the People's University for Police Officers, students often resorted to bribing officials in the hope of landing a better position.

Yet even those students who wound up with prestigious and coveted postings soon learned, if they were not already aware, of the disparities which so angered other intellectuals. A salesman hawking leather jackets to tourists could earn ten times more than could most scholars with degrees. One young man discovered the cruel truth when he placed an advertisement for a wife. "Of what use is studying?" one woman wrote back. "Scribblers are not even as good as beggars. You can't eat culture and you can't put ideas in the bank."

7

Graduates counting on studying abroad, meanwhile, were irritated by new regulations which seemed specifically designed to impede them from leaving. Many were told that they could not go until they had worked for periods of two, even five years. Rampant corruption only made things worse. Some students discovered that classmates with the right *guanxi*, or connections, were able to get the best jobs or obtain passports speedily. These factors, along with an aging and distant leadership, contributed to a growing sense of hopelessness, frustration and futility.

It should not have been surprising, then, that these feelings would manifest themselves at some point; perhaps at any given opportunity. Certainly, that had been the case in late 1984, when students at Beijing University used a "lights out" regulation as a pretext to launch a minor protest. September of 1985 provided another chance which the students in the Chinese capital seized.

The event was the fifty-fourth anniversary of the Mukden incident, when Japan had started its occupation of Manchuria. Big character posters began appearing on Beijing campuses, followed by what was described as the largest student demonstration in a decade. The unrest spread, with students taking to the streets as far away as the southwestern city of Chengdu. In Xi'an, two Japanese visitors were attacked. Although the students were initially protesting against the Japanese prime minister's visit to a war shrine, the scope of their grievances widened. Soon, they were protesting against everything from Japan's "economic aggression" against China to poor canteen food.

This was not dissidence on a mass scale, and the students did not publicly denounce the Chinese leadership, but the demonstrators continued their fledgling movement throughout the fall, using patriotic reasons as a platform to air other complaints. With December approaching, it appeared that the students were about to launch a fresh assault. This time, the justification would be the anniversary of the 9 December Movement of 1935. Fifty years earlier, militant students shouting "Down with Japanese Imperialism!" had demanded that the Nationalist Party (Guomindang) join forces with the Communists to oppose Japan. The government of 1985 was anxious to avoid a repeat performance, regardless of the slogans.

Party officials bustled to major campuses throughout the country, lecturing the students about the importance of stability and canvassing support for government policies. A meeting was also organized during which the younger generation of activists met with older Chinese who had taken part in that 1935 demonstration. Despite these attempts to diffuse their energy, the students went ahead with a planned rally in Tiananmen Square. It was fairly low key, however, perhaps because the protestors were ringed by police.

The next student movement would spring to life in December of the following year. This time it was not triggered by students in Beijing. Rather, demonstrations began at the University of Science and Technology (known as KeDa) in Hefei, Anhui Province, where a spirit of intellectual liberation had been fostered under the direction of its vice-president, Fang Lizhi, and other administrators. The students were no longer simply complaining about Japanese aggressors or mouldy rice. They were asking for, then demanding, greater democracy.

The demonstrations spread to other cities, including Shanghai, where several vehicles were overturned. In Beijing, a relatively small protest at Tiananmen Square on 1 January 1987 led to several arrests. Those arrests, in turn, prompted a large march that evening.

It was just before midnight when the soft strains of the Internationale began to drift up from the street. It was a cold night, and a thick layer of snow covered the streets. The rally was about four thousand strong; several rows of students at the front of the column linked arms in solidarity as they marched towards Tiananmen Square. It was a powerful display.

Although the students were determined to reach the heart of Beijing, the authorities were just as determined to stop them. Every few blocks along the route, hundreds of police set up human roadblocks to impede the marchers. The protestors did not miss a beat in their advance. They simply pushed through, singing all the louder as the lines gave way. These confrontations came to resemble well-rehearsed ballet as the students continued towards the square.

Yet while there was confidence in that youthful crowd, there was also fear. Public security agents lined the route, snapping photographs of the marchers. Some used low-light video cameras. Many of the students turned their heads, or moved towards the centre of the pack. Others stared defiantly back at the lenses. A Chinese would later remark: "When it comes to technology, China is far behind the rest of the world. But when it comes to public security, China is very sophisticated."

Near Diaoyutai, the state guest house where the government accommodates visiting foreign dignitaries, the authorities demonstrated that sophistication in a different way. A water truck parked close by flooded the snowy streets, creating an ankle-deep layer of slush. The thin canvas shoes worn by the students offered no protection against the icy mixture—they might as well have been standing barefoot. It was about 2:00 A.M., and some students started to turn back.

Moments later, the vice-president of Beijing University arrived by

9

car and addressed the crowd with a megaphone. He announced that those who had been arrested earlier had since been released and urged the students to return to their campuses. Many of the protestors interpreted that as a victory, and a huge cheer went up. Others urged their comrades to push on, and several hundred continued what had become a very uncomfortable trek to Tiananmen Square. They stayed until 6:00 A.M., then returned to their campuses on buses provided by the municipal government. A few students, freezing and miserable, declined the offer of a free ride and walked the fifteen kilometres back to their schools.

In the days to come, an American journalist working for Agence France Presse would be expelled from China; a young student who had talked to him would be sentenced to jail. The crackdown had begun.

The warning shot came after the last Beijing demonstration in early January 1987. It was an article in the *Anhui Daily*, a newspaper published in Hefei, which opened by saying that student "enthusiasm and concern about the fate of our nation and the future of reforms is understandable." The accompanying unrest, however, was less acceptable. The publication went on to suggest that the dissent had been caused by a "very small group of people who had spurred on the trend of 'bourgeois liberalization', . . . and taken advantage of the students' enthusiasm and lack of experience in society to achieve their political aims."

The government's countermeasure would come to be known as the "Anti-Bourgeois Liberalization Campaign," a drive to cleanse the masses of unwanted Western ideals; a communal exorcism to restore national purity. Day after day, the state-run media harped on the need to follow the socialist road and keep on guard against bourgeois elements. The Communist Party even went so far as to dredge up a role model used more than twenty years earlier.

He was Lei Feng, a People's Liberation Army soldier. During the early 1960s Lei was constantly promoted as the paragon of Communist ideals. A selfless (and some say fictitious) young man who dedicated his life to helping others, this socialist superman died a hero's death at a tragically young age. While assisting comrades at the scene of an accident, Lei Feng—model soldier and Communist—was hit on the head by a falling telephone pole. In the wake of the student demonstrations newspaper articles exhorted the nation's youth to follow his altruistic example once again. "Emulate Lei Feng," headlines blared. Many young Chinese privately ridiculed the propaganda effort; others displayed open cynicism. "Who wants to be a Party member?" one asked. "All you do is sit and around and eat apples and read the paper. I'd rather party."

Throughout the campaign, China Central Television (CCTV) and other media ran countless "happy" stories about China's wonderful students. It was as if the "hooligans and ruffians" bent on sowing instability had never existed. Instead, Chinese saw industrious and patriotic scholars who took time off from their busy schedules to sweep streets, visit the elderly and entertain members of the People's Liberation Army. The media had been given a state directive: one officially sanctioned piece on students per day until further notice.

The Anti-Bourgeois Liberalization Campaign was also carried out on a more grassroots level. At CCTV, staff were repeatedly lectured by the local Communist Party official. They were warned, on an almost daily basis, not to deviate from the socialist path. "You are responsible for broadcasting the news," he told them. "You must not become the news." It was also stressed that the young reporters had good jobs with bright futures—perhaps even the opportunity to travel abroad. Similar meetings took place at other *danwei*, or work units. The message was understood. "If you do something wrong in the United States," confided one journalist, "you lose your job. If you do something wrong here, you're black-balled for life."

Older Chinese who remembered the Cultural Revolution and other purges also heeded the government's words, but for different reasons. Some of the language used in the propaganda effort insinuated that anything but absolute conformity could mark a return to the dark and chaotic days of the Cultural Revolution. For a generation which had known much madness, it struck a powerful chord.

The campaign was intense for several weeks. When it finally began to fade, it did so erratically. In April of 1987, it was suddenly announced that students would have to meet political as well as academic requirements before being allowed to sit for university entrance exams.

During the movement's early phase, the state-run media took great pains to avoid coverage of other international events which involved protests or clashes with authority. Student demonstrations in Italy, along with labour unrest of any sort were not shown on Chinese television. The only images permitted were of cheerful pupils.

It was clumsy but effective propaganda. People outside Beijing—except perhaps for those with shortwave radios or trusted friends in the capital—never learned of the truth. What they did hear was a carefully worded announcement on Chinese television the evening of 16 January. After making "a self criticism of his mistakes on major issues of political principles in violation of the Party's principles of collective leadership," Hu Yaobang had resigned as General Secretary of the Chinese Communist Party.

Hu had been forced out—ostensibly for refusing to take a hard line against the recent demonstrations, for his tolerance of "bourgeois liberalization." Up until his dramatic fall from grace, he was widely considered to be Deng Xiaoping's hand-picked successor.

Born in 1915 to a peasant family in Hunan province, Hu had all the right stuff: a good class background coupled with selfless commitment to the Party. When he left home to join the cause he was only fourteen. At nineteen he was a Party member; by twenty-six he was with the Red Army. It was then, in the Taihang Mountains, that Hu was assigned to work under Deng Xiaoping. The men are said to have gotten along well—at least partly because Hu shared Deng's passion and talent for bridge.

By 1949, the year in which the People's Republic of China was born, Hu Yaobang was one of four people working directly under the command of the future Chinese leader. From that point until early 1987, when he was so abruptly discarded, the destinies of Hu and Deng seemed twinned. Both men were veterans of the Long March; both transferred to Beijing in 1952, and both saw their power and stature rise during the first sixteen years under Mao Zedong.

After moving to the capital Hu quickly became ranking secretary of the Communist Youth League (the Party auxiliary which Lenin referred to as the "transmission belt of the Communist system"). He remained a youth leader until he was a spry forty-nine years old, by which time he had held a position on the Central Committee, China's cabinet, for more than a decade.

Like Deng, Hu was purged during the Cultural Revolution. His head was shaved and he was sent to the countryside to tend livestock. When Deng returned to favour during the final years of the Cultural Revolution, so did Hu. When Deng was again purged shortly after the death of Premier Zhou Enlai in 1976, Hu went with him. Finally, when the Gang of Four was toppled, both men were welcomed back into the fold.

Hu was catapulted to the inner circle, becoming a member of the Politburo as well as the head of the Communist Party's organization and propaganda department. While holding those posts, he was in charge of rehabilitating 900,000 people who had been unjustly persecuted during the 1957 Anti-Rightist Campaign and the Cultural Revolution. It was a move which earned him the admiration and respect of millions of Chinese.

Hu's star continued to rise into the next decade. In 1982 he was named general secretary of the Communist Party and Party chairman (a position later abolished). On paper, he was the most powerful man in China. It was Deng, though, who remained "senior leader." The elder statesmen made that clear on a bleak January day in 1987,

12

when he sacrificed his comrade and bridge partner of more than forty years.

Hu never publicly supported the students, but it is believed he did not feel as threatened by them as did other Communist leaders. His final days were spent reading, practising calligraphy and taking long walks. An impotent member of the Politburo, Hu Yaobang never broke ranks with those who betrayed him.

* * *

The other prominent man to fall during this period was Fang Lizhi—then vice-president of the University of Science and Technology in Hefei, where the student unrest had begun. By the time Hu died on 15 April 1989, Fang was well known to the West as the man who could not come to dinner—the scientist Chinese police prevented from attending a banquet hosted by U.S. President George Bush when he visited Beijing in February. The Western press squawked about the incident; Bush labelled it a denial of human rights. Inside China, no one came to Fang's defence. Fang Lizhi was, in many ways, a man in the wilderness.

"A dissident is as strong as a government," he claimed in an interview given in September of 1988, held at the comfortable eleventh-storey apartment he shared with his wife, Li Shuxian, near Beijing University. He had just returned from Australia, where he had claimed that many Chinese leaders squirreled away millions of dollars in foreign bank accounts. It is believed that Deng Xiaoping had personally phoned Fang to demand a retraction, but Fang had stood by his statement. His punishment would be denial of a visa to attend a December conference in the United States.

Fang occupied a curious position inside China. It was quite clear the leadership was obsessed with him, angered by what he said, yet reluctant to stop him. Fang himself believed the authorities wanted nothing more than to lock him up but were not willing to risk widespread condemnation over one man. Deng Xiaoping, in particular, seemed rankled by this voice of dissent. "I have read Fang Lizhi's speeches," said the elder statesman in December of 1986. "He doesn't sound like a Communist party member at all. . . . He should be expelled, not just persuaded to quit."

In early January 1987, four days before Hu Yaobang stepped down, the Party Central Committee and the State Council moved against Fang. He was dismissed from his post as vice-president at KeDa and transferred to the Beijing Observatory. Shocked students pasted up banners in protest; the dazibao were promptly torn down. Press at-

13

tacks against Fang intensified, culminating in a television announcement broadcast on 19 January: the Anhui Provincial Party Committee had expelled the intellectual from the ranks of its membership.

Later that year, Zhao Ziyang (Hu's successor) appeared more conciliatory towards the astrophysicist. He told NBC's Tom Brokaw in October that Fang was still a respected member of the scientific community. He was allowed to speak to journalists from Taiwan and still permitted to hold the beliefs which got him expelled from the Party. "I don't think you could call this a crackdown," Zhao said.

The Party was correct to oust Fang. He is no Marxist. "All countries which follow Marxism are unsuccessful," he maintained during that September 1988 interview. He claimed that he has no clear idea which "ism" he does follow, but to listen to him one thinks almost of a Chinese Thomas Jefferson—espousing such concepts as democracy, free markets and decentralization of political power. He spoke with astonishing directness and clarity—astonishing since the Chinese are masters at the fine art of implicit communication.

"Why is the government so stubborn in keeping the salaries of intellectuals so low?" he was asked. "Because they don't want too many intellectuals," he replied. "Because if there are more intellectuals, they will demand more independence. Yes, they need them in the economy, but they don't want them in the political field. This policy is the key to control."

Fang liked to laugh. He hid his vicious attacks on the Party behind a mask of mirth. He appeared to find delight in his analysis of Chinese society, of a Communist regime that was forced, against its nature, to sow the seeds of its own destruction. Communism, according to Fang, was inherently unstable; China's state-controlled economy had failed. He provided the economic miracles of Japan, Taiwan and Hong Kong as evidence: out of four regions with similar cultural backgrounds, China had been left in the dust. The failure, suggested Fang, was a direct result of the Party's inherent distrust of intellectuals.

He claimed that China spends just slightly more than two per cent of its GNP on education, the same percentage spent when the People's Republic was founded in 1949. "If people are in a position where they don't want knowledge, and are in fact kept in that position, then they're easier to control. . . . But if you want to develop the economy, you need educated people."

Fang believed that, while senior leaders of the Communist Party opposed political reform, they had started a process which would inevitably result in demand for such changes. Economic reforms would, as a matter of course, lead to calls for greater political free-

14

dom. Without some easing of restraints, said Fang, the economic reforms would be doomed to failure.

As a result of the 1986–87 student unrest, Fang stated, the pressure was on—both from within China and from foreign companies. He claimed many investors withdrew from the country during the Anti-Bourgeois Liberalization Campaign, fearing a return to the old days. "That, I think, also puts pressure on our government to consider the situation very carefully before there is another class struggle." He also noted that this was the main reason the government was being lenient with him: "Without reform, I must be in prison."

Although Fang was indisputably an activist, he placed much of his faith in the students. The demonstrations in 1986, he said, augured things to come.

"I think they made some changes in the concepts people think about. Because before that many people said 'everything should be given by the Party'. This was a typical slogan. Everything is given by the Party—even your body is given by the Party. Everything. Now we have rights, we have human rights. Two years ago, students would never dare to say something about Deng Xiaoping or the leadership, because they were afraid. Now if you go to some universities, they're criticizing Deng Xiaoping. Recently, there was a poster which said 'Corruption in Deng's Family'."

He did not see change coming overnight. "I think China needs at least one generation to change the situation. I have some arguments. First, we need the old generation out. The second is we need education. Even if we start to emphasize education now, it will still take one generation."

Fang knew he was being shadowed by the Public Security Bureau. He accepted it, and even joked about surveillance. "I think they watch very carefully. Even you—they know that you are here tonight. . . ." Pointing to the ceilings and walls, he smiled and joked about building a machine to detect listening devices. His wife, though every inch a dissident, did not take things as lightly. They were prepared, she explained, for the day they might go to jail. A handsome woman in her early fifties, Li Shuxian is also an accomplished physicist. Fang, however, thought arrest unlikely. "Sure, they could throw me in jail. It's very easy. Even tonight. But I think if they put me in jail, the response would be strong, very strong. And perhaps more people would become like Fang Lizhi."

The day after this interview, the family next door was moved out. Their apartment was taken over by the Public Security Bureau, which set up a committee to monitor closely Fang's activities—and his guests.

* * *

15

During the period between the Anti-Bourgeois Liberalization Campaign and the spring of 1989, there were signs that many Chinese were again willing to test the tolerance of the state. Journalists penned more liberal articles and editorials. Authors proudly declared that the period when literature had to "serve Socialism" was behind them. Western dress and music flourished among younger Chinese in the capitals; discotheques and Western-style bars sprouted near Beijing's university district. Controversial movies examined the legacy of Mao's Cultural Revolution.

There were also signs that the state was willing (albeit in a limited way) to deal with allegations of corruption. In July of 1987 the Party announced that any member guilty of accepting bribes would be expelled—regardless of rank. The resulting cases were well publicized, perhaps in an effort to convince the public that the regulation was being adhered to.

What many would define as the turning point marking that era of optimism came during October 1987, at "The Big Thirteen." It was the thirteenth National Congress of the Communist Party of China, a period which, by all accounts, pointed towards a brighter future. Zhao Ziyang, a perceived moderate, was confirmed as party secretary. His keynote speech, which described China as going through the "primary stage of Socialism," recognized some of the nation's problems and plotted economic and political solutions. Deng Xiaoping, meanwhile, retained his post as chairman of the Central Military Commission but resigned from the Politburo. He took with him the majority of elderly conservatives who had opposed reform (though the new members who were appointed, it turned out, held similar points of view). Nonetheless, it was a landmark Congress—one filled with debate and even dissent; one which bode well for future political change.

The following year, however, a broad base of Chinese would be less satisfied with their government. Allegations of corruption, though not always openly voiced, became widespread. Millions of average citizens felt frustrated by the elusive "back door"—a passageway through which those with the right connections could get almost anything: the right job, the best television, the best education. The government responded by trotting out another anti-corruption campaign. Hotlines were set up, and the media encouraged people to inform on those who were using their positions to profit. Well-publicized cases ended in dismissals, jail terms, even executions. But none of the "Big Potatoes," as Chinese call them, fell. Soon there was rampant talk that Deng's son, along with the children of other top leaders, was living in luxury. The rumours grew to the point where a new saying was coined: "The only thing that works [to get ahead] in China is a good father."

Inflation, spurred on by a booming economy, made things worse. Vegetable prices soared by fifty per cent during the first three months of 1988. The cost of eggs, vegetables, pork and sugar also went up as the government removed price controls in May. Workers at state-run enterprises and collectives began receiving a 10 yuan per month ($2.70 U.S.) government subsidy to help defray the rising cost of living. The leadership made vague promises to help slow down the "overheated" economy. In the local markets, consumers priced vegetables and muttered. Throughout it all, Chinese television news continued to show the daily parade of visiting foreign dignitaries—however minor—who were in Beijing to meet with the leadership. More often than not, senior leaders hosted lavish banquets for their guests. Living inside the closely guarded government compound at Zhongnanhai, they continued to alienate those they governed. No one could remember when Deng Xiaoping had last met with an average citizen.

In June of 1988, Deng revealed that he was delegating more power to Zhao Ziyang. Although the elder statesman was still the chairman of the Central Military Commission, it was Zhao who was now in charge of the People's Liberation Army. One year later, Zhao would be gone. Deng's soldiers would be firing on their own people.

By early 1989, the Anti-Bourgeois Liberalization Campaign seemed all but forgotten. In its place, artists and intellectuals were once again testing the limits of constraint. In Beijing, the country's first exhibition of art depicting nudes broke all attendance records despite its relatively high admission price. Later, in March, the Chinese capital would host the nation's first exhibit of experimental and performance art. Scheduled for two weeks, it lasted only five days. It was closed after a twenty-six-year-old woman sculptor from Guangzhou started shooting at her work with a pellet gun. The display consisted of two statues in telephone booths. She was questioned, then released, after convincing authorities that her actions were part of her work's intended message: alienation.

On 6 April, nine days before Hu Yaobang's death, Li Shuxian—the wife of Fang Lizhi—was invited to speak to two hundred and fifty BeiDa students at a self-styled "Democracy Salon." A spokesman for the university said it viewed such activities as "unhealthy" and had taken steps to stop the meeting. The outdoor gathering was attended not just by students: several men lurked on the fringes, taking photographs.

"This time I come before you courageously," Li Shuxian told the students. "For me, democracy is not something that can be divided into East or West. It is a fundamental principle." She asked for opinions from the students. There was silence until a young man wearing glasses and a Mao suit stepped forward. "We want to speak out," he ventured, "but we are afraid of all the people here listening. Graduation day is coming fast and jobs will follow."

Another student stood up. "It's not so much fear that I feel. It's just hopelessness. Our leaders don't listen to the people. They never will."

The day after Hu Yaobang's death was announced on 15 April 1989, the first banners and tributes in his honour started to appear. At Tiananmen Square, three hundred students, representing three universities, laid a huge wreath: "WE RESPECT THE BELOVED HU YAOBANG," it read, along with "YOU WILL LIVE IN OUR HEARTS FOREVER," and "YOUR ACHIEVEMENTS WERE MUCH GREATER THAN YOUR MISTAKES. IT'S BETTER THAT YOU ARE DEAD."

Far more cutting statements were starting to appear at Beijing University. Built hundreds of years ago, BeiDa is located in the northwest corner of Beijing, directly south of the Old Summer Palace that British and French invaders burned to the ground in 1860. At that time, BeiDa was known as Yenjing University and was staffed by missionaries who built elegant English-style houses for themselves and educated the children of privileged Chinese. After the Revolution, the missionaries moved out, and Peking University—which had been located near Tiananmen Square—moved in to educate the sons and daughters of Communist leaders. Today, the dozens of sad grey brick dormitories and classroom buildings built in the past forty years have not erased its beauty. BeiDa remains a peaceful campus of lakes, pagodas, willow trees and learning.

But in April 1989 people did not come to BeiDa to walk through its gardens or across to the island where a Qing dynasty stone barge serenely waits to ferry students to distant shores of contemplation. They came instead to a grimy convergence of three small roads, bordered by two dorms and a decaying canteen. This was the Triangle, a tiny island of democratic thought. Normally, the area is used for notices from the school authorities. In the days immediately following Hu Yaobang's death, however, it served a very different purpose.

"WHEN YOU WERE DEPRIVED OF YOUR POST, WHY DIDN'T WE STAND UP? WE FEEL GUILTY. OUR CONSCIENCE BLEEDS," read one of the hundred dazibao that had been hastily affixed to the student notice boards. The billboards, some measuring fifty metres in length, had been commandeered for a far greater cause than student schedules. "THOSE WHO SHOULD DIE STILL LIVE; THOSE WHO SHOULD LIVE HAVE DIED," declared one stark poster. Another went so far as to name the

Chinese leader: "DENG XIAOPING IS STILL HEALTHY AT AGE 84. YAOBANG, ONLY 73 YEARS OLD, HAS DIED FIRST." Still others made wry reference to the problems of inflation and corruption: "EVERYTHING IS GOING UP THESE DAYS, EXCEPT XIAOPING'S STATURE."

If Hu Yaobang could have witnessed what was taking place on the grounds of Beijing University during those few days, he might have seen something of himself in the young students. "I am not a man of iron," he once said. "I am a man of passion."

Indeed, passions grew during the next few days. The posters were joined by clippings taken from foreign newspapers. At first, these were articles from Hong Kong publications or the *International Herald Tribune*, papers sold at foreign hotels or subscribed to by some university departments. Soon, coverage of the student movement from as far away as London, Los Angeles and New York would be pasted to the tattered boards. Students, even those who did not read English, gathered to stare at the photographs and headlines. They were gaining strength, and the world was noticing.

The march to Tiananmen Square during the early morning hours of Tuesday, 18 April, when students draped the huge banner across the Monument to the Revolutionary Martyrs, was followed by a much more daring display. Thousands of students—some estimates range as high as ten thousand—took to the streets less than twenty-four hours later. This time, they took their grievances directly to the top—the central leadership's residential compound at Zhongnanhai, a kilometre west of the square.

It was an unprecedented scene: thousands of students planted outside the inner sanctum where the country's top leaders live and work, chanting for direct talks with the premier. "COME OUT, COME OUT, LI PENG!" they shouted. Hundreds sat down before the front gate. It was clear that they would not move unless someone came out and listened to them. Other students clambered atop the imperial stone lions which flank the entrance; still more curled up against the compound's massive walls to catch a few hours' sleep. A crowd of onlookers numbering thousands cheered their approval.

A few students were eventually allowed inside, where they presented lower-level officials with a list of seven demands. The functionaries accepted and promised to duly study the list, which included demands for greater freedom of the press, better treatment of intellectuals and a re-evaluation of Hu Yaobang's role in history.

By 4:30 A.M. the number of students had dwindled to about a thousand. An equal number of police arrived on Changan Boulevard and marched towards them. The protestors left quietly.

Watching the demonstration, one was reminded of an old Chinese proverb: "Newborn calves do not fear the tiger." The following night

19

that tiger would bare its teeth, when students staged another sit-in at Zhongnanhai.

The demonstration on the night of 19 April began like the others, with banners, chanting and singing. Some forty thousand people, including onlookers, filled Tiananmen Square. Students scaled the Monument to the Revolutionary Martyrs, calling for greater freedom and democracy. They also criticized some of China's top leaders, though not by name. To the west, on Changan Boulevard, other students again parked themselves in front of the government headquarters. Using their bodies as battering rams, they pushed and heaved against lines of soldiers protecting the entrance. "LI PENG, COME OUT!" they chanted.

The premier did not come out, but several thousand police did materialize near the square. They swept through Tiananmen, then pushed on towards Zhongnanhai. Most students ran away, but roughly two hundred sat down and refused to budge. Authorities surrounded the group, which continued chanting pro-democracy slogans in defiance. Restraint prevailed for several hours before the police actually moved in. Students said they were kicked, had their hair pulled and their clothes torn. Some said they were threatened with truncheons. Police loudspeakers blared, accusing the youths of chanting "reactionary slogans." One woman, face bleeding, was taken to hospital.

As dawn broke on Thursday, 20 April, a small crowd had reassembled at the base of the Monument to the Revolutionary Martyrs; the stone column was festooned with wreaths and other homages to Hu. One of the tributes was a six-metre-high black-and-white oil painting, an offering from the Central Academy of Fine Arts.

By Friday, students knew their part by rote: a noisy march to Tiananmen Square, some slogans and speeches, followed by a sit-in at Zhongnanhai. Despite government warnings to stay clear of the square, about ten thousand students took part in the demonstration. A driving rain drenched the spirits of most protestors, but a core group of one thousand continued to the government headquarters after delivering speeches from the Monument. They shouted a few slogans, waved a few flags, and left peacefully. The large contingent of police outside the compound did little but urge stragglers to keep moving. With Hu Yaobang's funeral scheduled for Saturday, it seemed they were under orders to avoid confrontation. Some Chinese surveying the scene were reminded of the death of another hero, Zhou Enlai, in 1976. His passing led to a similar outpouring of grief, which was eventually crushed with brutal violence in Tiananmen.

The remaining students returned to their campuses, only to

Faces of the democracy movement — hunger strikers huddle beneath a quilt at dawn, 17 May 1989. *(S. Simmie)*

Popular rock singer Hou Dejian during his hunger strike, 2 June. *(S. Troyer)*

Student leader Chai Ling addresses supporters. *(S. Simmie)*

Noted dissident Fang Lizhi at his home. *(S. Troyer)*

Famous ballerina Bai Shuxiang, persecuted during the Cultural Revolution. *(S. Simmie)*

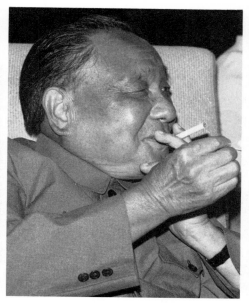

Chinese leader Deng Xiaoping. *(Reuters)*

Chinese Premier Li Peng . *(Reuters)*

Communist Party Chief Zhao Ziyang . *(Reuters)*

Young pioneers mourn deposed leader Hu Yaobang in front of the Monument to the Revolutionary Martyrs on Tiananmen Square, 22 April 1989. Beside them is an illicit banner calling Hu the "Soul of China." *(J. Annells)*

A lone soldier guards the Great Hall of the People during the funeral of Hu Yaobang. *(J. Annells)*

Spectators take to the trees to
glimpse the demonstrations.
(S. Lecker)

Students defy the government
in an early mass march.
(S. Simmie)

Disciplined students clear a space for a solemn display of their patriotism, Tiananmen Square, 4 May. *(S. Simmie)*

Lines of soldiers, arms linked, await the arrival of student demonstrators at the west corner of Zhongnanhai. *(S. Simmie)*

Bicycle brigade of students heads towards Radio Beijing offices to demand press freedom, 11 May. *(S. Simmie)*

The "Flying Tigers" motorcycle group parades past the Great Hall. *(J. Annells)*

Ambulance from Beijing Medical University Hospital cruises the streets of Beijing, 17 May. A front-seat passenger shouts slogans over the vehicle's loudspeaker. *(J. Annells)*

Factory workers from Shijiazhuang, the capital of Hebei, demonstrate, 18 May. *(S. Simmie)*

A truck full of jubilant demonstrators speeds down Changan Boulevard, 18 May, their banner proclaiming "Fear not expulsion." *(S. Simmie)*

reorganize for an even larger demonstration that evening. A government announcement that the square would be closed for Hu's funeral represented a direct challenge to the movement. On campuses throughout the university district of Haidian in northwest Beijing, students painted banners, slept and waited for nightfall.

By the time marchers began to set out shortly before 10:00 P.M. on Friday, 21 April, people were already swarming around Zhongnanhai. Thousands filled the sidewalk, hundreds more were perched on higher ground. They took up positions on any available vantage point: in trees, on streetpoles and on the roofs of nearby buildings. The main thoroughfare was jammed with bicycles, most parked in endless rows on the north side of the Great Hall of the People.

Soon, an estimated thirty thousand people were in the square. Most were squeezed around the base of the Monument to the Revolutionary Martyrs, which was now cloaked in hundreds of wreaths, posters and banners. Everyone seemed to be pushing towards the base of the obelisk, drawn to it like iron filings to a magnet. The human mass heaved and swayed with a mind of its own. The crush was incredible. Students trying to make speeches at the base of the Monument appeared to be ignored. Others attempting to lead the crowd in chants were echoed only sporadically. Organization appeared to have been lost, supplanted by an almost primal desire among Chinese merely to be there—to be near the wreaths and close to the forbidden stone. The human dominoes swayed from side to side, never quite toppling.

Amidst the chaos, there was intermittent order. Whenever groups of students arrived bearing a new wreath or tribute to Hu, the crowd would magically part—only to close in behind them like some fluid organism.

At about 11:30 P.M., the student demonstration was getting close. It stretched for several kilometres northwest of the square along a street called Xidan. It was a massive gathering, composed of groups representing all of Beijing's major universities. Students from each institute banded together like small regiments, with flag bearers leading the way. Some wore headbands identifying their schools. On the outer edges, rows of protestors marched with linked arms, creating a walking fence to keep out infiltrators and troublemakers. Besides excluding unruly elements and bystanders, the action seemed to have a higher purpose. The protestors wanted a certain element of purity to their march. This was to be a demonstration of students and students alone.

Xidan became a cacaphony of slogans and song as the march continued. Each school had its own chants, and the students took obvious delight and pride in trying to outdo other institutes. Particularly witty slogans were followed by an approving chorus of "Hao, Hao!" (Good, good!). It was, in a bizarre way, like high school fans preparing for the ultimate football game.

A handsome young medical student wearing his white lab coat shouted that he was marching "for democracy, for freedom." When asked what democracy meant to him he replied "Opposition parties!" He grinned, with obvious relish at the thought. "We want opposition parties to criticize the government, and newspapers to criticize the government—just like they have now in Hungary." That country had recently been in the news for its announced plan to allow non-Communists to run for its new parliament, though the Communist Party would still hold ultimate power. Asked if he thought that marching would achieve these goals, he answered "No. But we must show the government that is what we want." He seemed aware of the risk he and his fellow students were taking.

"I think there will be violence tonight. I think there will be bloodshed." He smiled, hiding his nervousness with laughter, and changed his mind. "No. It won't happen. No bloodshed. No violence."

At about 2:30 A.M. on Saturday, 22 April, demonstrators were shouting instructions and reorganizing for the final march to Zhongnanhai and Tiananmen. It was so crowded that some people had parked their bicycles more than two kilometres away from the square. Tens of thousands of Beijingers lined the streets, applauding as they passed by. The students smiled and waved back to the crowds in much the fashion that rock stars acknowledge adoring fans.

The applause was almost continuous, but few onlookers actually cheered. They seemed more interested in the electricity and vibrancy of the display, rather than the demands it represented. At least, that was the case until a group of about twenty people carrying a single banner appeared. Although this assembly was dwarfed by the larger demonstration, a huge roar of approval went up. Like an invisible marcher, it pulsed through the crowd as the entourage made its way forward. "Look," said a middle-aged man, "Workers!"

It took almost two hours for the procession to march past Zhongnanhai. Inside Tiananmen Square, the crowd swelled. Student marshals cleared an area in front of the Monument for new arrivals; a living rope of volunteers grew as classmates streamed in. Those who found themselves displaced from prime spots cheerfully gave way; no one tried to push through. In a nation where people routinely elbow their comrades to get a seat on the bus, it was a remarkable display of self-discipline.

It was obvious that police would not be able to clear the square. With every student or onlooker who arrived, this shared knowledge became more apparent. It was a scene of jubilation, of victory, as the tens of thousands realized the government had little choice but to back down.

Throughout that magical night, the number of people continued to swell. An ocean of smiling and hopeful faces shone under the bright lights of Tiananmen Square.

2

Their Purpose is to Poison People's Minds

When they walked out of the massive bronze doors at the entrance to the Great Hall of the People that Saturday morning, China's leaders saw for the first time the faces of rebellion. Although they could not distinguish the chants of the tens of thousands gathered in Tiananmen Square for Hu Yaobang's state funeral, those few who ventured briefly beyond the imposing doors appeared taken aback when they surveyed the sheer size of the crowd.

The service was subdued, a requiem for a fallen, but still respected, comrade. The forty-minute ceremony was broadcast live on state television and radio; flags throughout the nation flew at half-staff. Four thousand of the most powerful men and women in the country gathered to mourn their former colleague before the crystal sarcophagus containing his flag-draped body. As a band played a funeral dirge, elderly leaders stared sombrely at the spot where they, too, could soon be mourned. Most wore blue or grey Mao suits in sharp contrast to Hu's suit and tie.

Even Zhao Ziyang, the man who had replaced Hu as Party leader, wore a light blue Mao suit for the first time in recent memory. Zhao had been chosen to read the eulogy, and he performed the duty with detached efficiency. Most of his five-minute speech was devoted to Hu's career. The circumstances surrounding Hu's removal were brushed over with the comment that he had been "brave enough to admit his mistakes and to insist on what he thought was right."

The students had been invoking the dead man's name for their own purposes, and the Party was doing the same. With Hu gone, Zhao urged the nation to rally around the Communist Party Central Committee. He never deviated from the text, never lifted his head to share a personal anecdote with fellow mourners, never wavered from a stiff formality. The words were of loss and sadness, but Zhao Ziyang

25

found the appropriate tone elusive. He seemed like an actor thrust into a role he could not quite capture.

The band played the Internationale and the Chinese national anthem with sterile precision. In the square, thousands of students singing off-key provided a far more stirring rendition. Deng Xiaoping, President Yang Shangkun, Zhao, Li and the rest filed around the casket, offering Hu's wife and family formal condolences. In Tiananmen, where the students heard the service on loudspeakers, many simply wept.

Fifty thousand of them had spent the entire night in the square, learning only shortly after dawn that the government would officially allow them to stay. It was a prudent political move; perhaps the only plausible solution open to the leadership. The students were not going to leave of their own accord, and using even moderate force against them could have inflamed the situation. They were, after all, only there to mourn the passing of a party leader.

Both sides would play the charade for another day. Under the guise of mourning Hu, the students cried "Down with Dictatorship" and "Long Live Freedom," while the state paid official tribute to a man who was a political embarrassment. The students regarded the government's failure to act against them as a major victory.

Many wondered why the government had decided to clear Tiananmen for the funeral in the first place, particularly since students had regarded previous orders as challenges. Would so many have marched if the government had invited them, instead of banning them?

Police did manage to limit the number of protestors by closing the Tiananmen subway station and erecting barricades to keep others out. The move held back an estimated seventy-thousand people, who crowded against the police cordon. But if the government believed this would somehow ideologically quarantine the students from the masses, it was mistaken. If anything, the leadership's directives only served to pique the curiosity of Beijing's citizens.

The obituaries which appeared in the state media during the week following Hu Yaobang's death did the same thing. Why did they ignore the true reasons for his downfall, which were common knowledge? Why did they instead explain away his departure (when it was mentioned at all) with the excuse that he had stepped down for personal and political reasons? Why was the minor student crisis which had led to his resignation so studiously avoided? The strategy reflected a government that was nervous, a leadership that wanted to jog only selective memories.

This tactic found expression in other forms, too. On 17 April, newspapers had shown a group of art students laying the first wreath for

26

Hu Yaobang; later demonstrations were ignored. Any student activities which were reported had been coloured and tinted to create portraits of patriotism. When art students again marched to the square with a six-metre-high oil painting of Hu, for example, Chinese television was there and dutifully recorded the scene. That evening's newscast, however, did not tell the whole story—and what was not shown was far more telling than what was. Absent from the coverage was the fact that students had deliberately held their work directly in front of the famous portrait of Mao Zedong on Tiananmen Gate, symbolically replacing Mao's memory with that of Hu.

Such an omission should not have been surprising. When the Chinese media does give out information, it often does so in a curiously backhanded way. The Thursday morning sit-in at Zhongnanhai was not given any coverage, but a nasty rumour began circulating that a woman demonstrator had been killed when police moved in. The story spread that the woman, while fleeing a police charge on Changan Boulevard, had taken a look over her shoulder and been promptly struck by an oncoming truck. In order to stifle that rumour, the media had no choice but to acknowledge that something had taken place outside Zhongnanhai. A woman had died, went the official version, but she had been hit by a bus as she left a library late at night far away from the student activities. The rumour faded away, lending credence to the government version.

The squelching of rumours is a large part of Chinese reportage and often gives people their first hint of the truth. People have become accustomed to interpreting stories that begin "Relations between China and Argentina are perfectly normal," as a clue that there has indeed been a rift. A humorous example concerned the Beijing International Hotel, about four kilometres east of the Tiananmen Square (not to be confused with the older Beijing Hotel which is just a few hundred metres away from Tiananmen). The hotel, the first luxury lodgings to be completed without the help of Western engineers or architects, was said to be leaning. It was leaning so badly, according to hearsay, that the elevator could not reach the revolving restaurant on the twenty-fifth floor. After more than a year, Chinese newspapers finally announced that such rumours were not true, and an indignant hotel manager then refuted at length each one of the many slanders against his fine establishment.

Those who had not heard the chanting of the students, nor read their mimeographed and silk-screened messages that were sprouting on concrete lamp posts throughout the city, got their first hint of the real state of affairs on 21 April. It appeared in a sternly worded commentary in the Communist Party organ, the *People's Daily*. "Those who take advantage of the mourning for Comrade Yaobang," it read, "and charge, smash, rob or set fire to offices of the Communist Party or the government will be condemned by history. Up to now, in dealing with the very small number of people doing these unlawful activities, the government has been restrained. If some people consider this to be weakness, they will have to face the bitter consequences."

The article informed the nation that the mourning for Hu went far beyond what previous reports had indicated, but in this account, it was the government which was rumour-mongering: no actual smashing, robbing or arson had yet occurred. There had been no violence—not from the students, and not from any of the estimated two million Beijingers who lined the streets to watch Hu's funeral cortege proceed slowly to Babaoshan, the Eight Treasure Mountain cemetery, where he was cremated.

In the West, such government efforts to manage information are known as "containment" or "damage limitation"—attempts to minimize the political fallout from a touchy situation, such as a senator's drinking or sexual habits. As U.S. President Richard Nixon discovered during Watergate, the issue sometimes becomes the containment itself. Hu Yaobang's death created a delicate political crisis for the Chinese government; delicate because he had been disgraced and removed from power. That dismissal implied a difference of opinion on the handling of the student unrest in 1986 and 1987. The Communist Party, however, likes to maintain that it speaks with a united voice for all China. Its very existence depends on conformity. "You know," Fang Lizhi noted. "Even recently some top people in [the National People's] Congress said a good vote is three thousand to zero. So I guess if opposing votes are greater than zero, then it's unstable."

Hu represented a destabilizing factor, yet he could not be labelled an enemy. He embodied, within the top levels of the Party, an unwanted voice, a voice which had the strength to say "I disagree." Rather than bring this volatile dissension out into the open, the government chose to gloss it over—a strategy which made the student mourning that much more symbolic. They were not merely paying homage to a dead Communist. They were siding with Hu.

On the morning of Saturday, 22 April, shortly after the leaders left the Great Hall of the People, three students were allowed through the lines of armed police guarding the building. They carried with them a metre-long paper scroll, an intentional replica of those that had been presented to Chinese emperors for thousands of years. The three young men all had long hair; the youth actually carrying the petition wore acid-wash blue jeans and white tennis sneakers. The trio climbed solemnly up the wide steps leading to the Hall, then knelt before its granite columns. They bowed their heads meekly and thrust the petition into the air.

In Imperial days, a courtier would have taken such a scroll and presented it to the Emperor, seated on a throne in the Forbidden City just a few hundred metres from where this scene was staged. But China's leadership is not to be mocked, and on this occasion no one came out. Eventually the young men turned to face the crowd, remaining there until a minor government official finally showed up to accept the petition.

Most of the seven demands were of a general nature: press freedom, punishment of corrupt officials, more money for education, better treatment of intellectuals and public disclosure of the incomes of top leaders. But the first two called for a reappraisal of Hu Yaobang, and a reassessment of the 1986 student demonstrations and subsequent crackdown on intellectuals. The students were asking the Communist Party of China to apologize for what it had done, to admit that it had made mistakes. Acceding to such a demand could usher in a potentially destructive political environment—democracy.

Although the government knew of the demands earlier in the week, it neither acknowledged nor agreed to discuss them. The leadership's obstinacy the day of the funeral would deeply affect a then-unknown student who watched the trio on the steps. Her name was Chai Ling, a twenty-three-year-old student who would soon join the government's most-wanted list. "Everyone cried when they saw them kneeling," she remembered. "I decided to work for the movement when no one came out."

Even a Communist Party Youth League member who watched from Tiananmen Square said that he would join the craze. Lenin's 'transmission belt' was starting to slip.

In the city of Xi'an, students gathered to watch the funeral on televisions set up in the central square. Xi'an is an ancient capital of China, the site where the famous terra-cotta warriors—life-sized clay statues of soldiers fashioned for a Qin Dynasty Emperor around the time of Jesus Christ—were discovered in the 1970s. Xi'an is also the third-largest university town, after Beijing and Shanghai, and students there were quick to use Hu's death as a catalyst for democracy demonstrations.

Exactly what happened on 22 April is not clear, but according to the official version, a group of "lawbreakers" went on a rampage after the funeral service ended. The term "lawbreakers" in China is often used to describe tough young unemployed workers who pose a growing security problem in Chinese cities. The official New China News Agency reported that about two thousand of these young thugs, together with an equal number of students, charged police lines. The delinquents pulled down a wall in the courtyard of a government building, then set fire to ten buildings and twenty state vehicles. One hundred and thirty people were injured, the news service reported, most of them police. It took six hours of fighting before order was finally restored at midnight. Chinese television showed a youth hurling a Molotov cocktail beneath a truck to the cheers of bystanders. Official reports also said a bus carrying Taiwanese tourists was stoned.

But that is not how a Xi'an student interviewed in May saw things. In his opinion, if it was a riot, it was a police riot. "You could see the blood that was splashed on the walls on the back of the government building," he said. "That's true. I was in the demonstration. That day, I saw the police use the sticks with the armour, and they just went ahead and beat the students and the citizens." Several other students who made the pilgrimage from Xi'an to Beijing's Tiananmen Square would speak of incidents which seemed to support this account.

Eighteen people were arrested in Xi'an. On 6 May, one man would be sentenced to death for looting, throwing bricks at police and government buildings, and setting fire to cars and buses.

In Changsha, the southern city near the birthplace of Mao Zedong, police on 22 April arrested ninety-eight people after several thousand "lawless elements" attacked police and looted shops. Local radio said police had been injured. Later, the government would go to great lengths to say that university students were not involved. In a litany of statistics, it would state that thirty-two workers, twenty-six peasants, twenty-eight unemployed, six self-employed and six high school students had been caught. Damage was estimated at about $35,000 U.S.

Politically, these riots were good news for the government. They were so unexpected that even the students in Beijing were shocked. Student leaders counselled that the movement should be peaceful; that violence must be avoided. Given that sentiment in Beijing, Party leaders were probably more than hopeful when the *People's Daily* asked people on Monday, 24 April, to put the unrest behind them.

"Our duty is now to transform sorrow into strength, and put all our enthusiasm for patriotism, democracy and reform into concrete work towards the modernization and restoration of the country," a commentary said. It called on all Chinese to rally behind the Communist Party Central Committee and "actively protect" order in workplaces and on campuses. The paper did not mention that order on the campuses had already broken down.

Once students had recovered from their all-night vigil in Tiananmen Square on Saturday, 22 April, the Beijing, People's and Qinghua Universities once again became centres of dissent. In a week, the students had transformed themselves from a rag-tag group of protesters into a well-oiled marching machine. No longer were the democracy demonstrations the actions of individual campuses. Many students came from smaller schools to read the posters at BeiDa. Often, they would transcribe the dazibao or whisper them into cassette recorders before returning to their campuses to spread the word. At any given moment during the day, dozens of people could be seen recording the illicit messages.

Although guards posted at the school gates often turned away those without BeiDa student cards, no one made a move against the posters within the Triangle. Other schools did not enjoy the same freedom. When students at the Foreign Languages Institute began using their own notice board for political messages, the board—made of metal and anchored in concrete—was dismantled.

Students were angered that the government had refused to acknowledge their demands. One poster at BeiDa compared the leaders to "tortoises which hide their heads," the term "tortoise" being roughly equivalent in Chinese to the English phrase "son of a bitch." They planned to demonstrate again on 4 May, the seventieth anniversary of a Beijing University student revolt. But that was two weeks away, and many students simply could not wait.

On Sunday, 23 April, ten thousand BeiDa students filed into the school's soccer field. Chemistry students clustered around a flag identifying their department. Economics students rallied near their banner. Similar flags from other departments dotted the soccer pitch. Debate flourished.

"We have too many theories," one student shouted in frustration. "We need more action." The students decided to call a class boycott. Word spread to Qinghua and People's universities, and by evening the boycott was on. Students at the People's University set up a loudspeaker outside the school gates which blared their decision to passersby. At BeiDa, not one student in ten turned up for classes the following morning. Students at thirty other universities and institutes also stayed away. By Wednesday, only three of the sixty schools in Beijing would still be unaffected: the Public Security University, the People's University for Police Officers and the School for Diplomats. Even students at the Communist Party's own university stayed away.

The boycott went unreported on Monday as the official silence continued. This mute response was now deliberate policy. On Friday, the day before Hu's funeral, Politburo member Hu Qili had met with nine newspaper editors. He advised them not to report on the student activities. Chinese journalists who knew of the meeting said Hu claimed such reports would only inflame the situation.

Despite the directive, not every newspaper followed orders. A few days after Hu Yaobang's death, the Shanghai-based weekly *New Eco-*

31

nomic Herald had organized a seminar with a Beijing magazine, the *New Observer*. Prominent writers and scholars were asked to reflect on Hu's life. They complied willingly; indeed, with an abandon that seemed designed to refute the Party's version of events.

The *Herald* published some of those opinions in its 24 April edition, devoting the first six pages to remembrance of Hu. The government was not pleased, and understandably so: Dai Qing, a prominent reporter for the *Guangming Daily*, was quoted as saying that Hu's resignation was "a total violation of our organizational principles and procedures. Besides, he was forced to make a self-criticism against his will."

Wu Mingyu, an official with the State Council (the highest administrative organ in the government), had told the seminar that Hu had only two regrets in his life: his failure to protect a colleague who had been wrongfully accused during a campaign in the 1950s, and his forced resignation.

A political scholar named Yan Jiaqi went further. "The main problem China has today," he said, "is the lack of democracy. A handful of people can just talk among themselves and put aside the interests of the Chinese people and then reach an unpopular decision." In case the implicit meaning was not clear enough, the *Herald* also reported that Yan supported the students.

The editor of the paper was a seventy-year-old intellectual named Qin Benli. He had been in trouble with the government before and was almost forced to retire in December of 1988. That time, his offence was the publishing of a speech by a Marxist theorist urging more freedom of expression for intellectuals. The theorist, Su Shaozi, had contended that Marxism was in crisis in China. The fallout from that piece nearly cost Qin his job. Rumours circulated that he only managed to hang on to his position with the personal intervention of Zhao Ziyang. This time, nothing would save him.

The government banned the 24 April edition of the *Herald*. Politburo member and former Shanghai mayor Jiang Zemin told the editorial board that the paper could be distributed, but only if the offending articles were removed. The Beijing newspaper *Science and Technology Daily* was also banned for ignoring Hu Qili's warning and printing a series of articles favourable to the students.

Though neither muzzling was reported in the Chinese media, the students quickly learned of both instances. On Monday, 24 April, four thousand of them from the Central Nationalities Institute marched the twenty-minute walk north to People's University, chanting slogans condemning the ban on the *Science and Technology Daily*.

The foreign media got far more respect from the students; leaders ensured that they were informed well in advance of planned activities. From the reporter's viewpoint, the students certainly provided better stories than the weekly Thursday afternoon foreign ministry press briefings. In their eagerness to bring the world's press into their camp, the students often mistook Western journalists for political allies. Although the activists got sympathetic hearings, reporters were not willing to overlook their faults. On Monday afternoon, the students called their first news conference at BeiDa. Several thousand students came to the outdoor meeting to hear what the leaders had to say. But once the cameras were rolling, the students could decide neither on their message, nor on how best to convey it. Some argued that Premier Li Peng should resign for refusing to hold talks; others wanted to continue pushing for negotiations. The meeting degenerated into a minor shoving match, as students began quarrelling amongst themselves and grappling for the single microphone. Some began calling each other "government stooges." Most of those who were watching left; reporters expecting to hear the students' newest strategy departed with a different kind of story.

The next day, a group of mid-level Chinese officials went to Qinghua University to meet with students. It was supposed to be the first real encounter between the government and its detractors. The delegation included the deputy secretary-general of the State Council, a vice-minister of Education, a deputy secretary of the Beijing government and members of the official Student Federation—the only student body recognized by authorities. The government's invitation to meet was never accepted by student leaders.

Although the delegation was supposed to meet with "eighteen students," a reference to the organizing committee students had set up to co-ordinate their mourning activities for Hu, the rendezvous never took place. The official New China News Agency reported that the students could not decide who should represent them. The agency said the group of eighteen had requested the meeting to discuss democratization of the government. But no students showed up. After two hours of waiting, the officials drove away.

If the Xinhua report was accurate, that the students did fail to show up, their actions may have enraged Deng Xiaoping. It is believed that the senior leader convened a high-level meeting that same day during which the decision was made to crack down. The opening salvo was to be a strongly worded editorial in Wednesday's edition of the *People's Daily*.

A Chinese with close ties to the leadership said one man had been placed in charge of the campaign: Politburo member Hu Qili. But the source said Hu had taken the assignment reluctantly. "If I'm going to my grave," he reportedly said, "I'm not going in the old man's coffin."

Deng Xiaoping had no intention of going to his grave either. He was the most resilient politician in the world. A minor student rebellion was not something that would end his career, nor—as he referred to death—hasten the time when he had to meet Karl Marx. Just a few weeks earlier, he had explained his absence from the National People's Congress by telling a foreign dignitary that he was not working so hard anymore, because he wanted to live longer. But for the chain smoking eighty-four-year-old, an appointment with Karl could not be indefinitely postponed.

Deng once dismissed Communist hardliners' concerns about his reforms with the comment "We shouldn't shut the window just because a few flies come in." The student movement, however, threatened to become a pestilence he could not control.

"You see that little man there?" Mao Zedong said to Nikita Khrushchev during the 1957 Moscow celebrations marking the fortieth anniversary of the Bolshevik Revolution. "He's highly intelligent, and has a great future ahead of him." The man he pointed to was Deng Xiaoping. Mao would do much to nearly destroy that future, but at the time Deng was one of his most trusted confederates.

The little man had joined the Communist cause while still a teenager, in the 1920s Paris of Hemingway and Fitzgerald. He operated the mimeograph machine for another revolutionary, Zhou Enlai, who would later become premier. Both men returned to China, where they escaped the bloody 1927 repression of the Communists by the Nationalist government. By the early 1930s Deng was a guerrilla leader in southern China. He allied himself with Mao and was even stripped of his Party posts in 1932 when Mao's policies were out of favour. Deng survived the Long March, and during the long civil war he was a ready sounding board for the Helmsman.

After the Communists took power in 1949, Deng rose through the ranks to become party general secretary by 1956. By then, Mao had begun moving towards disastrous economic policies that were based more on ideology than common sense. Millions of Chinese starved to death during the Great Leap Forward—the forced collectivization of farms launched after 1958. Deng worked with Liu Shaoqi, the chief of state, to undo the damage. Mao complained bitterly that Liu and Deng's pragmatic economic policies were undermining his authority. In retaliation he used the Great Proletarian Cultural Revolution (1966–76) to strip the two men of their authority. Liu and Deng became the nation's top two "capitalist roaders," people accused of condoning the exploitive and bourgeois system of capitalism. Liu died in prison; Deng worked as a waiter.

34

By 1973, he was back in power. His old ally, Premier Zhou Enlai, was grooming Deng to be his successor. Zhou's death in January of 1976, however, set the stage for yet another power struggle to which Deng would fall victim.

The so-called Gang of Four, led by Mao's wife Jiang Qing, refused to allow public mourning for the dead premier. But Zhou's popularity did not die with him, and millions of people went to Tiananmen Square on 5 April—the lunar calendar day on which Chinese traditionally mourn their ancestors. Deng was accused of encouraging the public display, which the Gang labelled "a counter-revolutionary incident" and crushed with violence. He was stripped of all his postings and would remain in political limbo. When the Gang was arrested a few weeks after Mao's death in September, Deng returned to both favour and power. One of his first acts was to revoke sentences passed on those "counter-revolutionaries" arrested in Tiananmen Square.

By 1978, he was the most powerful man in the country, and he launched China on a program of economic reforms that would double the nation's gross national product within ten years. As the country's wealth grew, so did his popularity. At the time he rose to power, people considered themselves lucky if they had the "Three Bigs"—a bicycle, a wristwatch and a sewing machine. By 1988, the "Three Bigs" were a refrigerator, a washing machine and a television set. In the West, his Open Door policy was applauded by foreign investors eager for new markets and cheap labour. With his "Four Modernizations" (advancing science and technology, industry, agriculture and defence), he promised to make China a modern industrial state by early in the twenty-first century.

Where Mao had put "politics in command," Deng countered with putting "economics in command." He surrounded himself with people who held an equally pragmatic view on solving the nation's economic ills.

This pragmatism extended to the political field as well. Many saw in Deng a humanitarianism absent during the Cultural Revolution because he redressed the cases of those who had suffered under Mao. The move could also be interpreted as an economic measure: in order for the reforms to work, China needed intellectuals. Evidence that Deng was no democrat came during the late 1970s, during the short-lived "Democracy Wall" movement.

The site was a long, unremarkable wall near the Xidan intersection in downtown Beijing—not far from the Forbidden City. In November of 1978, big character posters espousing liberal and democratic themes started replacing the advertisements for tractors and other goods which previously adorned its grey surface. It seemed harmless enough; an innocuous outlet for a population only just recovering from a decade of repression. Deng seemed not just tolerant; he appeared to encourage the initial stages of the movement. He told a visiting Japanese politician that the advent of these dazibao was "a normal thing and shows the stable situation in our country. To write big character posters is allowed by our country's constitution. We have no right to deny this or criticize the masses for putting up big character posters. If the masses feel some anger, we must let them express it."

The posters became increasingly political over the next year; soon, a direct relationship developed between the number of people at the site and the tally of Public Security agents who watched them. When a poster calling for a Fifth Modernization—democracy—appeared, the government would no longer be tolerant.

The manifesto was the work of Wei Jingsheng, a former Red Guard then working for the Beijing municipal government. His poster said that without democracy, the much-lauded Four Modernizations were meaningless. Only if people could achieve "freedom and happiness" would they become masters of their own destiny.

The concept pushed freedom of thought, and Deng Xiaoping, too far. Wei was arrested in the spring of 1979 and brought to trial six months later. Charged with "counter-revolutionary crimes of a serious nature," he was convicted and sentenced to a prison term of fifteen years; his appeal was unsuccessful.

"You have read it yourself," said the prosecutor. "It is decreed in our Constitution that there is freedom of belief. You can believe or not believe in Marxism-Leninism and the Thought of Mao Zedong as you wish, but you are absolutely not permitted to oppose them. . . ." Today, Wei Jingsheng remains incarcerated near Beijing. It is believed that the years of solitary confinement have taken a serious toll. Some reports suggest he is now blind and insane.

Wei was one victim; soon the entire movement would be silenced. On 1 December 1979, the *Beijing Daily* announced that the municipal government had decided to close the Democracy Wall. That was followed on 16 January 1980 by a speech in which Deng Xiaoping insisted that the right to put up wall posters be deleted from the Chinese constitution. The privilege, he said, had been abused by a "handful of reactionaries with ulterior motives" to undermine China's "stability and unity."

Yet Deng's pragmatism still told him that without some easing of restraints, intellectuals would not work hard for his reforms. He dropped the Maoist dictum "Art must serve politics," which had stifled artists and writers by making their work the plaything of competing communist factions. Instead the slogan became "Art should serve socialism, serve the people"—a much broader domain. He instituted the 'Three No's'. No grabbing of pigtails, no beating with sticks and no putting hats on (three classical Chinese sayings that mean no picking faults, no attacks meant to humiliate or dishonour and no labelling people as enemies). This policy helped usher in a more relaxed intellectual environment during the 1980s. People were not so fearful of becoming targets of repression for expressing their opinions.

Deng knew this policy forced his government to walk a tightrope. Without constant control and vigilance, the nation could plunge into chaos. He maintained that everyone must adhere to the "Four Cardinal Principles"—the socialist road, the people's democratic dictatorship, the leadership of the Communist Party and Marxism-Leninism/Mao Zedong Thought. Whenever those axioms appeared threatened, he did not hesitate to crack down.

He did not hesitate at the end of April 1989. On Tuesday, 25 April, he decided it was time to exercise control. On Deng's orders, ten thousand troops were moved closer to Beijing. One Chinese with close connections to the leadership quoted him as saying "If necessary, some blood could be spilled and that repression would not seriously harm China's image in the world."

The propaganda machine geared up remarkably quickly: a stern bulletin condemning the student movement led the 7:00 P.M. national television newscast that night. The announcement, a version of the *People's Daily* editorial slated for the following day, was broadcast only hours after the New China News Agency reported that the students had snubbed the government delegation. Quoting the newspaper, an announcer called for a "grave political struggle" against the student unrest, which was labelled as a plot by a small group of extremists to topple the Party. "Their purpose," relayed CCTV, "is to poison people's minds, create national turmoil and sabotage the nation's political stability. This is a planned conspiracy, which in essence aims at negating the leadership of the socialist system." The campaign to undermine popular support for the democracy movement had begun.

* * *

Wen Huaisha knows all about repression.

When he was released after ten years' imprisonment in the late

1970s, a reporter from the Associated Press came to visit him. Wen's case had not yet been completely redressed and he was forced to rely on the generosity of a colleague to survive. His living conditions were miserable for so celebrated a scholar, and the reporter tried to take a photograph of him washing worn-out socks.

"I asked for his negative," Wen remembered. "I told him, 'I want your respect. I want you to respect me as a Chinese'."

The reporter apologized, and perhaps to mend things offered to get Wen a television set.

"How much money are you prepared to give me in exchange for my Qu Yuan, Li Bai and Du Fu? I respect *you* just because you come from a country which boasts Jack London. Jack London is not someone who could be exchanged for money."

The reporter left, and Wen decided not to speak to Western journalists again. He agreed, somewhat reluctantly, to an interview in November of 1988.

Wen is a classical scholar, one of the greatest authorities on the ancient philosopher Qu Yuan, who threw himself into a river in protest against the emperor's policies. Friends who tried to rescue him by boat arrived too late. As a last gesture of honour they threw rice cakes into the swirling waters, imploring fish not to eat his body. Chinese celebrate Qu Yuan's memory every May with dragon boat races that recreate the frantic efforts to save him.

Wen Huaisha has travelled the river of modern Chinese history with an equally reckless abandon. He has shot through dangerous rapids unharmed, only to be trapped by whirlpools. Yet, in recalling his life, he revels in the humanity of both his good fortune and his misfortune. The story of China, he believes, can be told in intensely personal terms. The great waves of revolution, of repression, of political campaigns and purges can ultimately be reduced to human passions.

"When Hu Yaobang was head of the Party's propaganda and organization department," Wen said, "he did a lot of things for the people. For instance, he took a personal interest in the redressing of many of my friends, and me. So if I want to express my gratitude to the Party, I must express this feeling in terms of individuals, not in terms of the Party as an abstract idea. If the Party is in good hands, I think the Party is good."

Wen Huaisha is not a man to take lightly. At the age of seventy-nine, his greying hair is thin and receding; wispy facial hairs flow down to his chest. He lacks only the robe to make him appear the contemporary of Qu Yuan, Li Bai and the other famous poets of dynasties long ago. He is quick with a cutting comment, and not afraid to offend. He once publicly called Mao's wife, Jiang Qing "worn shoes"—

the Chinese term for slut (he claimed he based that conclusion on facts).

He has never been a Communist, but during the 1940s his criticism of the Guomindang government forced him to flee into Communist-held territory, so the Party thought him an ally. When the People's Republic was founded he was given a responsible job editing books of literary criticism. It was in this position, in 1954, that he become part of the flesh and blood of history.

Looking back, the event seems almost unbelievable. It started when a friend of Wen's, fellow scholar Yu Pingbo, needed to borrow money to pay for his father's funeral. Wen lent him 200 yuan, but Yu was unable to repay the debt. All he could offer were a few un-published manuscripts he'd written thirty years earlier. One of them was on the ancient novel *Dream of Red Mansions*, the *War and Peace* of Chinese literature. Wen decided to publish the article, which would give Yu enough money to pay him back.

That likely would have ended it, but two students from Shandong province, a few hundred kilometres south of Beijing, read the work and did not like it. They wrote a criticism, which they sent to publish-ers in the capital. Although it was rejected by the editorial staff of the *People's Daily*, it was accepted by the students' local university paper. The next issue of that paper would set into motion a truly bizarre chain of events.

"Since Jiang Qing (Mao's wife) was also a native of Shandong prov-ince, the university mailed a copy to her," recalled Wen. Jiang Qing showed it to Mao, and the Great Helmsman was incensed. He was furious that the students' article had been rejected in Beijing. " 'When they venture to criticize Yu Pingbo in a Marxist perspec-tive'," Wen quoted Mao as saying, " 'they should not be suppressed'."

Mao ordered a meeting of the writer's union to denounce those who had rejected the students' article. "You are all Communists," he said, "but where are your Communist identities?" That question was very serious. The People's Republic was less than five years old. The Korean War had just ended with the loss of one million Chinese soldiers—including Mao's son. The country was still in the midst of a campaign to "Wipe out Counter-Revolutionaries," those Chinese who were believed to actively support the Guomindang. Mao warned the writers that their works must serve the political ends of the state.

For a small group of young Marxist writers, Mao's words were good news. It meant almost certain publication for their works, and grow-ing political influence. They were led by a man named Hu Feng—an unconventional Marxist who had locked horns with orthodox com-munists for years. He saw in Mao's speech a developing freedom which he could exploit by claiming that he and his followers had been suppressed. In reality, Hu Feng was after artistic and cultural license—free from the bonds of the Party. That was not what Mao had in mind.

A Judas in Hu Feng's group of followers came to Mao's rescue. He had in his possession some letters in which Hu Feng revealed his private thoughts—some of which ridiculed the Party. When these were published, Hu Feng was labelled a representative of bourgeois ideology. Later, he and the "Hu Feng Clique" became known as political subversives, agents of the Guomindang and imperialism. By 1955, Hu had been arrested as a counter-revolutionary. He spent the rest of his life in prison and died a madman in the early 1980s. Many of his followers ended up in psychiatric institutions.

What began with Hu Feng quickly became a much wider movement. In March of 1955, the Party came to realize that Hu Feng might not be the only one to hide his heresies behind a shield of Marxism. So began a Movement to "Wipe Out *Hidden* Counter-Revolutionaries." No one was above suspicion. Inside the Party alone 150,000 cadres were investigated. Tens of thousands were sent to labour reform camps to correct their thinking.

"The movement was intended to wipe out counter-revolutionaries all across the country," Wen claims. "According to a conservative statistic, there were altogether about 800,000 people who were shot. This figure was probably released by the Party. So you can see what part I played in the whole process. In the beginning, I helped Yu Pingbo with 200 yuan. At the very end of that process 800,000 people perished." Historians are divided about how many people actually were killed during this era, but no one disputes that these events destroyed many lives.

* * *

The message was clear: intellectual conformity was the key to survival in the new China. Although this tendency weakened during the 1980s, many still knew what to expect when bulletins of the *People's Daily* editorial were broadcast. To call the unrest "a planned conspiracy" was virtually a declaration of war.

On the campuses, students were shocked, hurt and angry. A sombre atmosphere descended over Qinghua, where several thousand students met on the evening of Tuesday, 25 April, to decide on a course of action. Many were shaken by the broadcast; there was even discussion of ending the boycott. In the end, students agreed to remain away from classes but stressed that anything more radical should be put on hold. Under no circumstances should the government be given a pretext to use force.

Some students cautioned that there could be arrests; others felt the authorities would not dare—there were just too many people involved in the movement. Most students, however, were simply incensed. Other than a few slogans and posters denouncing top leaders, the movement had been very patriotic. Suddenly, their nationalism had been labelled subversive. It was a stinging slap in the face. "We must persist to the end," blared a student-controlled loudspeaker that evening, "and the victory will be ours!" They continued to organize; large-scale demonstrations were planned for 1 and 4 May.

The next day, Wednesday, 26 April, the Beijing municipal committee of the Chinese Communist Party met at the Great Hall of the People. It was no small get-together: the city's ten thousand Party secretaries had been called in for a briefing on the student demonstrations.

The leader of the group, Li Ximing, said the students were "stirring up turmoil" which had to end. "We must firmly stop such riots," observed Li, "or there will be disturbances." Far more telling was his warning to fellow cadres: stop your children from attending illegal activities. That same day, the *People's Daily* hit the streets.

> ... A very small number of people with ulterior motives continue to make use of the desire of young students to mourn Comrade Hu Yaobang. They fabricate rumours to poison people's minds. They make use of posters to libel and slander and attack the leaders of the Communist Party and the government. They wantonly violate the Constitution, (and) incite people to negate the Party's leadership and the socialist system. In some universities, they have set up illegal organizations and taken power from official student associations. In some universities they have incited students and teachers to boycott classes. . . . All comrades of the Party, and the whole nation, must understand clearly that if we do not resolutely stop this unrest, our state will have no calm days. . . . A promising China will become a turbulent and hopeless country. . . . Our reform and modernization will depend on this struggle and the future of our state and nation will depend on it.

The dense text was not just directed at students. It was also a dark warning to everyone from doctors to peasants to stay clear of the movement. To ignore that call would be tantamount to conspiracy. At the same time, the editorial quietly dredged up shadowy memories of a grim period in Chinese history: the Cultural Revolution. Its lines clearly implied that unless the protestors were stopped, there could be a return to instability—"our state will have no calm days." Similar fears had been played on effectively during the student unrest in 1986–87. Finally, the message appeared to leave those who had been taking part with a face-saving opportunity to withdraw. They had been used, it said, by a minority with ulterior motives. The phrase intimated that those who stopped now could escape future consequences.

Students were enraged. It was bad enough to have the government insinuate that they were bent on destroying their country; that alone was an insult to their integrity. To suggest additionally that they were helpless marionettes was an insult to their intelligence.

One BeiDa student, Xiao Cong, was furious. "The government says it wants democracy, it SAYS it wants democracy. I think we will have to fight for it!" She said that students would not wait until 1 May to demonstrate. They would march the very next day. Hu Yaobang was no longer the focal point of the students' protest; now their target was the government.

It was a warm, sunny day—the kind of day when Beijingers are grateful for the shade provided by the huge trees which line most bicycle lanes. Confident the weather would bring good business, street vendors stacked bottles of soda on huge blocks of ice. Women clad in bulky aprons wheeled white carts containing popsicles and ice cream to busy intersections. Police directed traffic to the accompaniment of bicycle bells. On the campuses, students gathered in force to defy their government.

At BeiDa, on 27 April, they began organizing at 8:00 A.M. Students leaned out dormitory windows, using megaphones to urge all comrades to join the cause. For the next hour, banners, headbands and commitment coalesced in the Triangle.

The scene was different at Qinghua. There, the underlying message of the *People's Daily* editorial had not been lost on organizers. Shortly before the march was to begin, student leaders resigned. As they were part of the "very small number of people with ulterior motives," they clearly had the most to risk. Those they had led went ahead without them. The leaders then abandoned their fears and brought up the rear of the march.

All across the city, students poured into the streets. At one school, the university president stood at the gates and sobbed, pleading with his students not to go. They listened politely, many of them embarrassed by his commitment which rivalled their own, then headed toward Tiananmen Square.

Back at BeiDa, students surged past the institute's steel gates shortly after 9 A.M. They walked straight into police lines—and kept on going. At 9:30 they ran into a similar blockade just outside RenDa; again, they simply pushed through. The scene was repeated farther down the street at the Central Nationalities Institute. Bystanders cheered vicariously, almost victoriously, as the students continued on their march.

In publishing the *People's Daily* editorial, the government had seriously misjudged both the students' resolve and the sentiments of average Chinese. Rather than condemning the protestors, Beijingers mobilized as never before to encourage them. Hundreds of thousands of workers abandoned their offices to cheer and applaud from the sidelines. Thousands of others waved from windows and rooftops. Vendors donated food and drink, while bystanders nourished the marchers with unequivocal support.

Throughout the eighteen-hour march, the students capitalized on themes of corruption and inflation. They addressed the concerns of the common man and received an astounding response. The editorial, it seemed, had also struck a raw nerve within the general populace. The students eagerly exploited it, calling on workers to join their cause.

In a country where less than one-fifth of one per cent of the population gets to university, the issue of education was not about to mobilize the masses. But complaints which students voiced over the rising cost of living, widespread corruption and aristocratic privilege hit home. Why was it that China's leaders should be chauffeured around in Mercedes Benz limousines while the average man broke his back just to get by? Why couldn't you get the simplest thing done anymore without the right bribe, or the right connection? Why had the *People's Daily* labelled this movement a conspiracy? The students had raised valid points; the questions begged to be answered.

One scholar remarked that the Chinese people were demonstrating a political consciousness not seen since 1949. Indeed, people displayed far more than that. Workers often surged right into the streets, pushing aside police before the students arrived. On three separate occasions, thousands of people surrounded hundreds of officers to prevent them from moving towards the marchers. Each time the authorities were vanquished, a triumphant cheer went up. This was more than open defiance—it was confrontation; a direct and audacious challenge to the government. The workers, apparently, were not intimidated by Wednesday's edition of the *People's Daily*.

Depending on how one interpreted that stern editorial, it could be said that Beijing's streets were filled with hundreds of thousands of conspirators that heady day. By the time it was over, students had marched through eighteen separate police and army lines. An estimated half million Beijing citizens had lined the entire thirty-five kilometre route throughout the city to show their support. Efforts to stop the march had failed miserably.

The government said it was ready to talk.

3

The Actual State of Affairs

The threat had not worked. Instead of scurrying back to lecture halls carrying books, students had swarmed into the streets waving banners. Even worse, they had been supported by hundreds of thousands of average citizens. The government had little choice but to back off. And it did—that very day.

A spokesman for China's State Council, the country's highest government body, proposed direct talks with the students "at any time." The unidentified spokesman stressed that the Party and the state had always believed in dialogue between the government and the masses. This was a far cry from the editorial of 26 April, which had all but labelled the protestors as seditious traitors.

But the leadership was not exactly taxing itself to be conciliatory. The spokesman also outlined several preconditions which the students would have to meet if the talks were to proceed. Students were urged to "go back to their campuses at once," and "adopt a calm and reasonable attitude." Most significantly, the dialogue would have to be conducted "through appropriate channels." These 'channels' were the All-China and Beijing Municipal Students' Federations. The protestors, however, had already formed their own autonomous organization. They regarded the government-approved bodies with suspicion and, in some cases, contempt. To allow those groups to represent them would be like having young Republicans negotiate on behalf of young Democrats. New posters went up at BeiDa, one of which set out its own preconditions: the talks must be open to the Chinese and foreign press and broadcast live on television, and they must alternate between government and university locations. Another poster simply read: "We won't waver until victory."

Regardless of the provisos laid out by either side, the students had achieved much. They were no longer being denounced, and the government appeared willing to talk. Politburo member Hu Qili took things a step further by meeting with staff of nine major newspapers. He told them they were free to report "the actual state of affairs" so that people could decide issues for themselves. He also told them that the leadership agreed with many of the students' demands—that it, too, wanted an end to corruption and inflation. The government had, after all, mounted several anti-corruption campaigns in the past (though with largely superficial results). In addition, the leadership had taken steps to cool down the country's economy and to lower inflation.

A more cynical view would be that the state was merely looking for a quick way to put a cap on the situation. With a promise of dialogue and media coverage, the students might go back to class. By showing flexibility and conceding that the protestors had raised valid points, growing popular support might be quelled. While it appeared to the public that the leadership was being conciliatory and tolerant, privately there may have been a different agenda: channel the dissent into a controlled situation, make a few token concessions, and crush the movement as quickly as possible.

Changes in the government approach were mirrored in the state-run media the day after the protest. Friday's edition of the English-language *China Daily* described the huge march as "a peaceful demonstration" and reported that students had chanted slogans and waved banners calling for greater democracy. The paper did not mention that police lines had been pushed out of the way. In what was perhaps a compromise between its newly sanctioned freedom and its traditional role as a mouthpiece for the state, it said "no clashes have been reported . . . both sides showed obvious restraint."

It was the *People's Daily*, however, that would reflect the government's new thinking. "Stability and democracy are two sides of the same coin," said Friday's editorial. "Spreading rumours about state leaders, staging strikes and instigating turmoil can only plunge China into chaos." Some students might still have taken offence, but it was a welcome change from the harsh words which had appeared on Wednesday.

The coin analogy used by the paper says much about the Chinese view on democracy. In the West, spreading rumours, staging strikes and causing unrest are all viewed as legitimate, if sometimes disruptive, aspects of the social order. There are limitations imposed, but a truly democratic government does not merely tolerate dissent—it nurtures conditions which allow people to be heard.

The Chinese have traditionally held a different view, which Communist Party leaders found well suited to their needs. Since the days of Confucius, democracy has been considered an agreement between

46

the ruler and the ruled. Educated citizens could see the wisdom of placing the collective good before individual interests, thus allowing the ruler to create a strong, prosperous and peaceful state on everyone's behalf. Stability is the key to this type of government. Any turmoil would threaten the mutual prosperity of the collective; the common good outweighed individual rights.

Mao extended this logic to the point where anyone who displayed anti-social, individualist or "bourgeois" characteristics was not part of the "people." He or she could be publicly criticized, re-educated, jailed or even eliminated—all for the public good. Under Mao, the state in its urge for conformity went so far as to decide what clothes people should wear. The drab, full-collared "Mao suit" appeared to be the uniform of a nation, a symbol of collective homogeneity.

Throughout the democracy movement of 1989, the Party would repeatedly use the appeal for stability as an emotional weapon against the students. It was used to strike a psychological nerve, a feeling deeply etched in every Chinese citizen by thousands of years of tradition—and by the recent decade of darkness.

The students had a different view of democracy, but they were not complaining. The government had backed down to the point where it was now inviting their criticism. Even with preconditions, the opportunity was not to be missed.

More than thirty years earlier, another man spoke out at the state's behest. He has regretted it ever since.

* * *

"Have you read any Dostoevsky?" Xi Ruisen asked one day in 1988 as the birds sang in the spring sunshine outside his window. "He once depicted the psychology of those who got a long imprisonment. He wrote that those people are numb, because there is no hope for them. They don't think much of the future, because they do not know what fate lies in store for them."

Xi Ruisen did not need Dostoevsky to tell him what he was feeling during his years behind bars. He brings up the Russian only to help others understand what it might have been like, a literary yardstick to measure his own suffering.

In his green police uniform, Xi does not look like a man who has endured twenty years of political persecution. On his shoulder epaulets, he keeps the blue metal police badge with the red stars brightly polished. His pants and tunic are always neatly pressed, his cap spotless. When asked, he can snap to attention as fast as a new recruit. But Xi is rarely asked. He is not a policeman, but a professor of English at the Chinese People's University for Police Officers. "I am,"

47

he likes to say with a smile, "working for my former jailers."

The university is located outside of Beijing, about twenty kilometres directly south of Tiananmen Square. It is a pleasant place in many ways, offering the best of the countryside with easy access to the city. The area is famous for growing China's best watermelons. During the summer, peaches, apples and grapes hang heavy from branches and vines, tended by minor offenders convicted of assault, robbery and petty crimes.

Xi Ruisen is not the only former political prisoner at the University. Victims of many campaigns have found secure—if disciplined—refuge behind its walls.

Xi loves the English language, almost as much as he loves his own. He delights in its versatility, its wealth of expressions and even its pure nuttiness. At the age of fifty-nine, he continues to find new expressions to savour. "Isn't it a PEACH of a day?" he'll ask. His students sometimes learn that it is raining "cats and dogs" before they know they are watching a "downpour." Xi peppers his near-perfect English with a host of such colloquialisms, collecting phrases the way many Chinese collect stamps. He has never studied abroad; his English has been mastered entirely through his own diligence. Within easy reach of his livingroom work desk are more than two dozen dictionaries, thesauri, grammars and stylebooks. He takes his chosen profession very seriously.

Xi is now a valued and trusted member of the Public Security Bureau. When a delegation from the Royal Canadian Mounted Police paid a courtesy call to China in 1988, he was chosen as their interpreter. When his vice-minister toured Canadian police installations that fall, Xi went with him—the first time he had ever been abroad. He came back full of stories for his wife. "You should see," he told Zhang Anli, describing the wonders of Ottawa's Rideau Market. "They have RED peppers, and RED potatoes!"

By Chinese standards, Xi and his wife are well off. Their four-room apartment houses a new colour television, refrigerator and a video-cassette recorder. They have no bath—few Chinese do—and no hot water. Even Deng Xiaoping is said to start his day with a cold shower.

No worldly comforts, however, could ever erase the lost decades when Xi Ruisen was considered an enemy of the people, a counter-revolutionary.

The year 1956 was a good one for China. After relentless witch hunts, the People's Republic appeared to be inching away from the constant compulsion to expose enemies of the state. Deng Xiaoping suggested that the need for class struggle was dying away; Premier Zhou Enlai called for better treatment of intellectuals, noting that the party had treated them with "unnecessary suspicion." This apparent unshackling of intellectual restraints was endorsed by Mao Zedong himself on 2 May. "Let a Hundred Flowers Blossom," he declared, "and a Hundred Schools of Thought Contend."

At the time, Xi and his wife both worked at Xinhua, the New China News Agency, translating English reports into Chinese. Like many other intellectuals, they were cautious about taking the government up on its offer. There had been numerous campaigns in the seven years since New China was founded, and many people had suffered. Those suspected of supporting the former Nationalist regime and those with "bad class backgrounds" had been rounded up and dealt with harshly. It might not be safe to speak one's mind.

So Xi Ruisen and others were wary, nervous about testing the sincerity of Mao's invitation. The campaign was so distrusted at first that few people—if any—stepped forward and spoke out. It was not until almost a year later that people began openly criticizing the government. Even then, the criticism came only after the Party launched a "Rectification Campaign" in April of 1957. This movement was aimed at cleaning up bureaucracy and inefficiency within the Party infrastructure. People were encouraged to point out shortcomings within the organization and put forward solutions. It was within this atmosphere, in which dissent was being encouraged, that people began voicing ever-stronger complaints.

At Xinhua, regular political study sessions were transformed to fit the campaign. Communist Party members were told to keep quiet and listen. But the discussions did not concern the affairs of the Central Committee. Rather, they focussed on the internal workings of Xinhua. For Xi Ruisen and Zhang Anli, those meetings in May of 1957 became a forum for airing petty grievances.

Zhang complained about the lack of daycare for their baby daughter. Party officials listened politely but were far more interested in Xi's list of complaints. He said his salary increase was not as high as that paid less-capable workers; he claimed that some people got their jobs through nepotism.

It was relatively mild stuff compared to the "storm in the universities." At BeiDa, students stopped going to class. They began putting up dazibao on what became known as that institution's democracy wall. A Chinese version of Khrushchev's speech denouncing Stalin appeared for the first time on the wall. The speech had been suppressed by the authorities, who were furious that the new Soviet leader would criticize a man still lauded as a hero in China. Khrushchev's speech had been translated from the American Communist Party newspaper, the *Worker's Daily*. The translator had been Xi Ruisen.

The criticisms swelled from a ripple to a tidal wave. By late May, Mao decided to suppress dissent. In an article circulated to party leaders, he lashed out at those he now called "Rightists."

"They admire bourgeois liberalism," Mao wrote, "and are against the leadership of the Party. They favour democracy and reject centralism. They are opposed to what is essential to the realization of a planned economy, that is, leadership, planning and control in the cultural and educational fields (journalism included). . . ." With a logic that might have amused Kafka, he declared "The kind of co-operation they maintain with us is co-operation only in appearance and not in essence." By appearing to agree with the Party, one could be damned.

The storm broke on 8 June 1957, when an editorial in the *People's Daily* asked "What is this all about?"

"The editorial was a declaration of war," Xi said. It claimed that many people had been exploiting the campaign to attack socialism. So much had been accomplished since Liberation, the *People's Daily* said. Why did the intellectuals think otherwise? On the same day, the Party's Central Committee issued a directive ordering that the rightists be stopped.

The mechanisms required to conduct such a campaign were already well in place. In fact, they were institutionalized. It was a very simple matter to transform the regular political study meetings, which only days earlier had been used as a forum to air criticism, into struggle sessions against the rightists—Party officials simply changed the agenda. The *People's Daily* had served warning, and Xi Ruisen kept his mouth shut: "You see, it's a cardinal crime in China to be labelled anti-socialist, anti-government and anti-party. This article served as an ultimatum to the intellectuals. Why should we continue to speak out? What useful purpose would it serve?"

Big character posters began to appear denouncing Xi, claiming that he had slandered the government. He did not protest his innocence—"that would only invite more trouble."

Mao estimated that of five million intellectuals in China, between three and ten per cent were opponents of Marxism, representing what he referred to as an "antagonistic contradiction." People who had made constructive criticisms during the Hundred Flowers represented "non-antagonistic contradictions," and their suggestions were supposed to be given serious consideration. It did not work out that way.

"Within every department, you had to pick five per cent of your employees and label them Rightists," recalled Xi. "At the end of the campaign, many people became victims just because the quota was not fulfilled. Those in power had to choose someone to be the scapegoats. They had to tell the higher-ups 'our campaign was very successful. We fulfilled the quota'."

The problem for the Party bureaucrats, however, was to find enough rightists. There were not enough from the pool of participants in the Hundred Flowers, and the consequences of failing to fill the quota were serious. Their solution was both simple and frightening.

"Suppose you did not criticize a Rightist at several meetings," Xi said. "That means you must feel for them. You were sure to be labelled a Rightist yourself. If any agency failed to get enough Rightists, they were sure to be blamed for the mistake. If they didn't find enough, they themselves would have been labelled as Rightists." Some of Xi's best friends became his harshest critics.

Most of those branded rightists—and there were half a million of them—were sent to the countryside for thought reform. Punishment for Xi Ruisen was much worse. Together with five of his friends from Yenjing University, he was arrested in February of 1958 and accused of forming a counter-revolutionary clique dedicated to overthrowing the government.

Xi soon realized that it was pointless to defend himself. He was not believed. It was a case of an individual against the power of the State. "If they want you to perish, they can arrange for that to happen, by any pretext. There is no escape. Whether you acknowledge your crime, you accept your crime, you plead guilty or not—" Xi stops, searching for the correct words. After a moment, he finds them.

"You were doomed."

The Chinese legal system is not like the system in the West, but the Communist Party did not create it. During the days of the emperors, a prisoner was assumed to be guilty until proven innocent. He had no right to legal counsel, nor could he defend himself in court. There was no habeas corpus provision, which would forbid arbitrary detention. The Communist government, which worked so hard to distance itself from the past, had not tampered with that basic premise of Chinese justice.

There were no cameras, no reporters or citizens at the trial of Xi Ruisen and his accomplices. No one was called to give evidence. The six men stood in a row, their shaved heads bowed before the judges. No lawyers defended them, and they were not allowed to speak. One judge simply read from a text outlining their "crimes."

Xi Ruisen was sentenced to ten years in prison. The "ringleader" got life; the other sentences ranged between ten and twenty years.

"They were all honest guys, there was no conspiracy. We were not in any position to overthrow the government, even if we had wanted to. We were very minor, simple-minded young men. None of us had any political ambitions. We were innocent."

51

Only four of the men survived imprisonment. The "ringleader" committed suicide in 1962; another died of pneumonia the following year. When Xi was released from prison after nine years (his sentence was reduced because of good behaviour), he found he had no political rights. He was forced to spend the next eleven years in work camps and in the countryside.

His case was finally redressed by Hu Yaobang in 1978, twenty years after the nightmare had begun. Xinhua offered him his old job back, but he declined. He could not face, let alone work with, those who had denounced him in 1958. Instead he became a professor and began to translate Edward Gibbon's *The Rise and Fall of the Roman Empire*, which he now considers his life's work. He credited Deng Xiaoping with saving his life and believed that the terrible days of the past would never return. "You know," he said in early 1989. "We Chinese suffered a lot for mere words, for thought, not action. Twenty years—that has served as a reminder. It has made me even more cautious when I have something to say. But I think I can afford to speak my mind now. There are many things which are unsatisfactory in China today. Inflation, corruption in government, low pay for intellectuals. The West can talk about freedom of speech. I think I am entitled to state in detail my thoughts about the word freedom. I think the most important freedom is not freedom of speech, but freedom from want. It's nothing short of a miracle for a Chinese government to have a billion people housed, clad and fed. If you have nothing to eat, freedom means very little." Xi does think, however, that the years which spanned his loss of freedom have had a devastating effect on Chinese intellectuals. That period left behind, he believed a very detrimental legacy. "Even now," he says, "when the government has adopted open policies and asks for opinion, intellectuals like me still feel inhibited whenever we want to speak out. As the old saying goes 'Once bitten, twice shy'. Even with students today, the experience of their fathers, brothers and relatives will serve as an example."

"As an agonizing reappraisal of my life," reflected Xi, "I should not say anyone ever lured me out to say anything. I myself am to blame for whatever I have done. I think I was too naïve at that time. I didn't know it was a political manoeuvre. I took everything in good faith."

* * *

In 1989, the government was again asking for criticism. But if the students had learned from the experience of their fathers, brothers and relatives—the lesson was to be wary.

In 1956, it was the government itself which asked for intellectuals to state their grievances. Socialist governments in Hungary and Poland had been rocked by popular rebellions that year, and it worried Mao. He hoped the Hundred Flowers campaign would allow people to vent their steam in a controlled way. A more sinister analysis would suggest that the entire campaign had been an elaborate trap—that by encouraging free speech Mao could flush out and remove those he deemed to be potential threats.

In 1989, it was the students who were pressing for talks, and the government which was reluctant to meet with them. Obviously, there were advantages to holding discussions—it could defuse the situation by allowing the young people to voice their complaints (particularly troublesome students could, if necessary, be dealt with later). It could also deflect some of the growing criticism aimed at Zhongnanhai—that the leadership was unresponsive and uncaring.

But such a strategy was also fraught with risk. The student negotiations could rapidly lead to similar demands within state workplaces throughout the capital, perhaps even the country. The whole thing might escalate into a national chorus of disapproval (as had happened during the final days of the Hundred Flowers). What made the situation most troublesome was that Deng had already played one of his aces—the 26 April editorial—and it had been trumped by half a million voices the next day. The scare tactics which proved so effective in 1957 had been jeered at in 1989.

On Saturday, 29 April, both sides met for talks. The government was represented by Yuan Mu, a spokesman for the State Council. Officially sanctioned student federations sent members on their behalf, but, in accordance with the preconditions set out by the government, the newly formed independent students' union was not permitted to attend. Unofficially, however, the organization did have a striking presence at the meeting. In order to circumvent the government directive, many of the union's leaders went to the talks as individuals. Since they did not claim to be representing the illegal union, the state could do little but admit them. Out of fifty students at the meeting, roughly one-third were leaders of the illegitimate group.

The three-hour meeting was taped and later broadcast by China Central Television, coverage which the students had demanded. Throughout, Yuan Mu beamed a patronizing smile for the cameras. "Li Peng and the Communist Party have the same interests as the students," he happily declared, in a tone which suggested his audience was composed of young children. The students, found neither his words nor his delivery convincing. They began peppering the middle-aged bureaucrat with questions on everything from high-level corruption and student beatings to China's invisible leaders.

"We called on Li Peng to come out," challenged one student. "Why can't the people's prime minister meet with the people?" Yuan responded with slippery vagueness and went on to the next question. One student walked out.

"The official press says that there were no beatings of students," continued another, "but a student in our university was seriously wounded."

"We are investigating it," came the polished response, "and the investigation is time-consuming." Yuan answered other questions more directly, though always with the same tone—a syrupy mixture of conciliation and condescension. He confirmed reports that the government would no longer import luxury cars for its officials. He assured students that the leadership's summer convention would not be held at Beidaihe, a resort on the seacoast east of Beijing. He also promised to forward complaints about the extravagant leisure activities of Chinese leaders (Zhao Ziyang is an avid golfer; Li Peng and other leaders regularly enjoy playing tennis at an indoor facility reserved for the national tennis team).

Yuan Mu also passed along a message from the elusive premier. In a written statement, Li Peng called on students to safeguard social stability and help the government overcome the current difficulties. They were urged to end their boycott and return to classes. In addition, Yuan told the students that their demonstrations were disrupting traffic and hurting the economy. As he spoke, ten thousand students were protesting in Tianjin, a coastal city east of the Chinese capital.

Although his words reflected a government which wanted compromise, Yuan's manner did not. His saccharine style mocked the seriousness of the dialogue. Even his appearance—the slicked back hair, the feigned gestures of sincerity—made him appear untrustworthy, almost reptilian. The students had wanted honest answers from a credible representative of the leadership. They received little more than crafty platitudes from a dialectical fox.

Wang Dan, a slender twenty-four-year-old history student at Bei Da who was emerging as a prominent activist, termed the meeting "regrettable" and said it could not even be described as a dialogue. Instead, he likened it to a news conference with the students acting as reporters. Another organizer called the talks "useless", saying the government had shown no willingness to change. Few argued when the students called for the boycott to continue until 4 May.

The students did not shut the door entirely on discussions with the government. It was agreed that there should be another attempt at dialogue. Students decided to allow the state until 4 May to start meaningful negotiations. If the deadline was not met, they would respond with a massive demonstration. The next few days would be used to organize and consolidate the movement.

Until then, it had been largely a fragmented crusade. True, an independent union had been formed shortly after Hu Yaobang's death, under the guise of a "mourning committee." But more often than not, the various campuses had their own groups, their own leaders, their own strategies. The movement was in a fluid state, its nature constantly evolving.

The students understood the synergistic value of combining forces, but finding credible, assertive and willing leaders presented a problem. Some students were unwilling to stand for elections out of fear. It was one thing to march with tens of thousands of others; quite another to be leading them. Chanting with a crowd might be safe, but what about making speeches outside Zhongnanhai? The penalty, many knew, could be prison—a nightmarish possibility. For a few, the dream of democracy was worth that risk. The United Association of Beijing Universities was established.

One of the students willing to gamble his own future was Wang Dan, who had no illusions about the stakes. Asked of his post-university plans, the olive-skinned young man replied that there was no longer a guarantee he would graduate. Sounding much like Fang Lizhi, he even speculated on his own arrest. He was philosophical about that possibility, saying the movement could continue without Wang Dan. "There will," he told a Western reporter, "be more and more people after me." Wall posters denouncing him started to appear at BeiDa, part of a small intimidation campaign by authorities.

The students, meanwhile, were at work on their own propaganda machine. Even with the government's softened stance, it remained crucial to spread the word if the movement was to gain strength. At BeiDa, RenDa and other campuses, student loudspeakers trumpeted democracy and patriotism. Miniature brass-coloured megaphones became trendy fashion accessories, with students turning into impromptu orators whenever the spirit moved them. Dazibao continued to go up even before the ink on them was dry. It was still small-scale. There were no fax machines or walkie-talkies, no guarantee the university telephones were not bugged. But after a lifetime of state-run media, even this rag-tag free press was a stunning accomplishment.

At the Central Academy of Fine Arts, the message was spread in other ways. Students there staged an exhibition of two hundred black-and-white photographs and colour slides taken during the previous two weeks. It chronicled the democracy movement, from those first daring marches to its present state of power. There were pictures of protests, sit-ins—even the attempt to storm the government head-

55

quarters at Zhongnanhai. The institute's liberal authorities allowed the show to go ahead but drew the line at twenty pictures which showed police hitting demonstrators.

Someone visiting Tiananmen Square on Monday, 1 May, however, would have seen little evidence of unrest—the government went ahead with scheduled celebrations to mark the May Day annual holiday. In accordance with tradition, a huge portrait of Sun Yatsen was set up in front of the Monument to the Revolutionary Martyrs, facing Mao's likeness on the Tiananmen rostrum. But unlike past years, the usual pictures of Marx, Engels, Lenin and Stalin were not there. When this point was raised, an official explained that it was the practice in other countries to honour only national heroes—not international figures. He emphasized it "did not indicate any change of political attitude towards Marxism." Thousands lined up for a pilgrimage to the Great Hall of the People, paying one yuan for the privilege. There was no organized parade.

Although students did not demonstrate that day, it was clear that few of them had heeded the sweet words of Yuan Mu. The unrest was spreading to institutes outside the Chinese capital. At Tianjin University, it was reported that seventy per cent of students boycotted classes; the figure was ninety per cent at the city's Nankai University, where authorities warned seniors that they would not be assigned good jobs if they joined the boycott. In Shanghai, several thousand marched until they were forced back by police. A group of student leaders from that city travelled to Beijing to discuss coordinating efforts with their northern comrades. Rumours circulated that police in the city of Wuhan had crushed pro-democracy activities with a combination of tear gas and cattle prods. In Beijing itself, the number of university students boycotting classes was estimated at seventy thousand, slightly less than half of the total enrolment.

Although students had been warned not to attack the reputation of Chinese leaders, criticisms and slurs continued. One Beijing student openly accused the mayor of Tianjin, Li Ruihuan, of getting his job through nepotism. Li is the son-in-law of Wan Li, the chairman of the National People's Congress. The student said Wan had pulled strings to secure the post.

The government wanted to put an end to all this, and so the talks continued. But like the first session, subsequent efforts proved fruitless. The students accused the government of not taking them seriously; the government, in turn, tried to placate them by stressing that it shared their concerns. Students fumed; Yuan Mu smiled. By Tuesday, 2 May, students had met with high-ranking officials on three separate days without making any real progress.

Many were not just disturbed over the lack of headway. They were also angry about the media coverage, charging that the government had edited videotape of the first talks before broadcasting them. In frustration, representatives of the United Association of Beijing Universities delivered copies of a petition to top government and Party organs. Dozens of students took the documents to the Standing Committee of the National People's Congress, the State Council and the Central Committee of the Chinese Communist Party. This time, they did not have to kneel on the steps of the Great Hall of the People. Their petitions were accepted.

Accepted, but not welcomed. Their charter listed twelve demands concerning dialogue with the government.

The first point addressed the issue of fairness, saying "Equal opportunities for speeches and questions should be guaranteed for both parties." This was, perhaps, a dig at Yuan Mu—a man who seemed to thrive on monologue. Other demands would be much more difficult for the government to tolerate. For instance, the state had already made clear its position on the status of organizations formed during the unrest: they were illegal and would not be recognized. Yet the students demanded not only that such groups be included in the dialogue, but also that the government disregard established, legal federations. "We absolutely refuse," read the petition, "to let such associations designate student representatives. We also refuse to recognize the representatives of those who were unilaterally and secretly invited by the government to be student representatives without the permission of the masses of the students." Another point outlined how the rogue union would go about choosing delegates for future talks.

The document also reflected the dissatisfaction many students felt over the conduct of government representatives. It asked for delegates "at or above" the level of Politburo member, vice-chairman of the National People's Congress Standing Committee, or vice-premier of the State Council.

Two of the stipulations dealt simply with protocol: how long each question should be, time limits on responses, invited guests, venues and so on. Others laid out strict guidelines to ensure free and unbiased media coverage. "Both Chinese and foreign reporters," read one passage, "should be allowed to do on-the-spot coverage of the event. The Central TV Station and the Central People's Broadcasting Station should broadcast the whole dialogue live. . . ." Another demand stated that after each round of talks, the results "must be truthfully reported" by the state-run media (exactly who would determine the 'truth' was not dealt with). Almost as an afterthought, the peti-

57

tion said that if the two sides came to any agreement, they "should make joint statements on them, with signatures signed by the two on the documents."

The petition ended with a menacing caveat: "If we are not given a reply before 12 noon on 3 May, we shall reserve our right to continue our demonstration." The first round of talks, it suggested, should commence on 4 May, at 8:30 A.M., at BeiDa.

The students were driving a very hard bargain. Their demands were not so much calls for political flexibility as they were a declaration of political independence. In addition, the petition carried a threat: give in by the deadline or face another demonstration. It would be asking a lot of any government—let alone one as authoritarian as China's—to accept a document of that tenor.

The same day, the United Association of Beijing Universities held a press conference at the BeiDa library. The event, staged to bolster both the coverage and the credibility of the group's new petition, was predictable: a spokesman roundly denounced previous talks as a sham and called for a balanced dialogue. More revealing was a brief statement made by an association leader. The activist accused the state of trying to "deceive public opinion by appearing to concede to student demands." The words reflected the same deep distrust voiced by Mao Zedong some thirty years earlier: "The kind of co-operation they maintain with us is co-operation only in appearance and not in essence."

A cool player was soon to enter the fray. During the coming month, students would regard him as many things: an adversary, a saviour, a hero and, ultimately, a martyr. That man was Zhao Ziyang.

A popular couplet in the southern province of Sichuan during the 1970s went "If you want *liang* (grain), go get Zhao Ziyang." Throughout the 1980s Zhao carefully cultivated that popularity by overseeing the bold economic reforms designed to make China a modern industrial nation. Fond of quoting American futurist Alvin Toffler, he was, in a sense, China's visionary. He saw the potential for high technology and encouraged its development; he dreamed of the day when China could be counted as a modern industrial power.

Just as important, Zhao was also a man with whom Western politicians and business executives felt comfortable. His easy manner, Western suits—even his passion for golf—made him more approachable than the country's aging leaders. In 1987, American television viewers saw him as both the patron saint of reform and as a relaxed and affable man who enjoyed a beer while being interviewed. He inspired confidence in China as a good trading power, made the growing nation appear as dynamic as himself. He seemed the man Deng needed for the job, a smooth-talking sophisticate with his eye on the horizon.

Innovation was his specialty; he was in no way shackled by Marxist orthodoxy. "We must not bind ourselves," he said in 1979, "as silkworms do within cocoons." For Zhao, as long as the principle of public ownership of production facilities was maintained, anything else that promoted economic growth was acceptable. His words echoed those of the pre-Cultural Revolution Deng Xiaoping. "It hardly matters if a cat is white or black," Deng once said: "As long as it catches mice, it's a good cat." Zhao's drive was matched by his competence. Someone once remarked that if he had been an American, he would have become the president of IBM.

Zhao was born to wealthy, landowning parents in 1919—not the kind of lineage smiled upon in socialist circles. In spite of that background, he had joined the Communist Youth League at the age of thirteen, the Party by the time he was nineteen. Although his first revolutionary work was in his native Henan Province, it was in Guangdong—the province to which Hong Kong is appended—where he made his reputation. At forty-one, he was designated party secretary of the province, the youngest man to win such a post. During the early 1960s, Zhao supervised the implementation of Deng's agricultural policies—strategies which had helped end the disastrous famines of the Great Leap Forward.

Politically, Zhao was an opportunist. During the 1950s, he dutifully orchestrated a purge against those party and government workers who were accused of being corrupt, opposing land reform or harbouring ties with Taiwan. During the anti-rightist campaign, Zhao helped send eighty thousand people to the countryside for "rectification." When the Cultural Revolution struck and Deng was labelled a "capitalist roader," Zhao Ziyang denounced his mentor in order to save himself. The attempt failed, and in 1967 he was paraded through the streets of Guangzhou (Canton) wearing a dunce cap. For a period of four years, he disappeared. But by 1971 he was back in favour and on his way to Inner Mongolia to serve as the region's party secretary. Soon he returned to Guangdong in his old post.

It was in Sichuan Province where he made his mark. A mountainous southern region, renowned as much for its poverty as its spicy food, Sichuan is China's largest, most populous province. When Zhao arrived to take command in 1975, Sichuan's 100 million people were suffering from food shortages; the provincial Communist Party seemed more interested in political infighting than in solving the problem. Zhao took charge like a corporate manager, giving the vast region a thorough shakeup. He disbanded the inefficient People's Communes and fostered free markets, cottage industries and greater autonomy for larger industries. In four years, he created 600,000 new jobs, increased industrial output eighty-one per cent and boosted agricultural production by twenty-five per cent. When he was summoned to Beijing in 1979, as a vice-premier and Politburo member, his programs in Sichuan became the model for the nation. Within six months, he had replaced Mao's anointed heir, Hua Guofeng, as premier. For the next six years, the triumvirate of Zhao, Hu Yaobang and Deng Xiaoping basked in economic growth and near-universal popularity.

But, as Zhao soon discovered, there can be too much of a good thing. Economic growth spurred on inflation, and in the mid-1980s cracks began to appear in the facade of modern industrial progress. Prices crept up slowly but steadily during 1986-87; by 1988 the official inflation rate had hit a staggering thirty-six per cent. It was simply too profound an increase for government subsidies to cover.

Zhao Ziyang was at least partly to blame. With his participation, the government had eliminated most agricultural price controls in order to stimulate the economy. When prices went up, peasants would produce more, and then with an abundance of supply, prices would go down again. It was pure market economy thinking. But the prices did not go down. By early 1989, some Beijingers said they were spending eighty-five per cent of their salaries on food. (This is quite possible, as Chinese danwei usually provide heavily subsidized housing and medical care for employees and their families.)

To soften the effect of inflation, the government refused to let the price of some products rise. Companies were told that they would have to cope by lowering their production costs. Many did not listen. Instead, they simply stopped production rather than lose money. Students throughout China found in the autumn of 1988 that they often had to share textbooks. The reason was simple: publishers were forbidden to increase prices; paper manufacturers were allowed to hike them. The presses stopped running. Farmers, too, felt the pinch of price controls. In many cases, they switched their production to more profitable crops, causing shortages of other goods.

In August of 1988 a wave of panic buying swept the nation. People snapped up whatever they thought might become more expensive. One woman bought a twenty-year supply of matches. More people began to purchase foreign currency illegally, rather than watch the value of their own money decline. The reforms Zhao had championed for more than a decade were not so popular anymore. Forced to react, he pledged in a New Year's address on 1 January 1989 that the government would slash inflation. By March, the state had cancelled or postponed hundreds of construction projects as it attempted to "rectify the reform." In its race to modernize, China had outpaced itself.

The economic difficulties also bred social problems. Beijing, Shanghai, Guangzhou and other major cities saw the arrival of millions of "floaters"—restless, jobless, young people who had come from the countryside in search of jobs that did not exist. Uneducated and unmarketable, they often turned to petty crime.

Zhao had earlier tried to deal with a separate problem. In late 1988, he launched an anti-corruption campaign designed to rid China of those officials who had taken advantage of the reforms. Telephone hotlines were set up for citizens to lodge complaints. More than a hundred thousand people were investigated; a few were executed to press home the government's seriousness. In the streets, however, there was grumbling that the campaign only extended to mid-level cadres. Zhao's own sons were reported to be making a fortune in southern China, and he had to apologize to the Central Committee for their aggressive business practices.

The Party leader was not the only target of such rumours. One of the more interesting denials on the pages of the *People's Daily* concerned Deng Pufang—the son of Deng Xiaoping. The younger Deng had become a paraplegic during the Cultural Revolution when Red Guards threw him out of a third-storey window. By the mid-1980s, he headed a national organization for the handicapped and a mid-sized tourist company based in Shanghai. It was rumoured, however, that he used the charity to funnel money into his own pockets. The story was so persistent that the *People's Daily* finally gave it widespread currency by issuing a denial early in 1989. "I can account for every penny," Young Deng said. The story did nothing to end the rumours.

When the pro-democracy movement continued into early May, a black joke concerning Zhao and Deng started making the rounds in Beijing:

"What can we do to end this?" asks a worried Deng. "Nothing seems to work."

"There's only one way to stop the unrest." replies Zhao. "Two people must die."

Deng looks up in alarm. "Two people?" he asks, fearing the worst. "You mean. . . ."

"That's right," Zhao says. "Your son and my son."

Actually, the Party leader did not have the same fears about the student unrest as did his patron. He felt that there was room for genuine conciliation and hoped a compromise could be reached. With the right candour, the government might be able to keep everyone happy.

He also knew that nothing would stop a demonstration on 4 May. Even before Hu Yaobang died, students were planning to march on that day. To ignore such an important anniversary, many students felt, would be a disservice to their predecessors.

On 4 May 1919, about five thousand BeiDa students had marched to Tiananmen Square in protest against the Versailles Treaty that followed the First World War; they believed that the agreement had sold out China. True, it did force Germany to give up its Chinese outpost in Shandong province, but the concession was then handed over to Japan—on even more humiliating terms than before. Students demanded that Chinese representatives to the Peace Conference refuse to sign the treaty, saying it would be better to have its terms forcibly imposed than to submit to them voluntarily. The demonstration on 4 May was an outburst of public frustration which sparked a nationalist intellectual revolution throughout the country. The Chinese Communist Party, which was formed in Shanghai in 1921, still traces its roots to the "May Fourth Movement." Seventy years later, state-run newspapers admitted that the official goal of that movement, "a new culture featuring Democracy and Science," was still a distant dream.

The Party had its own May Fourth activities planned, and it was to one of these that Zhao took his peace offering. On 3 May he addressed three thousand hand-picked young men and women at the Great Hall of the People. They were officially considered to be the best and brightest of China's youth and included seventy students who were honoured for "their outstanding contributions to socialist reconstruction and reform." Although Deng was not present, almost every prominent leader was. It was a clear display of party unity. President Yang Shangkun, Li Peng, Wan Li and Hu Qili all applauded Zhao's words, words which had been carefully chosen to appease. Zhao's speech would be the lead item on television that night; his job was to convince the nation that the Chinese government was full of good intentions.

"When we have stability we sometimes aren't aware of its value," he began. "But once we lose it we feel deep regret. . . . Stability, sober-mindedness, order and legality are required not only for economic construction and reform, but also for democracy and science."

He admitted that the party had made mistakes and said that student demands to end corruption, promote democracy and improve education were goals the government shared. Like wayward sheep, he called them to return to the flock: "Let's understand one another in the future, do a better job and cross rivers in the same boat in stability and unity."

Reform, said Zhao, could not come overnight. There were no

shortcuts. He asked the young people to merge their personal responsibility with the destiny of the nation, and each individual's role with the collective. If the disruptions continued, warned Zhao, a country of promise would be turned into a country of hopelessness and turbulence.

Just a few hours before Zhao attempted to win the students' sympathy, Yuan Mu was doing what he could to antagonize them once again. The spokesman told a news conference that the government had rejected demands for more talks. Yuan Mu could scarcely conceal his contempt for the students' petition. He noted that the document demanded that both sides be treated as equals, yet the students were deciding who the government could choose to represent it. He called it, with some justification, "unreasonable, emotionally impulsive and menacing to the government in the form of an ultimatum." He also rejected demands for official recognition of the student union, implying that the association was unrepresentative and riddled with factions. "If, because of one single event, some part of the students can declare the establishment of an organization, then I think it will lead to greater disunity among the students," Yuan maintained. "When the students are divided under these circumstances, it is not appropriate to establish organizations through illegal or non-democratic processes."

But when asked if the government would take action against those responsible for such illegal and non-democratic institutions, Yuan said no: "There are students and other people who have engaged in behind-the-scenes activities. Those people are very vicious. But at present we are not planning to take any action. At present the good and the bad are mixed together. These conditions are not favourable for detentions or arrests. . . ."

"One of the basic reasons," Yuan oozed, "is that we really love and cherish our students from the bottom of our hearts."

Yuan named names. He said Fang Lizhi and the U.S.-based Chinese Alliance for Democracy were playing a role in the unrest. The Alliance had been declared a "reactionary" organization by China, which claimed that anti-communists in Taiwan funded it. The leadership was so hostile towards this group that students who had participated in its activities were sometimes jailed upon their return to China. Pressed for details about Fang, Yuan would only say "His remarks and future facts will show what a role he is playing in the current unrest." Fang denied any involvement, and student leader Wuer Kaixi declared that neither Fang nor the Alliance were influencing their activities.

The press conference ended with Yuan admitting that students might ignore government appeals and march on 4 May. "I think more and more students will come to seriously consider the remarks that we have made," he said. "And we hope there will be no massive demonstrations tomorrow." Yuan Mu paused briefly. "But maybe my hope will not come true."

A middle-aged woman and two soldiers stood at the entrance to BeiDa the following morning. The uniformed men guarded the gate and tried to wave off foreign journalists, many of whom simply waved back before walking in. The woman had the reporters sign a register before allowing them to pass.

At 7:30 A.M., the campus had neither the look nor the feel of unrest. Students, many still yawning, walked slowly to and from the shower house. Others sat on steps or leaned against buildings, eating their breakfast from tin bowls. A few gathered in small groups for seemingly casual conversation. The nervous energy one might have expected to find was absent. Demonstrations, it appeared, were becoming almost routine.

By 8:00 A.M., the pace began to pick up. Clumps of students started to gather at the Triangle to read the daily offering of dazibao and foreign press clippings. Loudspeakers played the Chinese national anthem and the Internationale; megaphones crackled to life. Smiling young men and women strode out of their dormitories with placards and cloth banners. They gathered near a makeshift podium, chattering amongst themselves and grinning for news photographers. A few of the protestors held up their banners for comrades to admire. But it still did not look like a demonstration. There were maybe two or three hundred students in all, hardly the thousands reporters had anticipated. Then, from somewhere, the rapid staccato of firecrackers was followed by the clash of a gong. The cluster of students started to march.

"And so it begins," remarked one journalist to a colleague. And so it did. Within moments, throngs of students carrying megaphones and banners joined in. They seemed to appear from nowhere, yet from everywhere. Students carrying banners from institutes in Tianjin and Guangzhou and other cities popped up in the crowd. Soon, there were about four thousand people. Beaming, they sang the Internationale as they headed towards the street.

Thousands of people were waiting for them, cheering them on as they passed through BeiDa's main gate. Foreign cameramen and photographers climbed on crates, bicycles and each other to capture the scene. Some had even set up on the roof of the building directly across the street. The students waved and chanted as they turned east.

When they reached the first major intersection, the marchers turned south towards RenDa. Thousands lined the streets, smiling and clapping as the youths turned the corner. Traffic was impossible. Cars and taxis could not move; public buses were similarly stranded. But few people seemed to mind. Passengers waved their approval, and in some cases got off buses to shout support for the students. Several truck drivers invited photojournalists to use their vehicles as platforms. The march continued to swell.

RenDa provided the protestors with an emotional and physical boost. Thousands of students carrying banners and school flags answered the call of the Internationale, flowing past the gates and towards its source. The song, it seemed, had become the movement's Pied Piper. Again, the students were cheered on by an equally sizable crowd of regular folk. Factory workers, food vendors, secretaries— even older Beijingers wearing traditional Mao suits—all looked eager to join the parade, but as on 27 April, the march was shaped to be a statement made by students and students alone. Marshals flanked the edges of the protest, allowing only journalists or those with student cards inside. Advance men rushed ahead with megaphones, urging cameramen to take their shots but keep their distance.

At the intersection just past RenDa, a traffic policeman stopped vehicles to allow the protest to move through. Scores of other officers, some of whom had been trucked to the corner at 7:00 A.M., watched silently as the students marched by. A few kilometres south, rows of police were taking up their positions. They spanned the street in tight rows, waiting on a tiny bridge that spanned a narrow canal near the National Library. The students pushed on.

As this marching mass moved forward, a similar group was advancing from the eastern end of the city. Students from institutes in that area had arranged with their northwestern counterparts to meet at Tiananmen Square.

A very different event was taking place at the hallowed square: ten thousand high school students were lined up in rigid rows, taking their vows as new members of the Communist Youth League. They promised to abide by Party discipline, study hard and struggle for Communism—everything their older brothers and sisters were at that very moment defying.

Fifteen kilometres and an ideological world away, tens of thousands of students from BeiDa, RenDa, Qinghua and smaller institutes struggled to get past police lines. It did not take long. The barricade stretched like putty, weakened, and collapsed. A mighty roar drowned out the megaphones.

Some of the students wore headbands identifying their university; others appeared satisfied to march with their classmates behind their school flag. Several carried banners in English and other languages for the benefit of foreign journalists. "Hello Mr Democracy," read one. Another, with the simple message "Thank You BBC," underlined the gratitude many students felt for shortwave radio coverage. A few students opted for more symbolic and cryptic displays. One young man carried a heavy piece of cardboard attached to a stick. Affixed to the cardboard were a pair of regular shoes, a belt and a pair of green runners worn by People's Liberation Army soldiers. They were linked by a mathematical equation: shoes + belt ≠ army runners. Bystanders and marchers alike laughed, hooted and cheered wherever this banner went. Many journalists could do little but scratch their heads and snap pictures. A protestor deciphered the bizarre placard as a reference to the beating of students at Zhongnanhai the previous week. The shoes and belt represented a student; the runners, the PLA. In other words, soldiers should not beat students—it does not add up.

Much more accessible was the ten-metre-long banner of white cloth which a number of students carried. In its centre was a single black square. "It means we have a mouth," explained a student, "but we have no voice."

For a movement without a voice, the students made a tremendous amount of noise as they strode towards the centre of Beijing. Near Tiananmen Square, there was a flurry of police and army activity. Jeeps and trucks ferried soldiers up and down *hutongs*, or alleyways. Police double-marched through side-streets, heading to unknown locations. On some tree-lined lanes, young policemen and their commanders merely sat down in the shade. It was difficult to tell whether the authorities planned to stop the march, or merely wanted extra security near the square.

The answer came as the students neared the downtown core. When they were about two or three kilometres from Zhongnanhai, still heading east, hundreds of police appeared. They linked arms at the last major intersection before the government headquarters, hoping to stop the students from reaching their goal. The police were young, in their late teens or early twenties. They spanned the entire width of Changan Boulevard, bracing themselves for the coming assault. There were fourteen separate rows, with a space of perhaps one metre separating each. All but one row faced the demonstrators; the last lines of defence had their backs to them. On the eastern side of this fourteenth line were an additional two rows of people. These were not police, or at least did not appear to be. They looked more like workers—middle-aged men and women wearing regular civilian clothes. All of them had special work cards pinned to their shirts. A Chinese observer speculated that they had been assigned the job to show that workers did not side with the students. Tens of thousands of bystanders, however, did. They swarmed into the intersection well in advance of the demonstration, showing both support and defiance. At one point, they massed towards a traffic island where a policeman was trying in vain to keep lanes clear. People tugged at his sleeves, straining to pull him off. They were not malicious but seemed instead like youngsters playing "king of the castle." The policeman managed to restore order, only to have a group of people actually mount the pedestal and push him off. He got back up and briefly convinced others to get back down. Once again, they climbed back up. The policeman finally gave up, and with a smile, left his post. An enormous cheer went up among onlookers.

Many of those watching this drama unfold had superb vantage points. Hundreds of people were perched in trees, on billboards, walls and roofs, looking like exotic creatures in a zoo exhibit. An officer tried to order them down from one building but gave up when few complied. Workers not already in the street, meanwhile, leaned precariously out windows, straining to see all the action.

Such curiosity does not always mean support, for China is a nation of watchers. Many of its citizens are accomplished voyeurs of even the most mundane occurrences. Everything from bicycle accidents to broken eggs routinely draws large crowds; the drama of human conflict is a bonus. When arguments occur in the street or market, many Chinese cluster around, often interrupting the dispute to offer their own opinions. When police pull over cars for traffic violations, accusor and accused are often surrounded in a smothering embrace of instant jurors. Some younger Chinese find such practices repulsive, saying they only serve to demonstrate how meaningless and dull life has become.

On 4 May, however, the tens of thousands of people filling the streets were not staring blankly from the sidelines, nor did they find life tedious. They were cheering, shouting, even giggling, as they surged into the intersection.

The excitement increased as the students approached the intersection; the applause and shouting became a continuous roar. Defiant energy pulsed through the crowd, as the watchers and the watched became one. The wave swept forward. "It's tough for you police!" chanted some.

The front lines held for a moment, then began yielding like taffy. Students and bystanders kept on pushing, testing the pliancy of this human elastic. The first row snapped; the second, the third. There was no stopping the students. Many of the police began a rapid retreat to the sidewalk. The remaining rows tried in vain to hold their ground. Some of the young officers appeared uncomfortable with

67

their role: they were the same age as many of the demonstrators, and a few, finding themselves face to face with former classmates, averted their eyes to the ground.

Behind this last line of defence were dozens of journalists, photographers and camera crews. Many stood on short ladders, in order to take pictures over the green police hats. Reporters and others, Chinese included, braced themselves around the bases of these ladders. They were not just worried about the impending crush of students; they were on the lookout for what they termed "kickers." These were reportedly agents of the Public Security Bureau who had been told to make the lives of correspondents as miserable as possible. About two weeks earlier, one of them had given the ladder of an NBC cameraman a well-placed boot outside Zhongnanhai. The man had broken his leg when he toppled to the ground with his camera. Another photojournalist was said to have suffered an arm injury under similar circumstances. Cameramen were no longer taking chances.

Even with these defensive huddles, it was still chaotic when the crowds broke through. Exhilarated, the students rushed forward with abandon; ladders began to sway despite the protection. Photographers hurriedly clambered down, only to be promptly swept away with the masses. It was like trying to fight against turbulent river rapids.

The noise was deafening. Camera crews and journalists shouted desperately at one another, relaying meeting points as they floated separate ways in the churning mass. Radio reporters had to yell directly into their microphones to overcome the sound. It was no mere cheering. It was an instinctive, almost guttural cry of victory as the marchers flowed past the police and towards Tiananmen Square. They were about one kilometre from their goal.

A roughly equal distance to the east of the square, tens of thousands more continued their trek. The two rivers would soon converge on the north side of the square, directly in front of Mao's portrait.

When the two sides did meet, the frenzied mood was replaced by one of patriotism and discipline. Those holding the lead banners from each march walked slowly towards each other, stopping about twenty metres apart. Students formed two lines along the edges to complete a rectangle. Then they sat down, leaving the centre clear of demonstrators and bystanders. Several students acted as public relations coordinators, seeking out camera crews and inviting them inside the clearing. When the television equipment had been set up, two students marched solemnly to the centre of the rectangle. They carried the Chinese flag. The Chinese national anthem, followed by the Internationale, rose from the crowd. It was a powerful and cleverly orchestrated climax.

After roughly fifteen minutes, the symbolic display ended. Megaphones cued the crowds, which dutifully chanted as they moved into Tiananmen. Although police had earlier been in the square, no serious attempts were made to stop the students, who milled about, listening to speeches, reading banners and talking democracy under the hot sun. One of their leaders, Wuer Kaixi, told the crowd that students reserved the right to stage future demonstrations. They responded enthusiastically. Cheers also went up as a group representing a Hong Kong students' association made the rounds.

As the sweltering afternoon dragged on, many decided to head towards the Qianmen district, to the south of Mao's tomb. The shopping area is filled with small shops and food stalls—the perfect place to buy a cold drink and a quick snack. At the southern boundary of the square, two rows of traffic police stood across the roads that flank the square. They allowed the students to leave, but when those same students tried to get back they were refused entry. Chinese and foreign journalists were also denied permission to return. One Westerner managed to convince the officer in charge that he was working for China Central Television. "These drinks are for my comrades," he told the man. "If I can't get back inside my leader will be very angry. What is your name?" The officer let the reporter pass. Other journalists were not so lucky.

Those who could not get back into Tiananmen Square did not miss much. The demonstration was winding down. The students had made their point and the heat was starting to take its toll. Tired but satisfied, many began the long march back to their schools. They had again defied their government and won.

Yet, even as they walked back to their campuses, Beijing students could not resist taking one more jab. Thousands of marchers heading towards the Haidian university district stopped outside Radio Beijing long enough to accuse the state-run network of broadcasting lies. Farther west, they parked themselves outside of China Central Television, where they called for greater freedom of the press. CCTV, in turn, called for the police. The students were gone before they arrived.

It had been a remarkable day, one filled with thousands of indelible vignettes: an old man applauding and cheering with the vigour of forgotten youth, a middle-aged woman hiking up her skirt as she triumphantly climbed a traffic pedestal, a young student, his hand held high in victory.

That white banner with the black square no longer seemed needed. On 4 May, the students had found a voice; a collective voice which spoke on behalf of hundreds of thousands—people who cheered them every step of the way.

4

A Revolution is Like a Bicycle

The sound of laughter rippled down the street as the singing got nearer. At first it was hard to distinguish the tune; only a few notes could be heard above the chanting and the recurrent strains of the Internationale. But as it came closer to the Beijing National Library south of the university district that 4 May, the melody was unmistakable. Some students were singing "Frère Jacques." But they were not crooning about a sleepy brother; they had changed the words to suit the occasion and the crowd giggled and cheered. The students marched on, endlessly serenading an appreciative audience.

> *People's Daily, People's Daily,*
> Really strange, Really strange.
> Always printing lies, Always printing lies.
> Really strange, Really strange.

For the next week, the melody would be sung throughout the city in a variety of forms. Students would tailor the lyrics depending on which state media outlet they were targeting, but it was a popular tune each time. Bystanders smiled knowingly and applauded the audacious inventiveness of the students. The songs seemed to capture the infectious innocence of the whole student movement, a youthful enthusiasm so often employed to mock and shame the government. On some occasions, they did not even have to change the words. As the students sang the Chinese national anthem, they savoured the irony of the original version:

> The Peoples of China are in their critical hour.
> Everyone must roar his defiance.
> Arise, Arise, Arise. . . .

They loved the lively Communist folk melodies from the war of Liberation. Gongs and drums would sometimes accompany them, as they might have done when soldiers from the Eighth Route Army marched more than forty years before. This song echoed through the streets to the festive accompaniment of an accordion:

> Workers, peasants and soldiers unite,
> All of one mind march together.
> We unite to struggle for democracy and freedom.
> The victory belongs to us.

When they were not singing, the marchers were inventing new chants and slogans. This chant began slowly, then accelerated to a frenzied staccato: "XINHUA TELLS LIES. IT SHOULD GET RID OF THIS BAD HABIT." In Chinese, the sound was electrifying.

Increasingly, the songs and chants concerned China's state-controlled media, but by the time the refrain from the Frère Jacques song became well known, it was virtually out of date. Even on 4 May, what was "really strange" was not that *People's Daily* printed lies. What was strange was that it was actually beginning to tell the truth.

When Hu Qili told newspaper editors on 28 April that they could report on the "actual state of affairs," every media outlet was slow to test the waters. Just the day before, the government had fired Qin Benli from the *New Economic Herald* in Shanghai for going too far. The offering of editorial latitude was so sudden and so unexpected—many did not know how to deal with it. For the next week, reporters showed more caution than independence. The English language *China Daily* newspaper, for instance, offered this tepid description of the student meetings with Yuan Mu on 2 May. "While many students and Beijing citizens felt relieved and satisfied to see the dialogues going on, quite a number of students expressed their dissatisfaction over their results and the way they had been organized."

Even that watered-down version was rare for Chinese reportage, since it stated explicitly that the two sides remained at odds. When it comes to domestic issues, Chinese journalism has traditionally shown a restraint bordering on toadyism. The media faithfully report whatever happens to be the current government line, but the Communist Party has charted a zigzag course through the years, and its direction still continues to change. Wen Huaisha found past inconsistencies hilarious: "Let's divide every ten years into a period, 1957, '67, '77 and '87. The party has had four different interpretations of the word 'socialism'. You see, the final authority of interpreting socialism rests on the Party Central Committee, not on me. So when we say

'Stick to the socialist road', I don't know what you are referring to. The socialism of what period?"

Most journalists try to evade this problem by refusing to interpret the significance of a specific event or policy. Usually, they diligently convey the latest official party or government version—with a total absence of critical or opposing views. Such reportage may lack dynamism, but it is certainly safe.

The tendency to err on the side of caution is pervasive. In 1988, for instance, a high-ranking government minister made a frank admission at a news conference that the state was not doing enough for education and might have to shake up its bureaucracy to improve the situation. A newspaper reporter attending the briefing found it all rather exciting. "Wasn't he being brave?" she confided to a foreigner, later adding "There's no way I can use any of that."

Many Westerners weaned on the attitudes of the McCarthy era might imagine that, in "Red China," party bosses make daily dicta to their journalistic minions—who then dutifully brainwash the masses. True, even in 1989, reporters were sometimes explicitly told what to write. But for the majority of stories, there is a far more insidious form of control.

As the newswoman demonstrated with her comments, reporters exercise a degree of self-censorship that goes against the grain of the Western news tradition. Given the chance to report on an admission that might prove controversial, the reporter chose to kill the story and write instead the usual platitudes for which such news conference are renowned. It did not matter that it would be the minister—not she—who would be held responsible were there repercussions. She still decided to take the easy route.

Mao Zedong once said that what people write is far more serious than what they say, and he filled the jails with thousands of such scribblers. Little wonder, then, that few took chances even during the leniency of the ever-changing 1980s. Although newspapers had dropped the ideological idioms of the Cultural Revolution days, when phrases such as "imperialist lackeys" and "capitalist running dogs" were in vogue, they still filled their pages with the government's terminology of the day. Catchphrases like "reform," "modernization" and "democratic dictatorship" could be found in almost any issue of a Chinese paper. There were exceptions. Some publications, such as the *Guangming Daily* and the *World Economic Herald*, gained increasing respect from intellectuals for their independence. Before the democracy movement took hold, even the government seemed quite content to relinquish a portion of its monopoly on thought. In fact, the *China Daily* frequently quoted controversial words from both papers.

When the winds of state began to change, however, Qin Benli discovered that even limited autonomy can be swept away with a single gust.

The fear that journalists must always dodge the storm clouds of the Chinese political scene inspired one Chinese writer to demand a better way. The journalist, a man named Ah Min, suggested in the *Press and Publication Journal* of September 1988:

> The worry [that reporters might lose current press freedom] apparently comes from the fact that the climate for the press keeps changing from clear to overcast and back again. In order to avoid or reduce the cloud cover I believe something must be done when the sky is still clear. . . . We should make the best of the current democratic atmosphere. I suggest that our newspapers become more open-minded and leave some room for opposing views, so that we can clarify some questions through debate. As the Chinese saying goes 'it is better to resolve a feud than to create one'.

Perhaps Hu Qili had that saying in mind when he made his dramatic announcement to the newspaper editors. Soon, the caution and reluctance gave way, and by 4 May, increasing numbers of reporters were beginning to drink in a new-found independence—and were thirsty for more. One week after the *People's Daily* denounced student activities, its reporters joined in with them.

Some people were shocked when they learned that one hundred of the paper's employees were planning to march with the students. It seemed inconceivable that reporters from the Communist Party's own newspaper—the voice of the Politburo—could be allowed to take such a step. Even more incredible was that the Chinese media actually reported it, and that there were not one hundred people, but *two hundred*, who chanted "The people have the right to know." Every issue of the major newspapers showed new signs of this journalistic emancipation. Reports quoted students declaring theirs to be the "largest patriotic movement in the last seventy years." Photographs showed protestors carrying banners and placards with democratic phrases. Written accounts described "a sea of white flags and slogan banners" that read "DIALOGUES SHOULD BE SINCERE," "GIVE US HUMAN RIGHTS," "THE NEWS MEDIA SHOULD TELL THE TRUTH" and "OPPOSE OFFICIAL PROFITEERING." The clouds had parted too late for Qin Benli, but the sun was now shining over China's journalistic skies.

Xinhua's reports remained lacklustre, and many outlets ceased to rely on them. Instead, they sent their own reporters and photographers. The *China Youth News* reported demonstrations in eleven other Chinese cities, including marches of more than ten thousand people in Shanghai, Xi'an and Wuhan. The *People's Daily* wrote "several hundred thousand spectators watched the students march along the streets. Many of them donated cold drinks and food."

To student leaders, this attention gave them a sense of increased legitimacy that had yet to be granted by the government. Although courting the media, particularly the foreign press, would ultimately become a serious liability for the students, in early May the media and the students thrived on a symbiotic relationship. Little wonder, then, that students would spend the next week emphasizing the need for a free press. Reporters would do their own share from the inside. Together, they formed an implicit alliance that was sealed under the spring sunshine in Tiananmen Square. "Long live journalists with a conscience," the students chanted. "Long live the students," came the reply.

"Have you seen the petition?" an excited reporter asked at CCTV on Friday, 5 May. "We're demanding press freedom and talks with the government." She was asked if she had signed it. "Oh no. Of course not. I want to, but only three people in the whole building have signed so far. Maybe if fifty people, or a hundred people sign here, then I will too." She smiled and slipped away. She had to go to the Asian Development Bank meeting at the Great Hall of the People.

Chinese journalists are skilled at the art of interpreting the veiled messages implicit in the words and actions of government leaders. When Zhao Ziyang was flanked by the other leaders as he spoke to selected youths on 3 May, it was obvious that the state had reversed its position since the 26 April editorial. Zhao was in charge, and it seemed his words would set the tone in the future. So when he spoke to the Asian Development Bank on 4 May and urged extensive consultations and dialogues with students, workers, intellectuals and others, journalists were quick to seize the opening. A petition began circulating within twenty-four hours of Zhao's speech. It called for talks with party and government officials "following promises by the authorities to conduct broad contacts and dialogues with people from all occupations."

Li Peng was also restrained when he spoke to the Development Bank meeting. The premier made stability the key theme of his speech, saying it was close at hand. "Now that the students have resumed classes and the dialogue between the government and the students will continue, I am very happy," he said. Li also stressed that the situation was under control. "The government has adopted calm, proper and correct measures, which have helped to prevent the unrest from spreading," he said. "I can tell you responsibly, that the political situation in China is stable."

75

That was the message he wanted to convey to the four thousand bankers, industrialists and financial experts who had come to the annual meeting. This was the first time in its twenty-two-year history that the Asian Development Bank had held a meeting in China. Delegates and observers were on hand from more than one hundred other nations. Understandably, Chinese leaders were concerned that social unrest could drive away much-needed investment dollars. A large part of the restraint shown on 4 May and earlier was aimed at convincing these moneyed men and women that the student movement was a minor disagreement which would be mutually resolved. The strategy appeared to pay off.

Zhang Xiaobin, a Chinese businessman who had helped set up China's first venture capital company in 1985, spent a lot of time discussing the investment climate with delegates and bankers. The question of the student protests was controversial, and he played the nation's tolerance to its advantage. "Most of the foreigners say to me they feel very comfortable," Zhang said. "They say 'Here are these students. They can peacefully go down the street and demonstrate, and the government shows an attitude that they will try to talk to them. A dialogue channel'. The progress of this society is a big step forward in the democratic system."

China's democratic and economic progress was being eyed particularly carefully by Shirley Guo, Taiwan's minister of Finance, the first official representative of the Taiwan government ever to visit the mainland. Her presence at the Asian Development Bank meeting was a reflection of how much things had changed inside both the People's Republic of China and the Republic of China (Taiwan). Taiwan businesses were rapidly establishing manufacturing plants in China's Special Economic Zones along the coastlines, using Hong Kong corporations to bypass a government ban on such activity. China was eager for a more maternal bond. The dream that all Chinese people might one day be reunited within a single border was still very much alive. For years, Deng had wooed the Taibei regime with promises of "One country, two systems." You can keep your capitalism, Deng promised, if you relinquish your claim to be the legitimate government of China.

But China had far weightier concerns in early May, and the Asian Development Bank only heaped extra portions on the leadership's already full plate: lure investors, pacify students, convince the world China is stable. In his speech to the bankers, Li Peng seemed happy that the student boycott had ended. In fact it was far from over. On the night of 4 May, hundreds of students had rallied at BeiDa calling for the strike to continue. In the Triangle, one poster said simply "GOING BACK IS WRONG." Activists phoned foreign reporters to stress that their movement was not flagging. On campuses throughout Beijing, students debated what their weeks of marching had won them. The answer remained precious little—some inconclusive talks with the government, a bit of television and radio coverage and worn out shoes. On Saturday, 6 May, the same day a man in Xi'an was sentenced to death for his part in the riot on 22 April, students at BeiDa voted to continue the class boycott. Ballots had been distributed to each of the twelve hundred dormitories on campus; the vote was two to one in favour of staying out.

Some students ignored the decision and returned to class. A professor of computer science at BeiDa continued lectures when four of his ten students returned. The vast majority, however, stayed away. A few students used the calm to read or study in empty lecture halls; most classrooms remained quiet. Neither the elation nor the commitment of the past few weeks was wearing off. It had become like an addictive drug, offering an intoxicating high. As one student put it, "I feel a very great power from the people. I think it can save our country."

There was also a growing conviction among the students that if anyone within the leadership could be part of that deliverance, it would be Zhao Ziyang. Although many Chinese wondered privately about his political strength, they clearly liked his recent proposals for compromise. The idea that people from all walks of life could actually become part of the political process was soon being championed by the media. A lengthy *China Daily* editorial on Monday, 8 May, described the students' goals as patriotic and praised both sides for the tolerance they had shown.

> Looking back on the past two weeks, one can be amazed by the wisdom of the authorities and campus activists as well, in avoiding a head-on clash when it was almost certain to happen. The students clearly expressed willingness to strengthen the socialist system. The government, for its part, acknowledged the message as a show of patriotic enthusiasm.

The editorial, entitled "Reason Grows," cautioned that it was still too early to predict if the "much-needed political maturity" was in place to prevent the debate between the movement and the government from degenerating into chaos, but it noted that the discipline of the demonstration on 4 May—and the leadership's response to it— were encouraging signs. The paper found comfort in the words of Zhao Ziyang, which were touted as a political panacea for the nation: ". . . a diversity of opinions and problems remain in this society. The only way to solve them, as General Secretary Zhao has proposed several times, is in dialogues through all democratic and legal channels."

The editorial suggested that lessons could be learned from the student movement—lessons that could make future dialogues fruitful. One important fact, said the paper, is that "the leadership and the people have never questioned socialism and the reforms, on which China's destiny depends entirely." The recent challenges were described as a positive development which could lead to "experimental efforts based on this common ground." In other words, the country had perhaps reached a stage where the masses could have a say in the future of the nation. Although the paper couched that remark by saying that criticism of government mistakes "cannot mean a denial of its broad representation," it went on to say "nor do the criticisms, however sharp, necessarily indicate an anti-government plot." The carefully chosen words, while recognizing the supreme authority of the leadership, took aim at the Party's historical inflexibility and paranoia.

The *China Daily* also observed that the traditional way of dealing with "different ideas and voices"—class struggle—was archaic and destructive. It recalled that the Chinese Communist Party itself had denounced the method in 1978, adding that the logic and reason shown by both the government and the students in 1989 was yet "another proof of the validity of the historical change started ten years ago."

With a visionary eye, the editorial said that issues crucial to the nation's development will remain long after the students have stopped demonstrating. All Chinese, it submitted, will eventually have questions of their own: Will price subsidies bring inflation under control? Can guaranteed welfare promote productivity? Can farmers keep producing when they are earning next to nothing? Can teachers and researchers go on despite hardships? Can bureaucracy, corruption and irrational decision-making be contained without some sort of "public supervision mechanism"?

Such questions were already on the minds of many Chinese. The *China Daily*, which put them on paper, suggested that they could be answered by an honest and responsive government. It was a bold future based on hope, a faith inspired by Zhao Ziyang:

> There will be many dialogues on these issues. In the process, the leadership will do a better job if it is candid about the true situation, instead of covering it up—as if nothing had happened and nothing would happen. Only by being open will leaders be in a position to solicit enough support from the people. This is the reason behind democracy. It is often referred to as "political transparency" in the Chinese language.

There was nothing transparent about the editorial's final sentence, which went far beyond advocating mere dialogue:

> After all, no difficulty can be so powerful as to crush the nation's unity and stability, if only democracy is institutionalized and reason allowed to prevail.

Democracy was no longer being discussed as some abstract concept, no longer delicately framed within the confines of socialism. The paper had laid out specific preconditions for the growth of democracy in China, including a reference to the need for a watchdog group to keep an eye on the government. The *China Daily* had shown striking independence, simply by extending the proposals of Zhao Ziyang to their logical conclusion.

Zhao himself continued to talk of political reform. On 8 May, the day the editorial was published, he met with visiting socialists from Turkey. He told the guests that solutions to the problems raised by the students would be found through "democratic and lawful" means. The process, Zhao said, would help promote China's "democratic and legal construction." China already had drafted a press law which would give the media the legal right to report opinions at variance with the official government stance. The National People's Congress was scheduled to debate the law at its next meeting. Zhao also told the Turkish delegation that economic reform and political "restructuring" were mutually supportive concepts. This was yet another break with the past, since the Chinese government had since 1979 been fostering an economic renaissance while largely ignoring pressure for political change. Indeed, the student movement was the result of that obstinancy.

"It is impossible," said Zhao, "to carry out reforms and development without encountering troubles. But generally, China will not run into big troubles."

Or so it appeared on Monday, 8 May. But as Zhao spoke with the Turkish delegation, the journalists' petition continued to be passed around, and more and more reporters had the confidence to sign it. By early Tuesday, it bore the names of 1,013 people. Every one of them wanted to take the party leader up on his offer.

The reporters were from thirty different news organizations in Beijing. On the afternoon of 9 May, their petition was handed over to the All-China Journalists Association—an officially sanctioned organization. It called for dialogue with party and government officials, a privilege which Zhao had all but guaranteed during his speech on 4 May to the Asian bankers. Specifically, the document demanded "sincere and equal" talks on press reforms with leading officials from the party's Central Committee. It said recent coverage of the student movement was "far from enough and not objective." The lack of unbiased reporting, according to the petition, had exacerbated the situation and violated the principle that people should be informed of important news events. In addition, the journalists criticized the recent firing of Qin Benli of the *World Economic Herald* by the Shanghai municipal Party committee.

The text also challenged government spokesman Yuan Mu, who told students on 29 April that "news reporting in China is based on the system of chief editors in charge of everything in their units." Yuan's statement had come in response to criticism of the *People's Daily* editorial of 26 April and complaints about the absence of fair reporting on the democracy movement. The evasive spokesman had tried to redirect protests against what was clearly a Party directive by saying that individual news outlets were responsible for their own actions. Yuan Mu's explanation, said the journalists' document, "does not conform to the facts." The reality, according to them, was that they had been thwarted from telling the truth. "Some reports of the demonstrations," their petition read, "were extremely distorted and they have severely damaged the reputation of China's press both here and abroad. . . . Restrictions of every kind have prevented full, objective and fair reporting."

The statement ended by urging that the various problems it had raised be resolved in the process of wider press reform. Two senior members of the All-China Journalists Association accepted the document and promised to pass it on to the authorities. Outside, about a thousand students waved banners and shouted slogans in support of press freedom. They later marched to Tiananmen Square, then to the *People's Daily*, where they serenaded the compound with uncomplimentary chants.

Although the government did not react immediately, the journalists and their petition had very dangerous implications. As a direct result of Zhao Ziyang's speech, people apparently felt that they had the right to challenge the government openly. Even worse, the journalists, who had already been allowed to report the "actual state of affairs," were demanding still greater freedoms. Who would be next, pounding on the doors of the Great Hall of the People with some well-publicized petition? Doctors? Academics? Peasants? The possibilities were frightening.

It was a scenario which Deng Xiaoping was not willing to entertain. A source close to the Politburo told the Hong Kong *South China Morning Post* newspaper that the senior leader discussed the possibility of military intervention soon after Zhao's speech. The newspaper was told that Deng travelled to the southeastern city of Wuhan some-time between 4 and 8 May to drum up support among army commanders. The source also quoted Deng as saying that Zhao had expressed his own point of view, not the Party's, when he addressed the Asian Development Bank. There were other signs that factions within the government might be advocating a hard-line approach. Although most journalists were seizing the chance to report freely, some were not. Editors of several Chinese newspapers denounced Qin Benli for playing into the hands of foreign "busybodies". Dissident Fang Lizhi, meanwhile, said he was frequently phoned by reporters from the New China News Agency. The journalists asked for his thoughts on the student demonstrations. Fang complied, but the interviews never appeared in dispatches. The astrophysicist suspected that his comments were instead being reported to senior party officials.

The guiding hand would likely have been Deng Xiaoping's. The senior leader had long disliked the outspoken Fang, and Yuan Mu's earlier comments left little doubt that the scientist was being watched closely during the democracy movement.

It was a murky period, filled with political contradictions. Three sources close to the government said the Politburo held secret meetings on 10 and 11 May. At those gatherings, the elite group reportedly endorsed Zhao Ziyang's moderate approach. In addition, the Politburo was said to have agreed that China should chart a course of more rapid economic and political change. Yet only days earlier, Deng was allegedly scurrying about lobbying the military. It was incongruous, to Western eyes, but not unusual for China. If past campaigns and purges have proven anything, it is that Chinese politics are notoriously unpredictable. Shifting allegiances, erratic policy swings, hidden cliques . . . these volatile elements have long been an integral part of the political landscape. As the career of Deng Xiaoping himself vividly illustrated, there is nothing more certain in the Middle Kingdom than uncertainty. What would ultimately happen to Zhao Ziyang, though unfortunate, was not unnatural. That the party leader should enjoy the backing of his peers only to become an outcast was far from unprecedented. Just ask Hu Yaobang.

* * *

Or Yang Xianyi. He carries himself, at the age of seventy-four, with an aristocratic gentleness. He has kindly, intelligent eyes that seem constantly preoccupied with some amusing problem. His voice is soft and muted. Yang Xianyi is a man one instantly likes. Visitors are received warmly, yet with a formality that one quickly realizes is a rehearsed politeness. Good manners are important to him. A colleague once aptly described Yang as the "last surviving Mandarin Gentle-man." His is a civilized regimen that contrasts sharply with the tur-bulence, persecution and tragedy he has known. He once commented bitterly on his experience during the Cultural Revolution. "A totalitarian government is not one that burns your books. A totalitarian government is one that makes *you* burn your books." The number of books Yang Xianyi has produced would make a large bon-fire. He and his wife, Gladys Taylor Yang, have together translated scores of volumes of classic and modern literature.

Yang was born in 1915 in Tianjin, during the tumultuous time after the Chinese had thrown off thousands of years of Imperial rule. His grandfather, an academic, had served as a mandarin to the Emperors. His father was a wealthy banker who still adhered to at least one feudal custom—he had two wives and Xianyi was raised by both of them. In other ways, his father represented the progressive modern Chinese seeking contact with the outside world. Yang went to an English school in Tianjin. In the 1930s he was sent to Oxford University, where he met Gladys Taylor and brought her back to China where they married. Finding the Guomindang government of the 1940s corrupt, he secretly worked for the Communists and cele-brated when the Red Army forced the Nationalists to flee to Taiwan. The Communists offered the Yangs work at the Foreign Languages Press in Beijing translating the works of classical literature into English. He and his wife had three young children, and the future looked bright under the socialist banner.

Yang is a realist, and he was not troubled when tens of thousands of landlords and counter-revolutionaries were shot during those first years after Liberation. It was, he believed, absolutely necessary if China were to rise on new foundations. As for the victims, he maintained that "very few were innocent." He escaped persecution during the anti-rightist campaign of 1957 because "I had no strong criticism of the Party." He even escaped having to denounce others because he was on holiday at the time. Nevertheless, the anti-rightist campaign was a shock for a couple who had thought that the Party valued intellectuals: "I still had great admiration for what had been accomplished, and the Party's prestige at the time was very high. So even though we had doubts, we wondered whether we were the ones making a mistake." Only years later, after the death of Mao, did they realize the full extent of the suffering during those years, but shortly after the anti-rightist campaign ended, their misgivings became sharper. Mao announced the Great Leap Forward, a movement to catapult China toward becoming a major industrial power—as rich as Britain by 1972. Everyone, even translators, doctors and teachers were told to build backyard furnaces and produce steel.

"We smashed up all our iron things and sent them in. Finally we'd produce something like this," he said, holding his hand in a tight fist. "Something the size of a cricket ball. And then we'd celebrate."

"Thoroughly stupid," said Gladys Yang.

"Thoroughly stupid," echoed her husband. Six hundred thousand such furnaces failed throughout the nation.

Just as impossible were the production targets Mao demanded of everyone. Farmers and workers were asked to double their output in just one year. Even the Yangs were asked to do their bit. "We were working as quickly as possible already," said Xianyi, "but they would ask us to translate forty thousand words in one hour."

Even more bizarre was the Five Pests campaign. Mao felt that, in addition to rats, flies, mosquitos and bedbugs, sparrows were also a nuisance that must be destroyed. Children loved it. They spent days banging gongs and drums, attempting to keep the birds in panicked flight. The theory was they would ultimately fall exhausted to the ground and could be crushed underfoot.

"At that time," Xianyi observed quietly. "We were only persecuting sparrows. Not human beings."

That would change during the Cultural Revolution, when Mao mobilized millions of young people into "Red Guards" in a power struggle against the pragmatists in the Party like Deng Xiaoping and Liu Shaoqi. For the Yangs, the early days of the Cultural Revolution in the spring of 1966 were very exciting. Gladys Yang, a tall white-haired woman with a lively wit and a delightful habit of rolling her R's, remembers the day she first saw Red Guards who had come from the countryside to "make r-r-r-revolution."

"There used to be a lot of donkey carts in those days, and I used to go out every morning to collect donkey dung for my compost heap," she recalled. "I went out and a huge crowd of youngsters from the provinces came rushing out of the Ministry next to ours, which had been putting them up. . . . They surrounded me and said 'Comrade, are you Albanian?' Albania was the only friend of China at that time. I said 'No I'm not Albanian, I'm British.' They said, 'Well, you must be a fine internationalist. Up so early cleaning the streets of our great capital. We shall go home and tell everybody.' That was the sort of mood, you know. They were determined to find wonderful experiences in Peking."

It would be, for both the Yangs, the last happy anecdote for many years. The Cultural Revolution soon degenerated into an insane ideological tornado that sucked in the entire Yang family. All three of their children had been brought up to feel very patriotic and idealistic. "Our daughters would only wear navy blue or white," Gladys Yang said. "They tried to be as conformist as they could. My

83

daughter said to me on one occasion 'Our family is too rich'. . . . Foreigners had this special shop at which they could buy all kinds of things. So our Chinese family, and our friends thought we were doing well." Their son Ye, a twenty-four-year-old student, was the most radical of all and beyond their control. When Mao denounced the "Four Olds"—old ideas, customs, habits and culture—Ye came home and began smashing paintings and statues.

"We've been told to destroy the Four Olds," he said when his mother protested. "In those days," said Yang, "a lot of families had such troubles." The episode still irritates his wife. "He destroyed our old family photographs which had historic value. It was a great pity."

The troubles at home were compounded by troubles at work. Yang found himself being denounced by his fellow workers, being accused of countless crimes. He had said Khrushchev was correct to denounce China's friend, Joseph Stalin. He had also made insulting remarks about China's other friend, Albanian leader Enver Hoxha. Yang had also criticized the Great Leap Forward. In addition, he came from a "bourgeois" background. To the followers of Mao, Yang's actions and past made him a counter-revolutionary. He had to stop translation work on the *Dream of Red Mansions* and start carrying out demeaning tasks. Xianyi was assigned to clean toilets and sweep floors. He was, he said, "in a very precarious position."

"During the summer of '66 the real movement began. We called it Bloody August. People were being kicked, beaten and killed in the streets. In Peking, so many people were being killed they didn't have enough coffins for all of them. I didn't dare go out. They'd written thousands of posters denouncing me, the most of anyone. Some people wrote thirty or forty denouncing me. I was called a 'Running Dog of Khrushchev'. I was called a 'Hidden British Spy' because I had a lot of British and English friends. And I was called a 'Reactionary Literary Man', which could mean anything. I have been given all kinds of titles from 'revisionist' to 'counter-revolutionary' to. . . ."

"Corrupting the Youth," his wife added. "He used to offer them drinks."

Anything could be considered a crime. "Once a friend of ours found a hedgehog, and he made it a pet for a few days," Xianyi said. "He fed it some milk. A poster appeared saying he was 'so rich he can afford to feed hedgehogs'. . . . But I never took those things seriously, because you can't. They were just crazy young people, saying crazy, lunatic things." His work unit did take them seriously. The Foreign Languages Press organized mass meetings to denounce him. "Under mass pressure, you are told to stand there and lower your head and I had to lower my head—not very comfortable—for a long period. And then you are abused and given all kinds of names."

84

At home he began to hear voices. Gladys Yang recalled her husband would "hear distant struggle meetings when there weren't any going on. He wouldn't talk. He would listen to them carefully. I remember one afternoon an American friend stopped by. Xianyi suddenly called to him 'Can you hear shouting outside?' We listened. There wasn't shouting outside. It didn't last too long though. Xianyi is really quite a resilient character."

"I suppose," recalled Xianyi, "I had this idea that I could prove myself innocent, and revolutionary, by catching spies."

The persecution subsided as the struggle within the Party intensified. "The revolutionary groups had split into two big cliques, and they began to fight each other. We were left on one side. At our press many people got killed, they were persecuted so much. Twelve people died, jumped or pushed out of windows. They had secret interrogations, people were beaten to death."

In 1968, he and Gladys were arrested and accused of being foreign spies. Gladys was one of several dozen foreigners who went to prison during the Cultural Revolution. She was put in solitary confinement, considered better treatment than that given her husband, who was jailed in a single room with twenty other criminals. The Yangs' case was "under investigation" for four years. Gladys helped pass the time by cleaning her cell with a toothbrush. In 1972, they were released.

Xianyi was let out a week early to clean up their apartment. When Gladys arrived home, she was surprised to see he had brandy and chocolates ready on the table. "I said 'What are you doing with these things? I thought you would be reformed by now'. He said 'It's the party secretary's instructions. I have been ordered to give you a good welcome'."

Their children had been sent to the countryside. Ye, their son, returned home greatly altered. In 1967, with true revolutionary selflessness, he had asked his school to send him to an impoverished region, but the high-spirited young man quickly became deflated as villagers treated him with suspicion. He was only half-Chinese, the son of counter-revolutionaries. He came back claiming he was English, not Chinese at all, and that he hated communists. He was diagnosed a schizophrenic.

"He became really quite a lunatic," Xianyi said. "His going mad is obviously, entirely owing to the change of family fortunes, and how he was regarded—from being a progressive youngster, to being treated as suspect. . . . He wouldn't have gone mad without the Cultural Revolution, no."

They decided to send him to England for treatment. Lonely and disturbed, Ye killed himself in the late 1970s. The Yangs' two daughters, Ying and Zhi, managed to cope better than their brother under similar treatment. Ying became a professor of Chinese at Harvard University. She did not want to return to China. Zhi studied in Chicago and is now China's only professor of Assyriology, the study of ancient Middle Eastern history, at a university in Changchun.

Gladys Yang says she never once considered leaving for England. "I was much more at home in China—my family was here, my work was here. People did find that decision surprising."

The Yangs returned to the Foreign Languages Press and completed the translation of the *Dream of Red Mansions*. Unlike Xi Ruisen, Xianyi could face those who had denounced him. "A few of those youngsters, they looked more ashamed than myself. And it was nothing. There was nothing to be resentful about. They were all in a mad sort of dream. It happened in the past. . . . A lot of them were doing it because of fear for themselves; for their own safety." Against those who hurt him, he holds forth forgiveness and pity. "I don't believe in blaming people," he said in September of 1988. "You can't have perfect justice. You create a certain set of circumstances and someone else creates another. I don't believe in fate. I have no feeling of revenge, and even if I did, I couldn't lash back."

In 1978, during the rehabilitation of those who had suffered during the Maoist years, they were visited by people from the Public Security Bureau. "I remember them coming, and making the most flattering remarks," Gladys laughed. "It was like listening to our own obituary service. They also offered to burn all our files in our presence, if we wanted. And I said 'That's not necessary'. They could always keep a copy, couldn't they?"

In the 1980s, Yang Xianyi accumulated a modest amount of influence, joining the Party, the Writers Union, the Political Consultative Conference and other groups. Gladys Yang, who was born in Beijing and has lived all but fifteen of her seventy years in China, is still regarded by many as an outsider. She is used to that and does not mind. Her family was always what interested her. "If you were to ask me now about the current situation in China's economic reforms, I couldn't give you a coherent answer. I'm just sitting back waiting to see what happens and hoping for the best."

Yang Xianyi also believed in hope, and in May of 1989, the student movement gave him great hope. "I don't know where it is going," he said. "But I think it will lead to something good." Even before the student movement began, Yang saw the possibility of growing democratic reform inside China. He said in October of 1988, "we would like to have more *glasnost*, so that more dirty linen could be thrashed out; so we can take more measures, say, regarding corruption." People were starting to challenge authority, Xianyi had noticed, and to subtly push for greater freedom.

"And complain openly in a way we've never known before in China," Gladys added.

Asked what guarantee the Party could give to prevent another return to its dark past, Yang was quick to reply: "No guarantee at all. But people do learn from their own experience. If you try to arouse the people today, I don't think people will behave like they did. Young people are becoming rather obstreperous. . . ."

"And querying things," his wife broke in. "And not accepting everything the Party says as true—that's a very healthy development."

"Well, healthy or unhealthy," continued Xianyi, "I don't know."

* * *

Positive or not, the student demonstrations were a very real problem for the Chinese government in May 1989. But, as Yang Xianyi had hoped, it did not appear that China would again be plunged into turbid waters. Instead, the state had chosen a course of moderation, of tolerance. It was a reluctant choice, but once it had been taken Politburo members rallied behind Zhao Ziyang's temperate line. The solution had earned the Party leader—and the government—greater respect and much-needed time to deal with the crisis. Certainly, it had worked better than the hard-line editorial in the 26 April issue of the *People's Daily*. Even more conservative members of the leadership, while not enamoured with Zhao's proposals, may have regarded them as the only viable tactic. Threats had not worked; perhaps genuine compromise would.

Another factor which may have garnered support within the Politburo for Zhao was that backing him seemed safe. He was popular with the people and the heir apparent to Deng. Given the mercurial nature of Chinese politics, it would have been prudent to ally oneself with Zhao at such an opportune time. Deng Xiaoping, however, was not about to remain on the sidelines and watch his power slip away, but he could risk neither a brutal crackdown nor a major rift within the leadership. Soviet leader Mikhail Gorbachev would soon be in Beijing for the first Sino-Soviet summit in thirty years, an event marking the normalization of relations between the communist giants. Internationally, it was to be Deng's crowning glory, a diplomatic high point in his life's work. With the international media in the Chinese capital, an assault on the student movement could only tarnish the historic visit. Similarly, a move against Zhao would expose an open rift in the leadership at a time when a display of party unity was essential. As a result, Deng Xiaoping may have deliberately concealed the "actual state of affairs." In the shadows of Zhongnanhai, he watched, waited and prepared.

It was overcast on 10 May and for much of that Wednesday afternoon it threatened to rain. Dark clouds slid slowly over the Chinese capital like huge sheets of lead. A veil of grey cloaked Beijing. Students would not want to march thirty kilometres in weather like this.

So they did not. Walking was too time-consuming—and too tiring —for a movement with such momentum. They organized instead a huge cavalcade of bicycles, a living realization of the saying that "a revolution is like a bicycle—it has to keep going forward or it will fall over." Some ten thousand students, waving enough banners to rival a Shriners' convention, wheeled their way from the Haidian district towards the centre of Beijing. But their destination was not Tiananmen Square. This time, there would be no ambiguous mixture of pro-democracy and anti-corruption slogans. The students knew exactly what they were after that day: a free press. And they knew precisely where to take their complaints—the state-run media.

The convoy was a mosaic of colour and sound. Cyclists wore pastel headbands bearing slogans and the names of their schools. Banners and flags of every hue cut through the air as the procession moved forward. Many students were forced to ride with just one hand, in order to keep the flags flying. Others allowed friends to hitch a ride on the rear carrier in return for banner-waving duties. Some opted to tie red flags around their necks, becoming caped crusaders for freedom. A few students rode with no hands at all, waving to onlookers while shouting through megaphones. They chanted, sang and rang their bicycle bells incessantly.

There were seven targets: the *People's Daily*, the Xinhua news agency, Radio Beijing, China Central Television, the *Guangming Daily*, the *Beijing Daily* and the Communist Party's propaganda department. Thousands of people, in some cases tens of thousands, gathered to watch the students at every stop.

Outside Radio Beijing, the brigade completely disrupted traffic on Fuxingmenwai, the western part of Changan Boulevard. Buses and cars were immobilized by the crowd; passengers who got off only added to the throng. There were so many people clogging an overpass beside the broadcasting station that the structure began to shudder. Beijingers seemed to take the demonstration in stride, showing great interest in what the students were doing but little animosity towards their disruptiveness. They mobbed each other for the leaflets protestors threw in the air, scrambling for them as if they were hundred-dollar bills. While the cyclists chanted outside the Soviet-designed facility, a few employees peered out through its huge windows. One could be seen waving.

The demonstration did not last long, for the bicycle squadron had many more places to go and people to annoy. After about fifteen minutes, one young man with glasses stood up on the back of a flat-bed tricycle. "On to Xinhua!" he shouted. A great cheer went up, the bells began jingling and they were off. The protestors left in their wake dozens of crudely printed tracts glued to lampposts. Clusters of people swarmed around the poles, eager to read what might not be published elsewhere. When they began dispersing, police started tearing down the handbills.

It was a short ten-minute ride to Xinhua. Without a bicycle, how-ever, it was a difficult journey. Foreign journalists, most of whom had been using taxis or private cars to track the demonstration, suddenly found their vehicles a liability: there were just too many bikes. Even the hutongs, where drivers can sometimes take shortcuts, seemed filled with people rushing to see what was going on at Xinhua.

It was quite a sight. The news agency's building is a shining and massive structure which looks as if it were transplanted from the set of Fritz Lang's *Metropolis*. Towering above the street it cuts an impos-ing silhouette against the dark sky. The demonstration, though ten thousand strong, seemed dwarfed by its foreboding presence.

That did not deter the protestors. Those in the lead cycled right up to its gates and began chanting. The rest of the demonstrators joined in from the wide street, which they had jammed completely with their bicycles. Thousands of bystanders pressed forward. "Xinhua speaks false talk!" rattled a tinny megaphone. "XINHUA SPEAKS FALSE TALK!" came the chorus. The crowd liked this one, and needed no en-couragement. Soon it was applauding and cheering as the students denounced the state-run wire service. The demonstrators made a game of speeding the chant to a dizzying pace until no one could keep up. By the time they began ringing their bells to announce their departure, the students seemed almost delirious. Employees watched from Xinhua's roof and windows as they cycled away.

The caravan continued to the remaining media outlets. At each one, the scene was similar. Chants, slogans, a horde of bystanders and a new version of "Frère Jacques." The rolling odyssey lasted six hours. By the time it was over, Xinhua had issued a fairly accurate re-port. There was also word that Xinhua reporters had been granted permission by the government to write about ongoing corruption cases. Previously, journalists were restricted to reporting only on in-vestigations which had been completed. Although it is unlikely that the Communist Party's propaganda department altered its policy be-cause of that single demonstration, the changes were a clear sign the government was still willing to grant concessions.

The protest was unique for more than its bicycles. Certainly, the students had been calling for greater press freedom throughout their campaign. People had endorsed those calls by applauding or cheering from the sidelines. Now, with the journalists' petition, they had far more tangible backing. With the knowledge that they had solid support from such an important sector of society, the students were becoming bolder. It was the most focussed and clearly defined demonstration yet. Two days later, the 12 May edition of the *People's Daily* called for democracy, human rights and "government by balance of powers."

For the government to have shown flexibility on the issue of press freedom was conclusive proof of how far the campaign had come. Regardless of whether the easing of restrictions was a sincere move or a temporary measure to contain the unrest, it was undeniably a recognition of the strength of the democracy movement. Others might argue that the 12 May editorial illustrated that the strings binding the Party to the Press were becoming increasingly frayed. State monopoly of the media has been crucial to the People's Republic of China since its foundation—both as a method of control and as a means to mobilize its people. Since 1949, Chinese people have heard largely what their government wants them to hear. The students wanted them to hear something else, and journalists were giving them just that—whether the leadership liked it or not.

Just as much, the students wanted the world to hear and see what was taking place in Beijing. Hundreds of journalists were in town for the Sino-Soviet summit; many had arrived early to cover the democracy movement. The students quickly became astute at the public relations game. They chanted with increased vigour when the cameras appeared and knew when to flash a quick "V" for victory in the direction of the lenses. Many of those who spoke English would eagerly approach reporters and answer their questions. There was no interference by authorities; it seemed like nothing could touch them. This false sense of political invincibility would later become a serious liability.

At that time, there were few fears. The government was apparently bending beyond all expectations. The students came to regard themselves as an omnipotent opposition party. By Thursday, 11 May, they were even talking about meeting with Mikhail Gorbachev, holding their own "welcoming ceremony" for one of the most important politicians in the world. A petition inviting the Soviet leader to speak at BeiDa was circulated and quickly had twelve hundred signatures. Students planned to deliver it to the Soviet embassy, a sprawling facility said to be the largest diplomatic compound in the world. Privately, some expressed doubts that the offer would be accepted. But the Voice of America reported that Gorbachev himself had asked for a meeting with the students, only to have the Chinese government reject it.

China's Foreign Ministry dismissed the report as "groundless," adding that "China and the Soviet Union have never discussed the question." The spokesman did say that Gorbachev would make a televised address to the people of China during his visit.

Another demonstration took place on that Friday in Tiananmen Square, but for once people were not demanding democracy. Between two and three thousand Muslims marched in angry protest against a book entitled *Sexual Customs*. The work, written by two non-Muslims from Shanghai, said that mosques are modelled after phallic symbols and charged that Muslims participate in a host of unnatural marital and sexual practices. "DEATH TO CHINA'S RUSHDIES!" the protestors chanted, in reference to the British author of the contentious novel *The Satanic Verses*. Shouts of "Restore the dignity of Muslims!" echoed through the streets. This protest did not come as a surprise to Chinese authorities, as the Muslims had applied for and received permission to demonstrate. The display was timed to coincide with a state visit by Iranian President Ali Khameini. But the protest raised another spectre for the Chinese government. China's people are as diverse as the country's terrain. The Chinese most Westerners think of belong to the majority Han nationality, but the nation has fifty-five separate and distinct minority nationalities, comprising seventy million people. These range from Mongolians, who bear a strong resemblance to North American Indians, to the soft-featured Miao, who seem closer physically to the people of Thailand. Most of these minorities have their own distinct languages, dress and customs. The Chinese government says that it treats them well and respects their cultures, but there is resentment towards the Han nationality. Many of these groups feel that the Communist Revolution has taken a great toll on their traditions and independence. Any protest is harshly suppressed, as had happened in Lhasa, the capital of Tibet, in 1989, when dozens of Tibetans were shot during antigovernment protests.

So, while the Muslim demonstration of 12 May did not pose any threat of its own, the protest served as a reminder: there were other special interest groups, some of which were very united and had a great deal to complain about.

For the moment, however, the Chinese government was more concerned with the upcoming summit than anything else. A Soviet delegation, including press secretary Gennady Gerasimov, had already arrived in Beijing; Gorbachev would touch down in three days. Keeping the students quiet, making sure their demonstrations would not interfere with the historic meeting, was a priority.

"You misquoted me," Gerasimov told a foreign journalist at a press conference on Friday, 12 May. "I never said relations should be normalized. I said they should be restored." To many, the difference in terminology might have seemed one of semantics, but Gerasimov was pointing out a truth in Sino-Soviet relations. Ties between the two nations have never been normal, and ending a thirty-year rift between Beijing and Moscow would not make them so in 1989.

For a nation that shares such close physical links with its neighbour, China remains remarkably independent of Soviet influence. Traditionally, Tsarist Russia saw in China a vast hinterland of valuable real estate. Deftly combining their diplomatic skills against Imperial Chinese ineptitude, the Tsars managed to absorb vast tracts of China within their own border. The Soviet republic in 1921 had continued this policy of encroachment, encouraging the independence of Mongolia, which it continues to manipulate through a puppet government.

Since its inception, the Chinese Communist Party had quarrelled with the Soviet regime. Stalin gave Mao grudging support in the 1930s, only because his own tactics had failed miserably, but he considered the Chinese leader a Marxist heretic. The Soviets rankled Chinese communists by dismissing Chinese claims that Mao's theories on peasant revolution had added a new dimension to Marxist ideology.

After the Communist victory in 1949, the Soviets and the Chinese settled in for ten years of petulant friendship. Throughout the 1950s, a legion of Soviet advisors came to China to help build socialism. Many public buildings in Beijing were constructed using Soviet plans, grey thick-walled monstrosities that appear designed solely to withstand sustained artillery attacks. The Soviets helped with the construction of heavy industry and brought technicians to assist in the erection of Chinese nuclear facilities. Thousands of Chinese students, including Li Peng, went to the Soviet Union during the 1950s for technical training. Cultural advisors encouraged development of the arts.

But the Chinese grew increasingly irritated by an attitude of ideological and political supremacy demonstrated by Soviet leaders. Mao was angered by Khrushchev lecturing him on political matters. He was especially upset when the Soviet leader denounced Stalin in 1956 without first consulting him—particularly as Mao was then developing a personality cult of his own. He was incensed when the Soviets refused to discuss the return of more than a million square kilometres of territory claimed by China. Khrushchev also meddled in China's internal affairs, encouraging a defence minister to oppose Mao.

On foreign policy, the two communist giants were also at odds. The Soviets were attempting to reduce the possibility of conflict with the

West through their policy of "peaceful co-existence," while the Chinese considered a war between the capitalist and communist worlds inevitable. Premier Zhou Enlai is reported to have said that if the U.S. and the U.S.S.R. fought a nuclear war, China would come out on top. At the end of such a holocaust there would be "twenty million Americans, five million Englishmen, fifty million Russians and three hundred million Chinese left." By the late 1950s, Khrushchev felt that Mao could not be trusted and ordered home all Soviet nuclear technicians—together with their blueprints. The rest of the Soviet advisors had left by 1961.

Mutual hostility continued throughout the next two decades, reaching a low point during the late 1960s when troops from both nations clashed along China's northeast border.

By the 1980s, barter goods, not bullets, were crossing the border. In 1988, unofficial bilateral trade amounted to a billion dollars.

It was Mikhail Gorbachev who finally offered the olive branch. China had repeatedly said it would restore relations provided the Soviets met three stipulations: reduce troop strength along its border with China, get out of Afghanistan and help settle the Cambodian question. The Soviets pulled out of their futile war with the Afghanis in early spring of 1989. Troops were leaving the border in early May, and the Soviets seemed willing to pressure their Vietnamese allies to withdraw their invasion force from Cambodia.

The summit would be an achievement for both Deng and Gorbachev. Some Western media reported that the Chinese leader had told visiting Iranian President Ali Khameini on 9 May that he would retire after the momentous occasion. Deng Xiaoping would have overseen the normalization of relations with both world superpowers—the Americans in 1979, and the Soviets ten years later. For Gorbachev, too, China would be yet another feather in a cap already festooned with diplomatic plumage. It seemed that neither side could lose.

"I think we have some mutual benefits," economist Hong Junyan remarked on 8 May. "Maybe Gorbachev will learn some Chinese economic reform experience. And so we can learn some political reform from the Soviet Union."

Certainly, Deng could teach the younger Soviet leader a few things about economic success. China's gross national product had more than doubled since 1979, as had per capita income. The Soviet economy, starting from a more advanced industrialized base had grown by only twenty-five per cent during that same period. The Soviet standard of living remained higher than China's, but Deng's reforms had done much to end the sorts of shortages that continued to plague the Soviet economy. China appeared to be able to attract foreign investors for its big projects far more easily than could the Soviets. But Gorbachev's political reforms had eluded Deng. Many Chinese intellectuals felt that Deng could not hide behind his "socialism with Chinese characteristics" to deflect the Gorbachev political message. As political scholar Yan Jiaqi told *The New York Times* on 12 May, "If we want to keep out Western influence, we can say we're against 'bourgeois liberalization' or 'total westernization'. But we can't use that pretext against the Soviet influence. Nobody, not even Deng Xiaoping can resist the Soviet influence, because there's no ideological concept to resist it."

Another intellectual, Zhang Binjiu of BeiDa, was even more explicit, comparing the Gorbachev visit to that of U.S. President George Bush in February of 1989. "Both Bush and Gorbachev carried with them a democratic breeze," he told the paper. "When Bush was here, there was no fire in China. Now there is a fire already burning, and so the wind can make it spread."

The wind would make it scorch.

5

The Chinese People Have Stood Up

The poster at BeiDa announced a measure most students had never even contemplated: "We asked for dialogue with the government, but it doesn't work. The government attitude is cheating us. We again petition the government and ask for a clear answer. The government says 'we will try our best to give you a clear answer'. We are angry with the government. They delay and delay and delay. Now we will go on a hunger strike to present a petition to the government."

A hunger strike.

Food is something all Chinese take very seriously. Millions had died of starvation during the Great Leap Forward, and food rationing continues to be a part of life. Student dining halls ladle out endless dollops of carbohydrates: rice, steamed buns and fried dough. Every fall, huge convoys of trucks, all carrying cabbage, arrive in Beijing and other northern cities. Residents store heaps of it in hallways, on balconies and outside their homes and work units. The frozen and wilted vegetable is used for cooking throughout the winter. Those with builds a North American might consider healthy are often nicknamed 'Fatty' in China. Perhaps the most telling sign is in the way Chinese often greet each other. The phrase "Have you eaten yet?" is as common as "Hello."

Little wonder, then, that few students signed up at first. By Friday, 12 May, only forty had agreed to stop eating, but more joined when they learned that two hundred students from Beijing Normal University had decided to fast. In all, between three and five hundred students ate a final feast on Saturday afternoon and marched solemnly to Tiananmen Square. They donned headbands identifying themselves as hunger strikers; some even tied cloths over their mouths to symbolize their determination to fast. One youth wore a sandwich board that said in Chinese and English "I love life, I need food, but I'd rather die without democracy." As they marched the students chanted "Our country, our society. If we do not speak, who will speak? If we do not act, who will act? If we do not struggle, who will struggle? If we do not fight, who will fight?"

A crowd of twenty thousand people watched them at the square as they raised their fists into the air and took the pledge. "We vow for the promotion of democracy, for the prosperity of our country, to go on a hunger strike. We will not give up until we realize our goal." The fast officially began at 5:20 P.M., after the crowd had sung the Chinese national anthem and the Internationale. A huge flag, bearing the characters for "hunger strike" was raised between two flagpoles in front of the Monument to the Revolutionary Martyrs. Several students went to work on a crude public address system, unravelling wire and setting up crackly speakers. Banners bearing the names of various institutes marked the groups of hunger strikers.

That evening the students held their first news conference in the square. Students provided simultaneous English translation for reporters who had flocked to Beijing for the Gorbachev summit that would begin on Monday. Several hundred reporters, camera and sound operators snaked their way around clusters of hunger strikers who sat directly north of the Monument. As darkness fell, flashguns flickered, sun guns probed, and the huddled students tried to forget their growing hunger.

The strike was a bold stroke by student leaders, an effort to revitalize the flagging democracy movement. After two huge rallies, students had grown weary of the long march to Tiananmen Square. Even the bicycle brigades of the previous week had mustered only several thousand students. Some thought that the movement was dying. Perhaps it would have, but the coming Gorbachev visit offered an opportunity to breathe new life back into the cause. As long as the students kept their resolve, the tactic held few risks. The pressure would be on the government to agree to hold substantial talks before the summit began.

The students now made only two demands. They wanted a retraction of the *People's Daily* editorial which had claimed that their movement was creating chaos. They also wanted dialogue with the government, talks which must be broadcast live on television. The agenda for those meetings was left open and would never be made clear. Some of China's leaders no doubt regarded the students as vengeful children whose feelings had been hurt; troublemakers who now wanted the satisfaction of watching the government squirm on national television while they masqueraded as statesmen. One saw in many student leaders an unattractive posturing, and the sense that if the government ever asked them 'what do you really want?' they would not know what to say. To them it seemed enough to be defiant, to personify everyone's pent-up hostility against the state. When the Mayor of Beijing, Chen Xitong, visited the square early Sunday morning, students jeered him into a hasty retreat. They were holding Tiananmen hostage and were not going to be moved easily.

Word of the hunger strike spread rapidly across Beijing. By the afternoon of Sunday, 14 May, more than one hundred thousand people crowded into the square to see the students who had now gone without food for twenty-four hours. Five hundred students from Tianjin's two universities bicycled the 140-kilometre route to join the group. Two rows of student marshals ringed the hunger strikers, keeping the public well away. When students felt the call of nature, they went in pairs to one of two public toilets on either side of the square. "That's for two reasons," one student said. "First to make sure that those who go do not fall down from hunger. Second to make sure they don't eat anything before they return." The first students started fainting from lack of food and heat exhaustion at midday.

The government asked student representatives for talks at Zhongnanhai. Late Sunday afternoon about fifty student leaders from thirty universities met there with education minister Li Tieying and other officials. Li apologized that the proper channel had not been found for talks and promised to hold dialogue in the future. The meeting was not broadcast, and when the seven o'clock news showed only twenty seconds of the talks, the students' anger boiled over. "CCTV won't broadcast this meeting until later," a student leader announced to the crowd. "This is another deception. Should we continue to talk with the government, or withdraw?" he asked. "WITHDRAW, WITHDRAW!" roared the crowd. A new group was sent to Zhongnanhai, demanding that their classmates leave. The talks broke up at 7:20 P.M. The hunger strikers cheered and applauded when they heard that their leaders had walked out. The only channel the students would accept for dialogue, it seemed, was the television channel.

"I think maybe there are two choices," a young student marshal said. "One is the government will hold another meeting with students. The other is maybe the government will force the students back to their colleges and universities. I am afraid the government will use the police to force the students to the colleges at midnight, or maybe the early hours of tomorrow."

It was a very real fear for all students in the square. The government had ordered Tiananmen closed to the public on Monday; it would be the site of the official welcoming ceremony for Gorbachev. Military bands, honour guards, red carpets would usher in the Soviet leader to the very seat of Chinese power. Student hunger strikers were not welcome. Twelve prominent intellectuals, including Yan Jiaqi, tried to persuade the students to end their fast and go home, but many relished the challenge of testing the government's resolve once again. "I think this is a very good opportunity," one student said. "Mikhail Gorbachev arrives tomorrow. So this is a very good opportunity for democracy, for the students to ask for democracy."

The crowd numbered perhaps 150,000 when the midnight deadline to clear the square passed. No police were to be seen. Rumours spread that the square would be cleared at two o'clock, then three o'clock, then five o'clock. Student loudspeakers urged people to stay, but the numbers dwindled. By 5:30, perhaps as few as ten thousand people remained, but as the eastern sky lightened the exodus ended. By 6:30 A.M., supporters of the hunger strikers returned to the square. The students had won again.

The strikers did make one small concession. They moved from their position directly north of the Monument to the Revolutionary Martyrs to the eastern side about one hundred metres away. "We don't want to do anything to embarrass our government and Gorbachev," a young man explained as he shivered beneath a blanket. The government could still have its welcoming ceremony on the square, he said, because "we will stay well away."

It was a meaningless gesture. Even as the students moved, the space they had occupied was filled by a legion of people streaming into the square. By noon, more than one hundred thousand people were there; by six o'clock, more than a quarter of a million.

Beijing's Capital Airport is not in the city proper but about thirty-five kilometres northeast of Tiananmen Square and surrounded by farms of the People's Liberation Army. A long willow-lined avenue takes visitors past shepherds tending their flocks and fruit farmers taking their goods into the city. It is a busy road, and a busy airport. The modest terminal building had become too small to handle the growing tourist and business traffic heading in and out of the capital. When Mikhail Gorbachev arrived on 15 May it was undergoing a major renovation to help cope with the increased flow of passengers.

Chinese officials, meanwhile, were trying to cope with problems of their own: Tiananmen was choked with people. Near the square all but two of Changan Boulevard's six traffic lanes were being taken up by pedestrians who found the segregated bicycle lanes that parallel the street too small for their needs. Regular motor traffic was diverted by police. It was now not simply a question of whether to hold the welcoming ceremony for Gorbachev in Tiananmen Square— it was how to get him to the square in the first place. Gorbachev's itinerary had been planned months in advance, but the democracy

98

movement had become a disruption that the Chinese government could not possibly have anticipated. The first of several changes was made only a few minutes after the Aeroflot jet touched down. Realizing that an official function could not be held near Tiananmen Square, Chinese officials hastily put together a welcoming ceremony on the airport tarmac. President Yang Shangkun hid his embarrassment behind a façade of grandfatherly good humour. The eighty-two-year-old leader, another survivor of Mao's purges, beamed as he and Gorbachev strolled past the honour guard.

The Soviet leader and his entourage were forced to skirt the main roads into the city, where thousands waited in vain for a glimpse of his limousine. After a circuitous route, his motorcade was directed to a side entrance of the Great Hall of the People, rather than the main doors facing the square. There would be no red carpet outside the massive building, no military band, no youngsters waving red flags. The pomp and circumstance had been relegated to the airport, hardly the appropriate venue for such an historic occasion. Plans to have the Soviet leader lay a wreath at the Monument to the Revolutionary Martyrs were cancelled. Chinese officials would later comment, without a trace of irony, that "Mikhail Gorbachev arrived in Beijing smoothly."

Inside the Great Hall, the Soviet leader and Yang effused pleasantries, promised to forget past differences and pledged their two nations to a future of mutual friendship and co-operation. Then, the moment which had taken three decades to reach: Deng Xiaoping shook hands with Mikhail Gorbachev. Deng greeted him warmly but took the opportunity to lecture the Soviet leader on the dangers of superpower confrontation—words of wisdom from an old man who had known Stalin, Krushchev and a very cold war.

Outside, on the east side of the square, between fifteen hundred and two thousand soldiers double-marched into the Revolutionary Museum, an imposing building that resembles the Great Hall. Word spread that the military might try to clear the square. Students and bystanders rushed towards the steps leading into the museum. Some time later, a few soldiers wandered out of the entrance. Under the hot sun, they casually sipped soft drinks.

At one point during the afternoon, a group of soldiers did take action—but not the kind of action protestors feared. Instead of making a move on the demonstrators, they joined the students in a patriotic sing-song, their commander conducting. Tension in the square eased; it appeared that the military posed little threat. But the hunger strike itself concerned many academics. Five hundred professors and scholars from BeiDa signed a petition urging the government to adopt "all possible measures" to prevent the strike from getting worse. They marched to Tiananmen Square with the document, in which they asked the government to accede to the student demands. They even offered to act as a go-between in discussions.

On the roof of the Great Hall of the People, Zhao Ziyang pulled out a pair of binoculars and watched—no doubt amazed—at the people massed below. An enterprising foreign cameraman managed to capture him as he peered at the growing throng. The original hunger strikers were now joined by twenty-five hundred more students who took the pledge to fast. A crude printing press churned out leaflets, which bystanders snapped up as quickly as they were printed. By 6:30 P.M., student loudspeakers announced that 103 strikers had fainted. Those strikers who spoke English used a different expression. "Many students fall down," they would say. "But I feel fine, so I hope I don't fall down."

Supporters in Tiananmen, fully aware of the significance of the meeting taking place just next door, stood proudly and defiantly. Several held placards which made reference to the Soviet Union's political glasnost. "Where is China's Gorbachev?" read one poster.

"We like Gorbachev very much," explained a hunger striker. "He has really done some practical political reform—that's what we really admire." The young man stressed that it did not really matter whether the Soviet leader admired them. What mattered was that the Chinese government took note of Gorbachev's glasnost. "Yes, YES!" he exclaimed. "We like such people [as Gorbachev]. China has done a lot of things in economic reform, but we haven't made much progress in political reform." Asked how long he was willing to take part in the democracy campaign, he replied "We are prepared to struggle to the end." Questioned about his physical condition, he answered with two words: "Very hungry."

While the students prepared for another night of fasting in the square, the Chinese leadership and its guests prepared for a lavish banquet inside the Great Hall. Mikhail Gorbachev delivered a speech which, by necessity, touched on the issue of democratization very diplomatically. He praised Chinese economic reforms, making only a fleeting and discreet reference to his own political reforms. He spoke of a new era of relations between Beijing and Moscow, portraying a Soviet Union more interested in friendship than control. "The Chinese side," he said, "can count on our benevolent and unbiased approach to discussing any problem." The dilemma no one wanted to touch, it seemed, was the student movement. At a press conference, Soviet spokesman Gennady Gerasimov glossed over the issue, saying "We regard this with necessary understanding. We have similar experiences and have lived through some difficult times." Besides, said Gerasimov, the demonstrations were secondary to the importance of

Gorbachev's visit. "So the size of the problem is not very big," he said. "But the summit is really a big thing."

* * *

As she practised her pirouettes in the lime-green dance room of Number 3 Taiping Jie ("Peaceful Street"), Bai Shuxiang still moved with the grace she had shown thirty years before at that first performance of Swan Lake in Beijing. In 1958, at the age of eighteen, she was a symbol of Sino-Soviet friendship—the prima ballerina of a Chinese ballet troupe trained entirely by Soviet instructors. She was famous. She dined with Khrushchev, danced with Zhou Enlai, and stood with war heroes in Tiananmen Square at National Day parades. In 1989, she had again been invited to dine with a Soviet leader, at a banquet hosted by Deng Xiaoping for Mikhail Gorbachev and his wife Raisa at the Great Hall of the People. What a different world it was for her.

During the late 1960s she cursed her fate. "I asked myself 'Why did those Soviet experts hand-pick me of all people to be the prima ballerina?'" Even today, she cannot hide her longing to relive those lost years. "See those two," she said, pointing to a young couple practising a pas de deux from *Don Quixote*. "They won a competition at the Anderson International Festival in Denmark last year. Twenty years ago, it could have been me. But no. . . ."

In 1954, when China and the Soviet Union signed an agreement on cultural exchanges, Bai Shuxiang was one of about twenty students from a northern theatre school to join a newly created Beijing ballet academy. Soviet teachers came from the Bolshoi and Kirov companies to instruct the students. They created a performing company, and Bai Shuxiang was their first star. She played both the white and black swan in that 1958 production of Tchaikovsky's classic. She played the leads in *Giselle* and a traditional Chinese opera called *The Mermaid*. The Russians continued to instruct until 1961, when Moscow ordered them home.

Bai was sad to see them go, but an even darker cloud hung over the young dancer. She came from a bad "class background." Her father had been a high-ranking magistrate with the Guomindang government. Although he avoided early campaigns, he was arrested and shot in 1958.

She was not terribly close to her father. Bai had lived in theatre schools since she was ten and had faith in the Party. "When he was shot, I was siding with the government, and I believed it was correct." She does not think that today. In 1986, a court agreed with her that the execution was unjust. To make up for the grievous mistake it instead sentenced her dead father to fifteen years in prison. She continues to seek his full rehabilitation.

In 1958, she worried only that his death could cause her problems. "Premier Zhou gave a party and as I danced with him, I said my father had been executed. Zhou Enlai said 'Your father is your father. You can go your own way. So long as you draw a distinction between you and your father politically, there is no problem'." She felt reassured. "I didn't care about the political message. I was concerned about improving my skills. As a ballet dancer, what made me most happy was to play as many roles as possible."

But others did care. In 1965, Mao's wife Jiang Qing began to impose her vision of culture on the nation. In speeches she ridiculed Western classical music, dance, opera, the works of Shakespeare and other writers. Eventually, she would attempt to reduce Chinese cultural life to eight "revolutionary operas" which made class struggle the aim of art. One such opera was called *Red Detachment of Women*, in which Bai played the lead. It was the story of a slave girl named Wu on an island plantation run by an evil capitalist landlord. When Wu tries to run away, she is captured, tortured and left for dead, but revolutionary fighters find the girl and nurse her back to life. Wu joins a women's Red Army unit. At the crucial moment when the unit is about to attack the landlord's command post, her hatred is so intense that she acts impulsively and alerts the enemy. The attack fails. One entire act is dedicated to Wu's self-criticism. Her commander tells her that the Revolution is not meant for settling old scores. Instead, he says, the cause is to avenge the whole nation. Wu realizes that the interests of the Party must take precedence over personal feelings. Even when her beloved commander is captured and burned at the stake, she remembers her lesson: Wu suppresses her anger and unites with others for the love of the nation.

Jiang Qing, however, was not as selfless as Wu. She was soon taking such class struggle lessons directly into artistic troupes. The former Shanghai actress used her position to settle scores against former colleagues. Some have suggested that she specifically wanted to ruin the careers of those whose skills surpassed her own. As the Cultural Revolution began, Jiang announced that China must train more artists from "good class backgrounds." The sons and daughters of suspected landlords, capitalists, rightists and Guomindang sympathizers were denied entrance to art and theatre schools, universities and other learning institutes. Bai Shuxiang would be singled out by Mao's wife, who made frequent visits to Number 3 Taiping Jie.

"Once when we were posing for pictures," recalled Bai, "Jiang Qing asked me time and again to come closer. She stood opposite and told me over and over 'Go to the left' or 'Go to the right'. But I could not decide if she meant her right or my right. She accused me of disobeying her and that became one of my crimes."

Similar 'crimes' against Bai were quickly concocted. There was her class background and a diary entry in which she wrote that Mao's hand felt soft when she shook it after a performance. These offenses became the basis of struggle sessions against Bai Shuxiang during the summer of 1966. Day after day, she was taken to a practice hall.

"I was ordered to take the 'air jet posture' during them. Two people stood on either side twisting my arms back into the air. They beat me and forced me to double over with my head almost touching the ground, with my knees on the floor. They beat me on my feet. A ballet dancer needs her feet, so they were trying to ruin my career. I was forced to assume that position for the entire afternoon. When I was allowed to straighten up, I simply couldn't do it. . . . In that situation, I realized I had to confess to anything they said I had done. It was very hard for me to acknowledge things I hadn't done, but I realized it was the only way to save my skin." Such sessions lasted for two years. She stopped training, and was assigned to clean toilets and perform other demeaning chores.

Bai was completely isolated. Her boyfriend, another dancer, denounced her. Her best friend did the same. No one spoke to her. "I couldn't understand why they were doing it. Maybe they were doing it to show their loyalty to Chairman Mao. Or maybe they were doing it to show they were revolutionaries. Some were doing it to retaliate against me. For instance, one woman was on very good terms with me. But she changed overnight and wrote a big character poster, saying I was against Jiang Qing. Only in this way did she herself become the prima donna."

She wrote self-criticisms, "enough to compile into several books. . . . You know, the criticism of oneself was quite difficult. You could easily be labelled too shallow, or overdoing it." Jiang Qing accused her of being a member of the 16 May Clique, a fictitious conspiratorial group supposedly headed by close associates of Mao dedicated to seizing state power. In 1968, Bai was sent to a labour camp near Beijing filled with other leading dancers, singers and intellectuals. She dug ditches, tended horses, plucked fruit trees, wrote countless self-criticisms and continued to be denounced. It lasted five years. She became stocky and stiff, and thought she would never dance again.

The historic visit to China by U.S. President Nixon in February of 1972 led to her release. "The government gave a ballet performance in his honour. Premier Zhou was present. He was surprised not to see me taking part. He asked 'where is Bai Shuxiang?' He was told Bai

103

Shuxiang is an active counter-revolutionary, a member of a counter-revolutionary clique. He said 'you should educate her, rather than treat her like that'. People took the cue, and set me free." Although she rejoined the company, she did not give a major performance for another five years. Finally, at the age of thirty-eight, after twelve years, Bai Shuxiang once again danced in the spotlight. It was 1978. She was rehabilitated and rose to positions of influence. She danced in the United States, in the Philippines and France. Jiang Qing was arrested and jailed as a member of the Gang of Four, which took the blame for the excesses of the Cultural Revolution. A few top people in the China Central Ballet also went to prison. In 1984, Bai became director of the troupe.

About twenty other members of the company were persecuted during the Cultural Revolution. Two of them died, both suicides. Today the company has four hundred and fifty employees, more than half of whom participated in the struggle sessions during the 1960s. Only two people have ever apologized to Bai. "Those people who were still very powerful in the troupe were very afraid of my rehabilitation. But actually, temperamentally, I am not the kind of person who would retaliate against anyone. I understand their mentality through and through. You see, persecutors are afraid of being persecuted. . . . Even today, the new batch of people who came to power in the art troupe after the crackdown of the Gang of Four are still pretty much reserved to me. They are afraid the old batch will someday stage a comeback. It's unpleasant for me to work in such surroundings, in such an atmosphere. But that's something I can't help."

When she was interviewed in February of 1989, Bai Shuxiang thought such evil times were behind China. She could stage any play she wanted. In 1988, the troupe performed the opening act from *Red Detachment of Women*, even though its strident class struggle between good and evil seemed out of touch with the new atmosphere in China. Bai wanted it staged again. Of all her roles, it is the slave girl Wu with whom she most identifies.

As head of the China Central Ballet, Bai struggled to develop world class dancers, sending talented youngsters to ballet schools across China. No longer were there restrictions based on class. "Ironically," she noted, "those people who had the best class backgrounds are now all in the United States and other Western countries. All these people were members of the Communist Party. It shows class background has nothing to do with fidelity." Bai had trouble keeping dancers in China. The best talents often seemed to be snapped up by foreign troupes. She was hurt when a couple she had worked with for years were lured away by an American dance troupe. The pair left one day and she never heard from them again. The West often celebrates such events as defections, but the lure is often simply money and status. "In China," Bai Shuxiang said, "ballet dancers have not been regarded as queens, emperors, princes, as they have been in foreign countries. In those countries, they have been regarded as very beautiful beings, because they have created beauty. But in China, it's quite different. We have braved sufferings and hardships of all descriptions. We have tasted all the bitterness in human life."

* * *

As night fell in Tiananmen Square on 15 May, the hunger strikers were not alone. More than two hundred thousand people packed the huge plaza, swarming around them. Most of the supporters were young; a high percentage were students who wanted to help out in some way, but an increasing number of workers and academics came to show that they believed in what the hunger strikers were fighting for. Many of them carried flags and placards, marching in the square for hours under the moonlight. Spectators and students alike would shout excitedly whenever they saw particularly clever banners. Often they would rush forward and march alongside the carrier, only to be distracted by appreciative hoots coming from somewhere else. Flatbed tricycles, normally used to transport everything from coal to cabbage, carried instant politicians. Young men and women balanced precariously, preaching through megaphones as the trishaws slowly advanced. Occasionally these orators would topple to the ground, only to jump back up again to bursts of spontaneous but goodnatured laughter. It was like London's Hyde Park, only every corner was Speaker's Corner.

On the east side of the Monument to the Revolutionary Martyrs, the hunger strikers tried to comfort themselves. It was a chilly night and many huddled together for warmth. A few sipped tea or smoked cigarettes in a minor violation of their pledge. Some students played cards, others sang along while one of their comrades strummed a guitar. Pieces of cardboard or donated clothing offered limited protection from the cool concrete. Sleep was out of the question. Student loudspeakers blared nonstop; when they were not playing the national anthem or the Internationale they were urging the hunger strikers not to lose their resolve. Messages of support from students in other cities and provinces were often relayed over the speakers. The strikers would cheer when these messages were read, though the cheers grew steadily weaker. Chai Ling seemed to be on the loudspeaker system most of the day and most of the night. Her voice grew progressively hoarse and emotional as the hours passed.

The hunger strikers could not always hear Chai Ling, or the Inter-

105

nationale. What they could hear was the wail of sirens. Several ambulances were standing by in front of the Revolutionary Museum. They were put to good use; students had begun to collapse with alarming frequency. With very little body fat to sustain them, the hunger strike was quickly taking its toll. Medical students ministered to the weak with glucose and empathy. More serious cases were loaded onto stretchers and whisked away to hospitals. Although the crowd surrounding the hunger strike camp was massive, it parted like the Red Sea when ambulances needed to get through. On the street bordering the eastern side of the square, volunteers linked arms to keep an emergency lane open. Many of the students who were hospitalized returned to Tiananmen Square immediately after receiving treatment. In the camp, volunteers solemnly marched with a placard displaying the running tally of students who had collapsed. It was updated every hour.

There was concern that agents of the Public Security Bureau might be posing as reporters to infiltrate the camp. Because of this, all Chinese claiming to be reporters were asked to produce proper identification. If the protestors were going to ask their own comrades for such documents, they were certainly going to ask foreigners. The student marshals tried to solve the problem by developing a pass system. Any journalist in the camp was given a pass—usually a pair of initials scrawled on cardboard—before he or she left. Only if the pass could be produced later would he or she be readmitted. In addition, the reporter would have to return to the camp through the same "gate"—pieces of bamboo holding flags reading "entrance" and "exit." Once inside, they were not permitted to eat or drink out of respect for the hunger strikers.

Medical students tending the strikers were not just concerned about their physical well-being. They and other volunteers tried to shield the strikers from anything that might weaken their resolve. Once a young worker broke through the human perimeter with an armful of fried dough sticks. A dozen people pounced on him as if he were an assassin. The food, he protested, was for the volunteers, but he was roughly shoved back before he could kill the hunger strikers' resolve.

In the early hours of 16 May, Tiananmen Square was like a living cell. The hunger strikers were its nucleus, protected by a thick membrane of marshals. Throughout the rest of the plaza supporters flowed to and from this centre, nourishing it with chants, cheers and admiration. At one point, the cell threatened to divide. Someone with a megaphone urged supporters to push their way into the Great Hall of the People, and thousands surged towards its front steps. Within moments, hundreds of police filed out the front door and formed a protective line. Student loudspeakers pleaded with supporters not to do anything which might provoke the government. The crowd complied, returning to the square after a brief and peaceful standoff.

Tens of thousands left during the night, cycling through the streets to distant homes, but there was still a huge crowd milling about when dawn broke on Tuesday, with more supporters on the way. Students continued to faint, ambulances continued speeding to and from hospitals, loudspeakers continued blasting encouragement. The military did not come. Life in Tiananmen Square seemed nearly normal. People began erecting tents.

"All the comrades," said Zhao Ziyang, "hold that in the interests of the Party we still need his wisdom and experience." The man to whom he addressed this comment was Mikhail Gorbachev; the man he was referring to was Deng Xiaoping. During a meeting with the Soviet leader on Tuesday, 16 May, Zhao divulged a state secret which he might later rue having mentioned: he told Gorbachev that Deng was in charge of the country. The elder statesman, said Zhao, was still consulted on major issues—even though he had resigned from all but one Party post at the Thirteenth National Party Congress in October of 1987. The sole official position which Deng retained was chairman of the Central Military Commission, but Zhao made it clear that the aging leader was deferred to on all matters of importance.

Zhao's comments did not support what Deng had been claiming for some time—that he was easing himself out of power and relegating more and more responsibility to those below him. In June of 1988, for example, Deng had told a visiting Polish delegation that Zhao had been given full command of the military. The following month the president of Brazil listened as Deng revealed that all of his own duties had been turned over to others. On numerous occasions after that, he remarked to foreign dignitaries that he would like to retire in the near future. Even so, there could have been little doubt among the general public that Deng remained the biggest potato of them all. Chinese television and newspapers still called him the "senior leader" in almost all coverage; top billing was given to his meetings with visiting heads of state. Zhao merely confirmed what most people already knew. There could have been another, more strategic reason for the party leader's choice of words. Zhao Ziyang may have been trying to distance himself from any action the government might take against the democracy movement.

Gorbachev also met with Li Peng that day. The premier greeted him in fluent Russian, which the technocrat had learned while studying in the Soviet Union in the 1950s. The pair spent two hours talking, during which Li promised to improve China's record on freedom,

107

democracy and human rights. Capitalist countries, said Li, did not have a monopoly on such concepts.

Gorbachev maintained a busy schedule throughout the day, shuffling from one meeting to the next, but he took time out to perform what had become his trademark: talking to ordinary people. On a sidestreet well away from Tiananmen Square, Mikhail Gorbachev plunged into a small but enthusiastic crowd of Beijingers. "I like Gorbachev," remarked one bystander. "He likes to speak to people, you know? Not like the Chinese leaders. They don't care to speak to the people." He paused momentarily, then added: "I don't know why."

Deng was very interested, however, in talking to Gorbachev. He praised reformist thinking during that second day of the summit, saying "Sticking to the old fixed rules can only lead to failure." Gorbachev responded with great understatement: "We're watching with great interest what is happening in the People's China. We have learned a lot."

At a state banquet broadcast live to the nation, the two men sat side by side—the picture of conciliation. Gorbachev was shown deftly handling his chopsticks as the meal began. The camera then panned over to Deng Xiaoping, who was shakily raising a morsel to his lips. As he was about to take his first bite, Deng lost his grip and the scrap unceremoniously tumbled back to the table. The Chinese cameraman quickly averted his lens from the table and towards the ground, but the damage had been done. The leader of China had looked very feeble and very old. Outside Zhongnanhai, a banner read "When someone passes eighty, he becomes muddle-headed."

There was still enough clarity within the government to realize that the democracy movement had to be contained. Hundreds of thousands were out in the streets again, chanting and marching before the world's media. The protestors were stealing the limelight from what should have been the main attraction—the summit. The demonstrations, already a great embarrassment to the Chinese, were growing stronger and more humiliating by the hour. They were also becoming more threatening.

The government tried twice that Tuesday to placate the students with compromises aimed at getting them out of the square. In the early hours of the morning, Zhao Ziyang sent a message to the students on behalf of the Politburo. The dispatch acknowledged that demands for greater democracy reflected the patriotic spirit of the movement. It pledged that the government would "work out concrete measures to enhance democracy and law, oppose corruption, build an honest and clean government and expand openness." Later in the day, Central Committee member Yang Mingfu went to the square as an emissary. He asked the students to stop their hunger strike, promising that neither they nor their supporters would be punished in any way. Yang also said that the Party would soon convene a high-level meeting to study their demands. If they were not satisfied with the results, he said, the students could reserve the right to carry out future demonstrations.

Student leaders Wang Dan and Wuer Kaixi recognized what they thought was a golden opportunity. They felt that Yang was sincere, so they endorsed his plea and asked other students to believe him. Other representatives, however, voted down their proposal. Why should they negotiate? There were now more than three thousand hunger strikers with perhaps a quarter of a million people openly backing their demands. The military had not come and most students felt it would not come. "The government has no choice," said one defiant striker. "If it tries to quell the demonstration [by force] it is crazy. The whole country would rise up."

It was a dangerous feeling of omnipotence, but it was understandable. More and more Beijingers were siding with the students. Several professors from the Institute of Minority Nationalities joined the hunger strikers on Tuesday afternoon. Teachers, workers—even party members—were demonstrating on the students' behalf. When they were not chanting or marching, these supporters donated money, clothing and other supplies. Bands of protestors, whether on foot or on bicycle, moved through the streets all day long; Tiananmen and the surrounding area were a nonstop parade of people and banners. The students could not help but feel powerful. Said one young man: "Anyone who has witnessed this event would reach the conclusion that the people support us. There is no doubt about that. If one does not believe that, he should come here and see for himself." Asked why the leadership had not used force, he replied "I think there is a political struggle within the government itself. The officials are divided and a struggle is going on. When it is finished . . . it might be very favourable to the students." The student said that he and his classmates would leave only if their demands were fully met: "Otherwise I cannot expect that it will end very soon."

Tiananmen Square was taking on the appearance of a permanent settlement: several tents and lean-tos of bamboo, canvas and plastic were set up in the hunger strike camp. Institutes marked off sections for their own students, almost all of whom sported coloured headbands identifying their universities. Fresh banners appeared daily, as students from other schools joined the strike. Bigger and better loudspeakers were affixed to the Monument to the Revolutionary Martyrs. Volunteers distributed tea, water and medical supplies. Reporters and camera crews, foreign and Chinese, continued to spread the word. The world was watching.

The scene was not always pleasant. Amidst the hope and optimism in Tiananmen Square, there was extreme discomfort. In addition to fasting, the hunger strikers had to cope with blistering days, chilly nights, constant noise and growing squalor. "The weather is too hot," said one doctor, "and the air in the square too foul." Scattered bits of garbage, broken glass, cigarette butts and spit littered the area. Few, if any, of the hunger strikers had showered since Saturday. Their clothes began to smell. Merely being in the square, among the constant hordes, proved exhausting. Yet the hunger strikers remained committed, if not always cheerful. "I will not stop," said one RenDa student, "until I fall down and am taken away to hospital." By late Tuesday evening 342 students had collapsed. Many refused to be loaded into ambulances, opting instead for treatment in the square itself. A field hospital had been set up where medical students administered glucose and intravenous drips to the victims. Dozens of hunger strikers lay sprawled on mattresses under heavy green canvas. The seriously ill were lauded as heroes by fellow students; collapsing for the cause was considered a badge of honour. One student from a foreign languages institute proudly declared that the first person to be taken to hospital was one of his classmates. Not only that, he boasted, but a student from his school was in the worst condition of any of the hunger strikers. His classmates nodded their agreement that this was a significant indication of their commitment.

The rest of the strikers tried, as best they could, to cope with the difficult conditions. There was little space to move in the camp. Strikers often had to step gingerly over one another, avoiding garbage, banners and wires as they threaded their way through this human obstacle course. There was barely enough room to stretch. Those who managed to sleep frequently had to use their comrades as pillows. Low-slung sheets of plastic and cloth offered respite from the sun, but there were not enough to go around. Newspapers and scraps of cardboard were fashioned into sun hats. Umbrellas, many of them donated, were also used to shield students from the heat. Volunteers showed up on flatbed trishaws laden with blocks of ice. Pieces were chipped off and tossed, brigade-style, to the hunger strikers. They, in turn, would suck on the cool chunks or slide them over their faces and necks. One young faster, a woman, was hit in the head by a lump thrown by an over-enthusiastic volunteer. It sliced a gash across the top of her scalp and she obviously required stitches, but her classmates spent several hours pleading with her before she finally agreed to go to the hospital.

The arduous conditions on the square were compounded by the unceasing noise. Student loudspeakers droned on and on at a level which could not only be heard, but felt. Megaphones brandished by student marshals added to the assault, as did Orwellian government speakers which called on students to end their fast. Supporters surrounding the strikers never seemed to tire of chanting, singing or clapping. Only the sporadic howl of sirens was louder.

Daily necessities such as trips to the bathroom became an ordeal. It should have been simple—there were public washrooms across the street—but because of the huge crowds in and around the square, that simple walk from the Monument was often a ten-minute struggle. When hunger strikers finally reached their destination, they often had to wait in long lineups. Conditions in the squat toilets were appalling; the reek was overpowering as far as half a block away. As the strike dragged on, toilets which had been used during mass rallies in the 1960s were reactivated on the east side of the square. They were not washrooms as such but more like open cesspools. Slabs of concrete in the sidewalk which normally covered the sewer were removed; an opaque sheet of heavy plastic was strung up around the area and became an instant toilet. Huge puddles of urine spilled out from under the plastic and dribbled over the sidewalk. The stench was sickening. It was little wonder that doctors feared an epidemic.

There was no shortage of medical staff. By midway through the week there were about a thousand physicians or medical students on hand. "I may not agree with the actions taken by these students," said one volunteer from a Beijing hospital, "but as a doctor I must come to offer my help."

That help was in constant demand. On Tuesday one doctor estimated that students were fainting at the rate of one every six minutes. By early evening the next day, it was almost impossible to keep up with the number of casualties. Ambulances circulated continuously; the streets around Tiananmen were an alarming collage of wailing sirens and streaking blue lights. Some eleven hundred students had been taken to hospitals.

"I have been here since Monday," said one young woman from Beijing University. "I feel very well. . . . Seven of my classmates began on Saturday and they are very ill now. Some have gone to hospital. The environment is very very bad, and it's very noisy. Some of my classmates are in very serious danger"—she sounded confused, disoriented—"but they will continue." As for the support the hunger strikers had gained, the student of economic law replied: "I was not surprised. Yesterday I didn't see so many people. We stayed in the middle of the square, people surrounded us, and we could not see. But today, I think many people will come today.

"Many people send letters to us to try to persuade us to stop our strike. But I think we will stick it out to the end. My parents don't know what I am doing—I have not told them. But I think they would support me, yes. Maybe they would worry about my health or my safety, but I think they would support me. I think most of the people in our country support us, want freedom and democracy."

"The students represent the whole country," said one middle-aged man in the square. "My young children come here every day to support the students."

Another man identified himself and his colleagues as professors from the Beijing Institute of Finance. "Most of us are Chinese Communist Party members," he said. "Today we have come to support the students. We came today, yesterday, and the day before yesterday. All of our teachers and students come here. You know our school is very far from here. . . . But our students and teachers, all of them want to support our students." The man said that everyone—including the professors—had been boycotting classes for four days. Several students from the institute were fasting, he said, but "we cannot find any. . . . We know some have been taken to hospital."

He had also heard that some hunger strikers were planning to take more drastic action to pressure the government. Eleven students from BeiDa had pledged to drench their clothing with gasoline and immolate themselves if the leadership did not solve the crisis by midnight Wednesday. "Some of our students want to die," he said, "but most of the students don't want them to do this. They want them to prepare themselves. We hope our government leaders will come to Tiananmen Square to meet our colleagues and students and offer a solution." As an afterthought, he added "We think this movement is democratic."

The clamour for a government response to the students' demands was becoming deafening. The hunger strikers had garnered immeasurable sympathy. Men and women alike wept over their plight. Four of the nine legal democratic parties urged Zhao Ziyang and other top leaders to go straight to the square. The China Federation of Literary and Art Circles echoed the appeal, as did the All-China Women's Federation, which promised to do "what little it could" to get an appropriate response from the government. Even the state-sanctioned students' federation demanded that government leaders go to Tiananmen.

Although the government had made conciliatory gestures, the students and their supporters seemed to regard anything less than total capitulation as indifference. Calls for leaders to step out into the square were increasingly replaced with bold demands that they step down from power.

"Deng Xiaoping should resign," said one student. "Everyone wants that. Deng once said that he will retire when the people ask him to retire. Now the people ask him to retire. At the start of this movement, the students did not ask anyone to resign. But now the government—particularly Deng Xiaoping—does not react to the students and the people ask him to resign." The student also believed that a power struggle pitting conservatives against reformists was going on within the Party, and he hoped that Zhao Ziyang had the strength to take control. Indeed, many students felt that the huge demonstration taking place around them would force the government's hand. A protest of its size and scope simply could not be ignored.

"Today and tomorrow are critical," said one student leader, "because we expect top leaders to make significant compromises. If nothing happens, however, we will continue our hunger strike to the last man."

By Wednesday, thousands of students from other cities were flooding into Beijing to help their comrades. Some of them joined the hunger strike, but most were content to mill about the capital, exchanging thoughts on democracy and writing down slogans and ideas to take back to their own campuses. They camped out on the ground, or under the trees in front of the nearby Revolutionary Museum, or in the pedestrian underpasses on the north side of the square. Food was contributed by families, factories and small restaurants; other necessities were purchased with donated money. Vendors set up stalls all around the square, offering discounts to any student who could produce a university card.

In Shanghai, some sixty thousand students staged a sit-in outside the municipal party headquarters in People's Square. Five hundred of them were fasting. Big protests took place in more than twenty other cities, as well. And in the remote western region of Qinghai, one hundred thousand Muslims demonstrated against the book that they felt blasphemed their religion.

There had been rumours on Monday and Tuesday that the people of Beijing would march in support of the students. Word even spread that a general strike was imminent. There was much anticipation; a shared knowledge that something big was going to happen. But no one, least of all the Chinese leadership, could have imagined the scope of it. An astonishing force was about to be unleashed.

Wednesday, 17 May, promised to be a beautiful day. At 10:00 A.M. bright flecks of sunlight sparkled off the brass gong a young man was clanging vigorously at an intersection far to the west of Tiananmen Square. A friend stood beside him, beating a traditional drum. Both men were positioned on a traffic island. A few cars and buses honked in appreciation. About fifty doctors and nurses waved as they walked past, their white lab coats contrasting sharply with the red banners they carried. Fifteen minutes later, about a hundred young men and women in track suits marched down the street. They, too, carried flags and banners. The gong's piercing clash became louder. Another group of protestors materialized.

Inside nearby China Central Television, foreign journalists rushed towards the main entrance. Many television networks had set up headquarters at CCTV, which was helping to provide pictures of the summit meeting. The station was also the "feedpoint," where networks transmitted stories back home via satellite. The reporters took one look at the street and ran back inside to get their cameras.

Outside, bundles of demonstrators started appearing more frequently, now separated by half a block, sometimes less. Banners identifying their hospitals, factories and organizations were waved from bamboo poles. Although a few of the groups represented universities and technical institutes, the vast majority were not students. They were workers, academics, artists. . . . Each new cluster seemed to represent a different sector of Beijing society.

A van whizzed by, its horn blaring. The vehicle was packed with people, all of whom managed to wave or to hold banners through the windows. A woman in the front passenger seat held out a placard on which was painted a large broken heart. It bore the characters *Wo de zhongguo*, or My China. Demonstrators cheered and waved their banners in return. A small truck, impossibly jammed with young people, was next. They hooted, yelled and gave the "V" sign as they sped past. Not long afterwards, a city bus rolled down the street, so packed its rivets seemed ready to pop. A huge red banner calling for democracy was strapped across the front. Smaller flags streamed from the windows. A woman, presumably the conductor, was excitedly shouting democratic slogans over the vehicle's loudspeaker system.

From the twenty-fourth floor of a hotel on the western reaches of Fuxingmenwei, the wide street was starting to look like a conveyor belt, transporting the speckled mass towards the centre of Beijing. A continuous line of trucks, cars and buses was also starting to take shape, cutting a narrow swath through the demonstration.

Near Radio Beijing, a sixty-year-old man watched and smiled from the sidelines. Despite the heat, he wore a traditional Mao suit, buttoned right to the collar. He could not help but think back to a time long ago. He had been just twenty years old when China was reborn, and the afternoon of 17 May brought back powerful memories. A wave of joy, pride and hope was flooding the streets once again—a wave with the power to cleanse a nation. Yet the feeling was not quite the same as it was in 1949. "This time," he said softly, nodding towards the crowd, "they're trying to build an even better China." He was on the verge of crying.

At buildings and factories throughout much of downtown Beijing, work stopped completely. Hundreds of thousands of employees abandoned their offices and headed outside. Some were so eager to demonstrate that they started marching within the guarded brick walls of their work unit compounds while their comrades hastily fashioned banners and dazibao. When they were finished, they marched united into the streets. Thousands of them donated money to the democracy movement, stuffing hard-earned yuan into cardboard boxes held by appointed students on street corners.

Those who did not leave their offices, and there were many, often showed support in other ways. Hundreds and hundreds of banners and posters dangled from windowsills and rooftops. Flags were even strung from the Revolutionary History Museum, on the east side of Tiananmen Square. "Help, help save the students," read one.

By early afternoon, the entire length of Changan Boulevard was filling with people from every imaginable occupation and vehicles of every conceivable description. The students, realizing that there could be problems, quickly enlisted volunteers to control traffic. The volunteers would have made a sizable demonstration on their own: thousands of them linked arms for a distance of perhaps eight kilometres. Two rows of them stood back-to-back straight up the middle of Changan, creating a centre line. Traffic flowed on either side of this human divider while two more rows of volunteers kept protestors and bystanders clear of the cars and trucks. The linked arms were eventually replaced by an endless length of plastic twine. Volunteers acted as fenceposts, keeping the flimsy barrier in place.

There were few onlookers that day. Everyone wanted to be part of the parade, and they did not care how large or small a role they played. Even holding a piece of that pink twine and waving on traffic seemed to be enough for some people. No matter where one looked, the sight was unbelievable. Huge cargo trucks stopped along the route and let anyone clamber onto the back. Some carried more than one hundred people, all of whom waved and cheered like returning astronauts. City buses—one after another after another—tooted their horns down Changan, the "street of eternal peace," while conductors and passengers bubbled democracy through loudspeakers and windows. Construction trucks, complete with cranes, rumbled down the boulevard. Workers riding on them, still wearing bamboo or yellow plastic hardhats, looked like conquering generals despite their grimy coveralls. One truck carried a group of disabled people, most in wheelchairs, past the crowd. Another rolled by with about a hundred policeman who waved and displayed the victory sign. Motorcycles, hundreds of them, buzzed by with an air of Democracy's Angels. Scores of taxicabs ferried people free of charge; slogans had been painted directly onto many of the vehicles. One taxi driver hired by a foreign television network insisted on navigating with no hands. He rolled down his window, steered with his knees, made a "V" with his fingers and shouted "Good! Good!" with all his heart.

On either side of the Tiananmen rostrum, the grandstands normally used by Party officials and visiting dignitaries to review parades were filled with average people. Couples with their son or daughter, workers, the elderly—they all jammed in to watch the parade of the century. They clapped as truckloads of ordinary citizens like themselves shouted "Down with Deng Xiaoping! Go play your bridge!"

Outside Zhongnanhai, volunteers kept the traffic moving. They allowed vehicles to slow down long enough for their occupants to shout a few well-directed slogans at the government headquarters, then asked them to move on. They all complied.

At Tiananmen Square, hundreds of thousands swirled around the huge plaza like bees. One group of demonstrators carried a mock Chinese coffin, apparently meant for Deng. Another toted a skeleton effigy with small bottles clinking from its wrists. "Small bottle," although written differently from the Chinese leader's name, has the same sound: Xiaoping. Great cheers followed both these displays. A growing militancy was also reflected in chants: "We should not wait anymore!" shouted a large crowd. "We should fight!"

Chinese and foreign reporters estimated about a million people were in the streets. But how does one count a million? There could have been two million, perhaps three—who will ever know? The potential was there for chaos, if not total anarchy. The parade attracted truckloads of *liumang*, or hooligans. Small bottles were being tossed and kicked throughout the square, symbolizing the end of Deng. Motorcycles roared up and down Changan for hours. The only police to be seen were those who were marching with their neighbours. It continued into the night and through next day. One might have expected assaults, lootings, or worse. But there was nothing. Only hope.

For the people of Beijing, the summit had become a curious side show. Under other circumstances, Mikhail Gorbachev's announcement on 17 May of planned Soviet troop reductions in the Far East might have been big news. His hope that the Sino-Soviet border

116

Hunger strikers waiting to begin their fast, Monument to the Revolutionary Martyrs, 13 May. (S. Simmie)

Hunger strikers take their pledge. Tiananmen Gate is in the background. (S. Simmie)

Bas relief sculpture flanking Mao's mausoleum became a popular vantage point and public noticeboard throughout the demonstrations. *(S. Simmie)*

Students and their supporters defy government orders to clear the square for Gorbachev's visit, 15 May. *(S. Simmie)*

A student paints slogans on an umbrella in Tiananmen Square. *(S. Simmie)*

Supporters of all ages joined in the protests for democracy. *(S. Simmie)*

Student hunger strikers squat behind a banner . *(S. Simmie)*

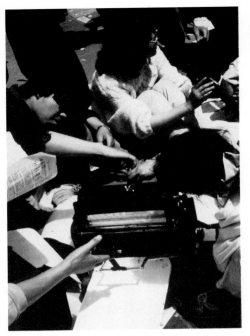

Propaganda the old-fashioned way. Student mimeograph machine on Tiananmen Square, mid-May. *(S. Simmie)*

Manual printing press used to produce leaflets. *(S. Simmie)*

Foreign camera crews survey the hunger strike camp from their perch at the top of the stairs to the Monument to the Revolutionary Martyrs. *(S. Simmie)*

Municipal transit buses provide temporary shelter for the hunger strikers. *(J. Annells)*

Heat and exhaustion weigh heavily upon the hunger strikers, 15 May. *(J. Annells)*

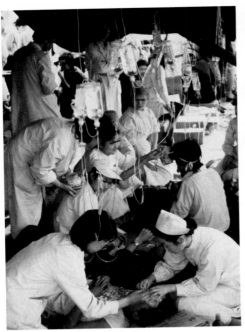

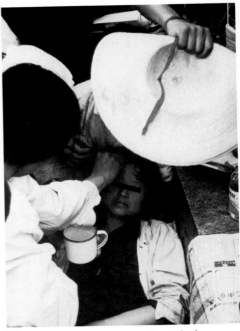

Medical volunteers on the square give intravenous aid to dehydrated hunger strikers. *(S. Simmie)*

Volunteers work to revive striker who has fainted. *(S. Simmie)*

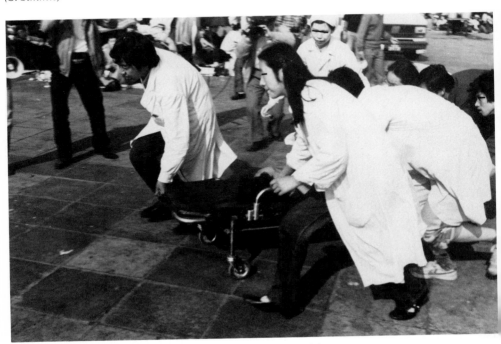

Medical students rush ailing hunger striker to care. *(S. Simmie)*

Workers spray the square with disinfectant to prevent the spread of disease. *(S. Simmie)*

After weeks of occupation, garbage piles up on the square. *(J. Annells)*

Journalists demand press freedom, outside the offices of Radio Beijing, 17 May. *(S. Simmie)*

Medical students march behind placard indicating their support for the students. *(S. Simmie)*

could be defended by "friendship" instead of soldiers might have been greeted warmly by the average Chinese. It did not work out that way. By late Wednesday there was far greater concern in the capital for the students. Not only were young men and women starving, but also it was starting to rain heavily; the hunger strikers had little protection. City buses, which had been carrying demonstrators the length of Changan all day long, provided the solution. Bus drivers drove directly into the square and opened their doors to the hunger strikers. Students piled in with whatever belongings they had and settled in for the long night.

The downpour continued well into Thursday morning, by which time Tiananmen Square had turned into a puddle of soggy garbage. Not all students enjoyed the comfort of the buses. Many sought refuge wherever they could; some slept on the ground underneath the vehicles.

Impossible as it seemed, demonstrations went on through the night. Certainly, there were fewer people on the streets than there had been on Wednesday, but motorcycle brigades and trucks filled with protestors continued plying Changan Boulevard and circling the square. Ambulances, too, streaked in and out of Tiananmen.

By dawn, action had slowed considerably. Busy ambulances still ferried hunger strikers to hospitals. Demonstrators were exhausted. Many of them had been in the streets all of Wednesday and half the night. Wearily, they unlocked bicycles and pedalled down wet streets. Some of China's top leaders, meanwhile, headed for a different destination.

Desperate to end the hunger strike and restore order, Zhao Ziyang, Li Peng, Hu Qili and Qiao Shi made a trip to the hospitals. Chinese television cameras filmed the men visiting with strikers, trying to assure them that the government shared their concerns. Li Peng seemed distinctly uncomfortable, moving stiffly about the beds and greeting students with formal reserve. Zhao, however, appeared genuinely concerned.

Back at Tiananmen Square, scattered bicycle brigades and bands of chanting people persevered, but for much of the morning there was a lull in central Beijing. The rain had almost ended. Mikhail Gorbachev had left Beijing for Shanghai. It must have been a relief for the Chinese government to see the summit end; demonstrations had prevented him from attending a performance of Beijing Opera and visiting the Forbidden City. Even his final news conference, scheduled for the Great Hall, was shifted at the last moment to the State Guest House. More demonstrators greeted him in Shanghai. Gorbachev had remained affable throughout his visit, and he deftly dodged all questions about the unrest. But when he left Shanghai for home on Thursday afternoon, the Soviet news agency Tass immediately reported that the Chinese authorities had lost control in Beijing.

Only hours after his visit to the hospital on the morning of Thursday, 18 May, Premier Li Peng endured a humiliating and exasperating sixty minutes with student leaders in the Great Hall of the People. Forced by the strength of a million voices, the televised meeting was a merry-go-round of futility. For Li, the shaggy-haired student leaders seemed to want publicity more than they wanted political reform. They seemed to find perverse pleasure in insulting him, ridiculing his role as premier of the nation. One can only imagine the rage Li suppressed as he listened to the rantings of these youngsters who had somehow managed to mobilize all of Beijing against him.

Li had tried to be calm and diplomatic throughout the meeting, but he failed when Wuer Kaixi interrupted him as he talked of friendship. The twenty-one-year-old hunger striker had come to the meeting from a hospital where he had been taken after collapsing earlier in the day. "Stop playing games and get down to business," Wuer shouted. Li called him impolite. Wuer replied, "Impolite? You've got a million people on the streets and you're calling me impolite?" The premier became flustered, and he later ordered that segment of the meeting edited out of the version which was later re-broadcast.

Li failed even to set the agenda for the meeting. As he sat with the students in a semi-circular row of armchairs, he thanked them for coming and announced "we will talk about only one thing: how to get the fasting students out of their present plight." He was quickly and rudely thwarted.

"Just now," Wuer responded, "you said we would discuss only one thing. But in fact it was not you who invited us to be here. Rather it was so many people on Tiananmen Square who asked you to come out and talk with us. So as to how many questions we should discuss, it is for us to decide." One could only marvel at such an arrogant display of confidence. As Wuer repeated the students' familiar demands he let slip an astonishing admission. The student movement was out of its leaders' control. "We really hope to ask students to leave the square. Over there it is not such a thing as majority rules; in fact ninety-nine per cent of the people must obey the will of the one per cent of the people—if only one hunger striker refused to leave, the other hundreds would never leave the square either." The statement indicated that the students in the democracy movement had a lot to learn about the concept of democracy.

Even if the government gave in to the student demands, Wuer continued, the students might not leave the square: "We may try our best, but can't guarantee we can make it." Shao Jiang, a BeiDa student, stressed the point: "The student movement may have become a people's movement. The students are relatively reasonable. But we cannot ensure that a people's movement can be reasonable."

Xiong Yang, another BeiDa student, asked the premier to be flexible: "As communist fighters, we are all people who have a conscience and a sense of humanity. . . . As long as it is a people's government, the people will still support it after it admits its mistakes."

After hearing such talk, Li was in no mood for compromise—especially if it might not bring results. He remained firm. He demanded that all hunger strikers be moved immediately to hospitals, whether they were ill or not. "Whatever common points and differences we have," he declared "the most important thing is to rescue their lives. In this regard, the government is duty bound. . . . What I want is not that the fasting students be brought to hospital only after they are critically ill. We must do it now."

Li denied that the government or the Party was responsible for the *People's Daily* editorial, but he made it quite clear that he stood behind what it said. In addition, he told the students that the government was about to act:

We have been affirming the students' patriotic enthusiasm, and many things you have done are right. . . . But the development of the situation does not depend on your best intentions, desirable expectations and patriotic enthusiasm. In fact, disorder has already appeared in Beijing and it is spreading across the whole country. I did not mean at all to let the students bear the blame. But the actual situation is there. . . . Beijing these days is basically in a state of anarchy. . . . I hope that you can think about it. What will come out of it, if things go on like this? The Government of the People's Republic of China is responsible to the whole nation. We cannot ignore the current situation. We will protect the students' lives, factories, the achievement of socialism as well as our capital. No matter whether you like this or not, I am glad to have such an opportunity to tell you. Turmoils have happened many times in Chinese history. At the beginning, many people did not intend to arouse turmoil. But finally it happened.

When Li refused to discuss the two demands of the students, Wuer Kaixi called the government insincere. Student leader Wang Dan said that the government must shoulder the blame for the social upheaval. The meeting broke up when Wuer collapsed again and had to be given oxygen. Li Peng walked out of the meeting with a determined look in his eye. Wuer Kaixi went back to hospital, where he told a *New York Times* reporter that the government had lost touch with reality: "They've been inside their offices too long. They don't comprehend the power of this movement."

But the youth was very, very wrong.

Outside, heavy clouds, fat with rain and dust, massed over the Chinese capital. The sky was almost pitch black at noon hour. A ripping wind tore down Changan Boulevard and through Tiananmen Square. Banners and flags shook ferociously. If there was any truth to the belief that the legitimacy of the ruler in China depended upon the Mandate of Heaven, this was surely a sign. In 1976 many Chinese regarded a catastrophic earthquake in the city of Tangshan as a signal that Mao Zedong had lost his decree to rule; he died shortly afterwards. The angry sky of Thursday, 18 May, appeared to augur an event of equal calamity.

But it did not deter the hunger strikers and their supporters. By early afternoon, hundreds of thousands of people were again in the streets. Convoys of trucks filled with chanting demonstrators raced the wind down the Boulevard of Eternal Peace. Tens of thousands of volunteers again stood guard, directing traffic and holding a twine barrier down the centre of Changan. As word spread of the failed talks with Li Peng, so did anger. Work stopped in many large state shops as workers abandoned their posts in protest. An official at the Number One Machine Tool Factory said the plant had "basically ceased production" after one-third of its ten thousand employees walked off the job. Parts of one of Beijing's largest engine plants also ground to a halt. By mid-afternoon an estimated million people were demonstrating, as they had the day before. The worsening condition of the hunger strikers gave the protest added urgency. Some two thousand had been taken to hospital; students were collapsing at the rate of one every two minutes. Medical tents were packed with victims. In addition to severe dehydration, students were diagnosed with such ailments as kidney deterioration, pneumonia and bleeding stomachs. Yet the hunger strikers did not give in. Several of them returned to Tiananmen over and over, leaving the hospitals as soon as they were well enough to walk. One young man was taken away for treatment eighteen times. A rumour, later found to be false, circulated that one young woman had died of complications.

Protests hit other cities, as well. There were marches in at least twenty provincial capitals. In Shanghai 200,000 had demonstrated despite heavy rain, an event timed to coincide with the visit of Mikhail Gorbachev to that city. Xi'an and Hangzhou reported rallies of 100,000 people. Hundreds of students began to fast in both those cities as a show of solidarity with the Beijing strikers. Chinese even

120

took to the streets in the relatively affluent and commercial city of Shenzhen, which borders Hong Kong. Although citizens in many areas broke through police lines to demonstrate, there were no reports of violence.

In Beijing, attacks on the Chinese leadership became increasingly vicious. Not only were several effigies of Deng Xiaoping being brandished, but many groups of demonstrators carried portraits of Zhou Enlai. It was a sign of their love and respect for the late premier, and a pointed display of their lack of respect for Li Peng. Pictures and badges of Mao Zedong were also dusted off. A group of teachers and academics took their protest right to the Communist Party headquarters. About thirty of them staged a hunger strike on either side of Zhongnanhai's front gate. Many of them appeared to have been fasting for some time and were in a weakened condition. Lying on blankets beneath an ornate overhang which decorates the main entrance, they looked very helpless and very sad.

Spanning the actual entrance were about forty soldiers. They sat cross-legged in front of the door, their eyes cast downward. Volunteers told journalists that the men supported the students but were under strict orders to guard Zhongnanhai. Many of the young soldiers looked like they were enduring some hellish punishment.

Facing all this was Changan, a thoroughfare no longer of Eternal Peace but of perpetual dissent. Rumours had spread all day that moderates were winning or had won the power struggle; that Deng Xiaoping had resigned or would do so shortly. The demonstrators were not about to let up the pressure. Even well after midnight, truckloads of mocking protestors rolled past continuously, denouncing Deng and Li. The two men had come to symbolize everything that was wrong with China.

"It's a crucial point," said one young volunteer outside Zhongnanhai. "Before now, people would just follow what the government said. Now people follow their own judgement as to what is right or not. And if it is not right, they want to criticize. Before this the government would say 'one' and everybody would say 'one'—just one voice. But now we have different voices."

A truckload of those voices drove past. "Down with Deng Xiaoping!" they shouted. "Li Peng step down!"

"Since the day before yesterday," said another young man guarding the hunger strikers, "the nature of this demonstration has changed. All the people—not just all the people in Beijing, but also in other places—all the people stand up to support the students." When it was pointed out that a hunger strike might be a dangerous political tactic, a woman volunteer defended the students' action.

"It's not like in Canada," she explained. "If we do not put on some pressure, no democracy. Democracy is gained by people; it is not delivered by someone." The hunger strikers, she said, were putting their own lives on the line "for me, for you, for all the people. We all need freedom."

A graduate of the China University of Political Science and Law jumped into the conversation. He said lawyers from "every part of China" had come to Beijing and they had reached a verdict: "Some people [within the leadership] think the students are guilty. We think they are not guilty; we think their demands are reasonable." He had less kind words for Deng Xiaoping: "I think he must collapse. . . . He is old enough. I don't think he is clear in his mind." Another man suggested that the government should rewrite its laws to guarantee democratic freedoms. "It must change its constitution and its State Council," he said.

There was one topic on which everyone seemed to agree: the talks between Li Peng and student representatives had been an utter failure. "I don't think they touched the core of the question," said one frustrated student. "I think Li Peng is still shying from the questions after nearly one month. We don't know why."

"What he said," interrupted a plump young man, "was very, very stupid. The result of such words is that a lot of people came to Tiananmen Square—because what Li Peng said was completely wrong. The people do not think he is right. . . . The situation is very, very serious. What the students need is a true dialogue," he continued. "Li Peng and the students must be equal, but from today's program on television it was not equal. Li Peng looked very, very serious and very angry."

For the time being, most shared the belief held by one of the many volunteers outside Zhongnanhai, who said "The government will give up. . . . I think it will give people more freedom with their own lives." They could already see it on television and read about it in the newspapers.

A revolution had taken place in China's media. Decisions were being made without any interference from government bureaucrats. "Even two days ago," a young reporter said on Friday, 19 May, "we could not decide what we wanted on the air. We had to report to the top leaders and see what their opinion is. . . . But yesterday, I don't know how and why, it has changed. We can use whatever we want."

Reporters by the hundreds threw off their self-imposed restraints and wrote freely about what they saw and heard. They opened their pages and airwaves to the voices of the people, and the people supported the students. The *China Youth News* conducted a random survey of people in the square. All but one of the seventy-five people it interviewed backed the student cause.

"The slogan of the students to oppose corruption enjoys the support of the people," said a Chinese businessman. "I think the government should have taken action long ago against corruption." A factory worker was quoted as saying "the students have good intentions and a demonstration like theirs is permitted by the constitution. If they do not resort to such means, the government will not feel a great impact." The lone dissenting voice came from a soldier. "The students have gone too far," he said. "What can they achieve in this way?"

Students had been angered by a lack of coverage on Monday, 15 May, but by Wednesday the hunger strike completely dominated the Chinese media. The 7:00 P.M. television newscast showed a full twelve minutes of events surrounding Tiananmen Square before Gorbachev's name was mentioned. Mothers were seen crying over their fasting children. The pictures showed medical units working feverishly on those who had collapsed, ambulances racing to and from the square, tens of thousands marching through the streets.

Throughout the week, the *People's Daily* published appeals for immediate talks with the students from professors, writers, factory managers. The newspaper reported that political columnists from several newspapers held an emergency meeting to discuss the crisis. Their recommendation: dialogue now. An old woman was reported to say "if Premier Zhou Enlai were still alive, he would have come out long ago."

Qian Xinbo of the Chinese Union of Journalism Societies commented: "newspapers are carrying more of their own staff-written stories, so papers are providing different news and voices to their readers. In the past they tended to carry Xinhua stories, all saying the same thing on controversial issues like the student movement." Although reports tended to offer a balanced description of each day's events, there was no doubt that journalists as a group were among the students' staunchest allies. At CCTV, two huge white banners backing them were hung from sixteenth-storey windows. Reporters from several media outlets joined in daily marches to Tiananmen Square to add their voices to the throng. They snaked their way through the packed plaza demanding press freedom; calling for the resignation of the Minister of Communications, Ai Zhisheng; demanding immediate talks between the students and the government. Then they would scurry back to their offices to write stories, edit videotape, develop pictures. Their own activities became part of their reports. One editor summed up what many were feeling. Fan Jingyi of the *Economic Daily* said "In the past I had thought reform of the

123

media must take a very long time. Now I believe that under the effects of the great movement in Tiananmen Square, many previously untouchable bonds can be broken."

Western television crews shadowed their Chinese counterparts to document this breaking of bonds. State control was gone. One CCTV reporter explained how it had happened at that office: "Ai Zhisheng normally comes by or sends someone from his ministry every evening at 6:30 to review the scripts. Whatever he doesn't like has to go. But on Tuesday when we demonstrated against him, he got scared. He phoned the Director of Television and told her to review the newscast. When the news editors phoned to find out where the censor was, she said 'well, whatever you decide is fine'. I guess she was scared of us too." It was the same everywhere. Xu Zhuqing, the editor of the *China Youth News*, said that he now based what went into the paper on his own judgement.

Few outlets abused their newfound privileges. They displayed a caution that reflected the precariousness and volatility of the situation. One poster that drew loud cheers showed an unflattering caricature of Deng and quoted words he had once used to rid the Politburo of some elderly members: "If the old don't step down, the young can't come up—Xiaoping set an example." Chinese reporters ignored such deliberately provocative messages. Instead, they increasingly concentrated on ways to end peacefully the growing crisis.

They gave great emphasis to those who counselled the government to give an "accurate evaluation of the student movement," a "prudent and humanitarian manner of dealing with it." *China Daily* pleaded with the authorities on 17 May: "Little time is left for the government to find effective ways to convince the fasting students of its sincerity. . . . It is hoped that political wisdom will lead to further compromise, much needed at this critical point. Such a compromise would help the government regain society's understanding and cement its authority. . . . Since the government and students both want democracy, why should they not start solving their problems in a democratic way on this very day?"

Such a course might also help cement some of the gains the journalists had won. Even if it did, most knew they still faced a long road ahead. One reporter said on 19 May, "we never have had any doubt that this censorship system will come back. It's going to come back. But sooner or later they will let people speak."

Zhao Ziyang had lost the confident glint in his eye when he boarded a bus containing hunger strikers from Beijing Normal University shortly before 5:00 A.M. on Friday, 19 May. As students crowded around him and a CCTV cameraman shone a bright light into his face, the general secretary of the Chinese Communist Party looked sad and pained. In his grey Mao suit, he looked more mournful than he had four weeks earlier giving the eulogy for Hu Yaobang. He was on the verge of tears.

Zhao had come to the square with Li Peng at a moment when the number of people in Tiananmen Square was at its low ebb. Student hunger strikers applauded and cheered as they approached the bus. A grim-faced Li Peng shook a few hands, encouraged students to end their protest, autographed a banner and went back to his limousine after less than two minutes. But Zhao lingered, and when a student draped in a checkered blanket offered him a megaphone, he took it and began his final public appeal.

"We have come too late, too late," he said. "We deserve your criticism. We are not here to ask for your forgiveness. You all want our country to become better."

Zhao stressed that things were complicated, that problems could not be solved in an instant. He appealed to the students to stop their hunger strike and promised to hold a dialogue after the fast had ended: "The channels for dialogue are wide open. . . . It could become too late if you insist on getting a satisfactory answer now. I am an old man. But you are young, and you should live to see the realization of the four modernizations in China." Zhao sounded dejected, knowing his words would not be believed, knowing his appeals would be ignored. When he finished speaking, a dozen students around him pressed for autographs. He signed pieces of paper, petitions, even their shirtsleeves. He left the bus before daybreak.

"There's a rumour," said a concerned Chinese journalist later that day, "that the Politburo had a ballot. The vote was thirteen to two in favour of a claim that the movement is a riot." Another version suggested that only the Politburo's five-member Standing Committee cast ballots; the result was four to one against Zhao. Rumours that Li had won a power struggle prompted fears that the military would be called in. The worried journalist said if Zhao was gone, the leadership "will try to convince soldiers from other parts of the country to come to Beijing and clean the students out. . . . I think it is possible." Another Chinese reporter, a woman, heard that the premier was going to place a ban on all demonstrations later that Friday. If he tried, she said, "then Li Peng is losing all the people here in China."

For the moment, the protests and demonstrations taking place in Beijing gave one the feeling that the entire country was awakening from a long and deep sleep. Mao Zedong's portrait stared silently out, past the roving trucks of demonstrators and into Tiananmen Square. Through a megaphone, one protestor shouted the very words with which the Great Helmsman had ushered in the People's Republic on

1 October 1949. "The Chinese people have stood up!" cried the excited man to the victorious cheers of thousands. "The Chinese people have finally stood up!"

6

We Were Tolerant and Reasonable for More Than a Month

A slender student grabbed a microphone and stood on the Monument to the Revolutionary Martyrs. "General Secretary Zhao Ziyang," he announced gravely to the crowd, "has submitted his resignation. His plan for dialogue with the students has been dropped. We are calling for a general strike in protest tomorrow." There had been no official word on Zhao's political demise, but the students and their supporters accepted the announcement as fact. "Long live Zhao Ziyang," shouted the throngs in Tiananmen Square. "Down with Li Peng!" The hunger strike should end, it was decided. They would all need their strength to continue the struggle.

Their vigorous chants were soon stilled by the rumble of government loudspeakers. It was just past midnight, a few minutes into Saturday, 20 May. The voice of Li Peng, which sounded thin despite the massive amplification, echoed off the walls of the Revolutionary Museum into a carpet of hostile ears. A shocked silence filled the square during pauses in the booming speech. The students and their supporters knew they were listening to a declaration of war and for some time they were hushed by a combination of disbelief, fear and mute rage. It was rage which won out, and before Li had finished speaking, the square erupted into a chorus of catcalls. "Come out here you big hooligan," a man screamed towards the Great Hall. The loudspeakers droned on. "Don't you students have any humanity?" Li Peng asked rhetorically. "You jerk," someone howled. "Hooligan government! Kill Li Peng," another yelled. Oaths and profanities pierced the midnight skies above Tiananmen Square. "We are fully against it," a student leader shouted to the applause of the crowd. "There are 300,000 people on the square. We should fight to the end."

One student dismissed Li's address as the rantings of a deluded man. "I think his speech is very silly," the youth said. "He is very silly. He doesn't know what the people think, what the students are."

Inside the Great Hall of the People more than one thousand senior Party and government leaders sat in Mao suits and military uniforms awkwardly applauding Li's call for a crackdown. They had been summoned to give support to his speech, to give it official sanction, to show the nation that the state would no longer tolerate the unrest. They wore the uncomfortable look of men expecting a visit to the dentist, willing to submit to some discomfort now in order to avoid more pain in the future. Their applause was unsteady, often missing Li's cues, sometimes coming as he made trivial points. In the days ahead, their performance would be the subject of much debate among the populace about the strength of their resolve. Those watching that speech on television as it was broadcast to the nation noticed a far more important sign. The head of the Communist Party, Zhao Ziyang, was absent.

It was the third day in a row that Li Peng had made a public appearance after midnight. He stood before his comrades in a charcoal-grey Mao suit, his owlish face grim and determined. Unlike the previous two nights, he was no longer a man attempting to reason with the students. Now he was a man ready to use all the resources of the state to send them home. "We were tolerant and reasonable for more than a month," he declared. "Perhaps no other government in the world would do that." The balance of his speech showed that he had not changed his thinking in that month. Li made the same characterizations of the student movement as had been contained in the editorial in the 26 April edition of the *People's Daily*. A handful of persons were using the hunger strikers as "hostages" he claimed, to coerce and force the government to give in to their political demands. He said it was clear that a very few people were attempting to create turmoil in order to negate the leadership of the Communist Party, overthrow the socialist system and violate the constitution. He outlined a conspiracy that had managed to dupe millions, of people who "establish secret ties, set up illegal organizations and force the Party to recognize them. In doing so they attempt to lay a foundation to set up opposition factions and parties in China."

That argument appeared to contradict another aspect of his speech, which had been inspired by student leader Wuer Kaixi. "Representatives of the hunger strikers said they could no longer control the situation on Tiananmen Square," Li said. "Crowds keep shouting demagogic slogans. Nationwide turmoil is possible." How conspirators could manipulate and lose control at the same time was not addressed by the premier. Li Peng was calling in the army and did not concern himself with the logical soundness of his argument. Instead, he produced a catalogue of reasons why military intervention was needed to end the chaos. Colleges were at a standstill, traffic was jammed, government work was affected, public security was deteriorating and the hunger strikers were in imminent danger. Coupled with the conspiracy to topple the government, the future of China was threatened; its reform, open door policy, socialist democracy and modernization would come to nothing. The government had been restrained in its reaction, he said, because it did not want to hurt the masses of good people. But because the conspirators took the tolerance as weakness, said Li, the state was now forced to take decisive measures.

The premier appealed to the students to end their fast, leave the square and get medical treatment. He asked everyone to keep working and resume classes. Dialogue would continue, he promised, with students and people from other walks of life. Students would not be penalized "for their radical words and actions."

The silver-haired crowd applauding Li's speech represented the old guard in the Communist Party, or rather those whose political authority had endured its turbulent history. Many had tousled Li Peng's hair when he was a boy, and he had sat at their side listening to stories. At the relatively youthful age of sixty-one, Li Peng represented an historic link to the very roots of Chinese communism.

He was born in Deng Xiaoping's home province of Sichuan. Li's father, a communist writer, was executed by the Guomindang when the boy was three. At the age of eleven, he was adopted by Zhou Enlai and his wife—one of many such orphaned children of revolutionary martyrs taken in by the childless couple. Li joined the party at seventeen, went to study in the Soviet Union when he was twenty and became an energy expert, as did his wife and three children. He worked his way up the political ladder to become minister of electric power in 1981. By 1983, he was a vice-premier and, when Zhao Ziyang took over as Communist Party chief in 1987, Li was the surprise choice to succeed Zhao as premier. Most had expected the more experienced Wan Li to assume the post. Li denied that his relationship to Zhou Enlai had anything to do with his promotion, but many felt that Li was underqualified to fill Zhao's shoes as premier. He was considered to be a conservative who might put the brakes to China's economic reform, a man with little tolerance for dissent. On 20 May, Party hardliners considered the latter quality an asset.

The marvel of crisis politics lies in the simplicity of its resolution. The leadership felt that the country had reached such a crisis on 19 May, and more delays and indecisiveness would only deepen the crisis—and increase the possibility of government collapse. It came down to one of two choices: negotiations or military intervention. Since neither Li Peng nor Deng Xiaoping were prepared to step down there was no third alternative. Li and his backers opted for the second option, with the obvious blessing and likely directive of Deng. The government had been tolerant and had tried dialogue. That approach had not worked. It had allowed ambulances into the square to take hunger strikers for treatment at government hospitals; that, too, had not worked. Neither had televised meetings with student leaders, nor messages affirming the patriotism of the student movement, nor any of the other measures taken to restore order. The student movement was like a ravenous monster that grew ever larger and ever more hungry each time it was fed. It had grown so large that the government did not know with whom it could negotiate to end the crisis. Student leaders admitted they were no longer in control, and still the monster grew. Young supporters from around the country flocked to Beijing. Thirteen thousand arrived at the capital's railway station in one four-hour period on Thursday, 18 May. Fifty thousand arrived on Friday.

By calling in the army, the leadership had abandoned all hope that the situation could be defused and decided instead that it had to be terminated. There could be negative international and domestic repercussions from such an action, but Li and Deng hoped to avoid these if the army could re-establish government authority without resorting to violence. The army enjoyed tremendous prestige among the population. Faced with such a determination to restore order, Li expected that the crowds would melt away. He couched his call to arms with conciliation, promising to respond to the wishes of the people once order was restored. That night, no one in the square took those promises seriously. They expected instead a crackdown. "I think top leaders like Deng Xiaoping and Li Peng think their power is in danger," one woman commented. "It is the traditional way for top Chinese leaders to take tough policies towards the people. Probably they feel they have no other way."

Trainloads of students continued to arrive in Beijing even during the speech. One group of students from Xi'an reached the city just before midnight, claiming that they had come with the blessing of their provincial government. They quickly learned of Li's speech. "When we marched onto the street," said one young man, "we heard that the soldiers would come to Tiananmen Square. But after that we heard people tell us they will prevent the soldiers from coming. Then we were encouraged and marched directly here."

Student leaders were undecided. Several of them, along with some teachers and academics, roamed around Tiananmen in a bus at 2:00 A.M. on Saturday, 20 May. At first, they pledged to reactivate the hunger strike and expand it to include everyone in the square—more than a quarter of a million people. Shortly after 3:00 A.M., they changed their minds and again called off the fast. Everyone, they said, would stage a sit-down strike until their demands were met. And they now had new demands: the withdrawal of martial law and the resignation of Li Peng. Ambulance sirens wailed through the night, chants rose above the square, and people waited for the soldiers to come. In one part of Tiananmen about fifty young women sang a beautiful melody—the Full Moon Festival song. The original version tells of a soldier who had to leave his love to fight the Vietnamese in 1979, but the lyrics had been re-written for the democracy movement.

For democracy, for freedom,
We should not hesitate,
We should not be silent.
For the people, for China,
We should work together as one.

Do you understand?
Do you realize?
I may fall and never rise again.

Above the Monument to the Revolutionary Martyrs, a full moon shone its pale fire onto an anxious plaza.

Even as Li Peng spoke, the "resolute and forceful measures to curb the turmoil and restore order" that he had demanded were already rumbling towards Tiananmen Square. Convoys of army trucks filled with soldiers moved in from the outskirts of the city. However, if the government expected people to be terrified, or even cowed, it was misguided.

Word of the troop movements flashed through the Chinese capital like lightning. Students and their supporters bolted towards the areas where soldiers were reported to be assembling. Many Beijingers jumped straight out of bed and rushed to the main roads leading into the city. At 2:00 A.M. on Saturday, more than one thousand students waited outside the gates of RenDa for four huge lorries to ferry them to the confrontations. It was the same all over Beijing.

Far to the west of Tiananmen, a few kilometres past China Central Television, at least fifty military trucks were being blockaded by tens of thousands of people. Middle-aged men and women, some carrying children, stood in front of the imposing convoy. Others swarmed right on top of the vehicles, pleading with soldiers not to move on Tiananmen Square. They were polite, but firm—careful to avoid violence, to avoid provoking the troops in any way. Several people offered the People's Liberation Army men tea or cigarettes. A few leaned over tailgates, explaining that the students were good; that they were patriotic and wanted only to help build the country. Some people, however, were less patient. All their lives they had known the PLA as an heroic and protective force, yet here were soldiers of the much-vaunted, much-loved army apparently preparing to march on their own people.

"Do you know what you are doing?" asked one agitated young woman. "You should be protecting the people, not cracking down on them." The soldiers stared back. "You cannot do this!" she continued. "You have a conscience!" Several demonstrators thrust pro-democracy banners in the troops' faces or stood on the hoods of trucks, waving flags. In some cases, slogans such as "The People's Army Loves the People" were written directly on the green military vehicles. In others, demonstrators crawled underneath the front wheels and cut fuel lines. Strangely, even these actions were performed with little animosity. They were instead carried out proudly, almost lovingly, as if each person were performing a great and patriotic duty. One elderly woman hunched down beside a truck full of troops, smiled warmly, and began letting the air out of its tires.

Similar scenes occurred in five other locations across Beijing, possibly more. In all cases, the soldiers were held back. Students and their supporters considered it a great victory. But was it? The PLA had neither brandished guns, nor made serious attempts to push through the lines of protestors. Certainly, the army could have made a greater effort if it were actually intent on clearing the square. There were some reports of minor scuffles, but from all appearances the soldiers seemed to have been sent as a warning. Some army men seemed surprised and confused by what they encountered. One group of soldiers at Liuli Bridge, two kilometres southwest of the CCTV building, told people that they had been forbidden to read newspapers or listen to the radio for more than a week. They thought that they were going on manoeuvres in northeast China. Others said that they had been told there was a massive flood in Beijing.

Word on the street was that they had indeed been ordered to clear the square, but that generals of the Thirty-Eighth Army, apparently stationed to the south, had refused to march against the students. The commander of the Twenty-Seventh Army was also said to be reluctant. Reports suggested that he would follow orders only if he received them, in writing, from Deng Xiaoping.

The end result was that the soldiers did not move—and many Beijingers wanted to keep it that way. They began constructing crude barricades at strategic intersections leading into the city proper.

People dismantled the concrete and pipe guard rails which normally protect the bicycle lanes. These barriers, along with heavy steel garbage cans, buses, cement sewer pipes and even metal vendor stalls, were dragged or pushed across roads. Large trucks filled with gravel were parked sideways to block streets.

In Shanghai, however, the struggle was already over. Police there swept through the People's Park and told students that their northern comrades had given up. The lie worked. Amidst confusion and bitter disappointment, leaders sadly told their followers to go home. The few who objected were dragged away.

In Beijing, they had not yet begun to fight.

"The bird is being pulled!" shouted a frantic Western television producer shortly after 9:00 A.M. on Saturday, 20 May. "They're going to pull the bird!" CCTV was a scene of bedlam. Foreign journalists and editors flew up and down hallways with precious videotapes, desperate to beam the night's events halfway around the world. The "bird" was the crucial satellite link they needed to do the job. For most networks, CCTV was the only conduit for such transmissions. That critical link was about to be cut: martial law had been declared.

It was to take effect at 10:00 A.M. and many of the Chinese who worked in the transmission centre did not like it any more than the foreigners. Tearfully, they pulled the plug at 10:03, in mid-transmission of a Canadian Broadcasting Corporation story. The Atlanta-based Cable News Network, which was beaming stories with its own satellite dish, refused to stop transmitting until it received the order in writing. North American viewers watched as a Chinese hastily scrawled a note outlining martial law provisions—all on live television. The coverage continued right up to the moment when a CNN employee was shown reluctantly turning off the uplink.

Foreign television journalists were not about to let martial law get in the way of a good story. At bureaus throughout Beijing, reporters and their producers stopped talking about "birds" and started discussing "pigeons"—people who could carry videotape to Hong Kong and Tokyo for transmission from those cities.

In Tiananmen Square, the State Council's declaration of martial law was being heard loud and clear. Government loudspeakers thundered the points repeatedly. The litany of regulations was also carried by the New China News Agency in consecutive bulletins:

BEIJING, MAY 20 (XINHUA)—CHEN XITONG, MAYOR OF BEIJING, TODAY SIGNED THREE ORDERS OF THE BEIJING MUNICIPAL PEOPLE'S GOVERNMENT. FOLLOWING IS ORDER NO. 1:

In accordance with the order of the State Council signed by Premier

Li Peng on enforcing martial law in part of Beijing, the Beijing Municipal People's Government issues this order with a view to quickly checking social turmoil and safeguarding the normal work, production, teaching, scientific research and social living in the capital.

1. Starting from 10:00 on May 20, 1989, martial law is enforced in the Eastern, Western, Chongwen, Xuanwu, Shijingshan, Haidian, Fengtai and Chaoyang districts.

2. Under the martial law, demonstrations, petition, class boycott, work stoppage and other activities of amassing people to impede the normal order are banned.

3. People are banned from using any form to create and spread rumours, establish ties, make public speeches or distribute leaflets to incite social turmoil.

4. It is prohibited to assault leading organs of the Party, the government and the army, to assault broadcasting, television communications and other key units, or to sabotage important public facilities. All disruptive activities, such as beating, smashing, looting and setting fire are strictly forbidden.

5. It is prohibited to harass embassies of all countries and agencies of the United Nations in Beijing.

6. Under the martial law, public security officers, members of the armed police and men of the People's Liberation Army on duty have the right to use every possible means to stop any of the above prohibited activities should they occur.

It is hoped that all residents in the city will observe the above.

BEIJING, MAY 20 (XINHUA)—MAYOR OF BEIJING CHEN XITONG ISSUED ORDER NO. 2 OF THE BEIJING MUNICIPAL PEOPLE'S GOVERNMENT HERE TODAY.

THE ORDER FOLLOWS:

1. Foreigners must observe all orders issued by the Beijing Municipal People's Government in accordance with the martial law order signed by Premier Li Peng.

2. During the period of the martial law, foreigners are not allowed to get involved in any activities of Chinese citizens in violating the martial law.

3. Men of the People's Liberation Army on duty have the right to adopt all possible means to stop any activities violating the above.

BEIJING, MAY 20 (XINHUA)—IN LINE WITH THE STATE COUNCIL'S DECISION TO ENFORCE MARTIAL LAW ON PART OF BEIJING, CHEN XITONG, MAYOR OF BEIJING, TODAY SIGNED ORDER NO. 3 OF THE BEIJING MUNICIPAL PEOPLE'S GOVERNMENT. . .

THE FOLLOWING REGULATIONS ARE MADE FOR PRESS COVERAGE:

1. Chinese or foreign journalists are strictly forbidden to utilize press coverage to instigate and incite propaganda.

2. Journalists from abroad, as well as from Hong Kong, Macao and Taiwan are forbidden to go to government institutions, organizations, schools, factories, mines, enterprises or neighborhoods to conduct interviews, take pictures or make videotapes without approval of the Beijing Municipal People's Government.

3. Those on duty have the right to stop those who violate the above regulations.

It was a very long list of prohibitions, one which made the situation sound much worse than it was. Students had not been sabotaging public facilities, nor had they been looting and pillaging Beijing. Perhaps the government feared they would, but it seems possible that some of those points were included in the draft to justify the imposition of martial law. For the millions of Beijingers who had not participated in demonstrations, who had not gone to Tiananmen Square, the orders implied that parts of the Chinese capital were in a state of total anarchy; that beatings and robberies abounded; that Beijing was under seige by terrorists. It was a scenario that Li Peng and his backers wanted the people of China—and the world—to believe.

The students and their supporters thought otherwise. Certainly, the prospect of a military crackdown frightened them. More pervasive, though, was a feeling of profound shock, frustration and anger. Less than two days earlier many had thought that the government was about to crumble before the power of the democracy movement; that Deng, or Li—or both—would resign. Yet now things were worse than ever. Much, much worse. Not only was the state calling out the army, but Zhao Ziyang had apparently fallen. The one man in power who seemed to sympathize genuinely with their cause was gone, and the students were to blame. It was like a nightmare, a sequel to the Hu Yaobang saga with a far more disastrous ending.

But it did not have to end. What was there to gain by packing up and abandoning Tiananmen Square? In the minds of the students, absolutely nothing. To quit the cause now would be to accept defeat, to relinquish everything they had gained. The government, they believed, had never made a sincere effort to end the crisis. With Zhao gone and Li firmly in control, there was even less reason to think that dialogue on an equal footing could take place. The solution was to use Li Peng's declaration to their own advantage; to unite in defiance against what they and their supporters believed was an unjust measure. Under the bright sunshine which warmed Beijing that first day of martial law, they rallied with renewed strength in Tiananmen Square.

The plaza was packed. Not only was it brimming with buses and students, but trucks and carts laden with food were appearing. There were scores of thousands of students from other parts of the country who had to be fed, to say nothing of the starving group which had just finished its week-long fast. Bread, steamed dough, rice and soup were dished out to seemingly endless line-ups. Much of the food was purchased with contributions, but a sizable amount had been donated. One family wheeled in a transport tricycle which carried a large vat of soup and several smaller pots of hot food. They cheerfully filled

135

plates, explaining proudly "We do this for the students."

The ambience in Tiananmen began to shift. During the previous week, much of the concern had been over the condition of the hunger strikers. The square had resembled a refugee camp, complete with tattered tents, harried medical workers, speeding ambulances and collapsing students. Now the fast was off and a new battle had begun. Although the banners and buses looked much the same, Tiananmen began to change drastically during the first days of martial law. Food, clothing and medical supplies were stockpiled on the lower level of the Monument to the Revolutionary Martyrs. Garbage details were organized to sweep the square clean of refuse. Printing presses churned out leaflets at a furious pace. More and better tents, some capable of sheltering more than twenty students, went up in many parts of the square. A new and reliable generator was installed to power the democracy movement's public address system. The student leaders moved to the south side of the Monument's upper level, where volunteers protected them like military commanders. On the north side, Chinese and foreign journalists started maintaining an around-the-clock vigil. The sit-in was being taken very seriously. As Tiananmen began taking on the characteristics of a small city, it was clear that students were there for the long term. Any who doubted that commitment needed only to look in their eyes or hear their voices.

Remote-control surveillance cameras, mounted to several lamp posts in the square, started to swivel. Slowly they panned back and forth, surveying the chanting crowd. Somewhere, a videotape machine was recording the faces of defiance. Big Brother was indeed watching.

And so was the People's Liberation Army. Minutes after 10:00 A.M. on 20 May, the distinctive sound of rotor blades heralded the arrival of five PLA helicopters. The camouflaged choppers swooped in from the northeast in low, graceful passes—whirring over Tiananmen Gate, the Great Hall of the People, Mao's tomb and the Revolutionary Museum. "Attention students," someone announced over the democracy loudspeakers, "Don't panic. . . ." They might have saved their breath. If the PLA mission was intended to menace or frighten the students it was an utter failure. Protestors began cheering and applauding the aircraft, waving to the pilots. Some climbed on top of buses and started swinging democracy banners in almost a beckoning fashion.

The helicopter formation was undeniably a dramatic and entrancing sight; many students looked like wide-eyed spectators at an airshow. The aircraft swept around the square majestically in long banking turns, the whine of their blades overpowering the student

136

loudspeakers. They circled Tiananmen several times, to continuous applause, before finally pulling out and flying low over the length of Changan Boulevard.

The rumour mill shifted into overdrive. The copters were coming back, students warned. They would be bringing commandos—paratroopers with weapons who would storm the square. Tear gas would be fired into the crowds, and people would be beaten. Nonsense, countered others. It was merely a reconnaissance mission, a way to gauge the size and strength of the crowd. Some students even believed that the helicopters were not on a mission at all; that they were piloted by men who had defected from the army to support the student cause. It was a rumour that many protestors—even if they did not accept it—wanted to believe was possible.

Hearsay was right about one thing: the helicopters would return. Over and over that day, the flying circus came back. On its second or third appearance, students tried to encourage at least one of the choppers to set down. Hundreds of them linked arms in a circle, leaving a clear landing pad opposite the Great Hall of the People. No pilot took them up on the offer, but they must have stared in disbelief, if not admiration, on a later pass. Not only had students cleared a circle, but they had set down huge posters in the centre—inviting the pilots to land. The PLA responded by passing along a message on behalf of the government. The helicopters swept lower, side doors opened, and thousands of leaflets were kicked out. They fluttered softly towards waiting arms. As soon as the students had read those pieces of paper, they stomped on them or tore them up in disgust. The leaflets contained stern words from the hated Li Peng: clear the square or face the consequences. Some students said that they received messages which warned that tear gas would be used at midnight unless Tiananmen was emptied.

They did not clear the square, but they did start taking the threat of an attack more seriously. Students began soaking bandannas and wads of cotton in pails of water. They believed that the damp materials could filter out tear gas, were it to be used. Volunteers also began distributing these crude masks to foreign journalists on the Monument. For some, it was not necessary. One television cameraman had brought a real gas mask—a souvenir from student protests in Seoul—and a Western photographer showed up with a pair of swimming goggles dangling from his neck.

On one of their later appearances, the helicopters swept so low they sounded like airborne chainsaws. They were roughly twenty metres above the crowd and some protestors covered their faces with damp cloth. A few, realizing that the choppers now represented the enemy, jeered at the droning formation. One woman, who was not a student, noticed a reporter holding his microphone to the sky, taping the sound. She rushed forward.

"Would you like to know what the average Beijinger thinks of all this?" she shouted over the roar of the helicopters. Her answer was quick and direct: "Down with Li Peng!"

The woman said that the military did not frighten her, adding "I think it will only make people more angry. People are people, they are not enemies. They [the PLA] just want to kill. . . . But people are not afraid nowadays." She started to leave, but the noise from a chopper, which was directly overhead, seemed to prompt her to make one more statement. "Down with the bastard Chinese leadership!!" she screamed.

As the day wore on, students returned from the suburbs with reports of clashes with soldiers. Forty-five people were said to have been injured while blockading troops to the north of Beijing. A column of tanks was said to be only a few kilometres to the south; thousands of volunteers quickly mobilized and began marching in that direction. There were also stories of fighting in the university district. One young man claimed to have seen PLA vehicles run down two people near Tiananmen Square. "There were two trucks travelling at high speed," he said. "They hit two people—one of them was handicapped. They went over them and did not stop. I didn't see the license plate, but they were army trucks." Sporadic reports of other skirmishes continued throughout the day. Word also spread that soldiers had taken over the Radio Beijing compound and were moving on other state-run media outlets.

Some protestors refused to accept that the army which had once liberated the people was now suppressing them. Said one man: "I believe, the students believe, the *people* believe that the People's Army cannot point its guns at the people." His thoughts were echoed by a young student who said "the policemen, the soldiers, cannot ignore the people's appeals." Others were more skeptical. "Most of the soldiers are good and won't turn their guns on the people," said another man in Tiananmen Square, "but I have no doubt a handful of people in the army are still loyal to Deng Xiaoping and Mr. Li. I think this small handful will become criminals. Historic criminals."

The students, meanwhile, drafted a new response to the declaration of martial law. It contained the following five points:

1. Avoid confrontation with the army. Don't do anything that will cause bloodshed.

2. We call for a national strike. No work, boycott class, stop teaching, close the shops.

3. The PLA are soldiers of the people. We should not fight with each other.
4. We demand a special meeting of the National People's Congress.
5. We demand a special meeting of the Communist Party.

They received a healthy endorsement from a workers' alliance claiming to represent thirty-seven factories. The group said that if the government failed to respond within twenty-four hours, it would back student demands for a general strike.

The students also began to put great stock in the National People's Congress and its chairman, Wan Li. He was then in Canada on a state visit, and students believed that he supported their cause. Although the Congress has relatively little power, it does have the authority to force the resignation of the country's premier. Students began talking of a scenario in which Wan Li would return to China and back Zhao. A special session of the Congress could be convened, they said, to denounce Li Peng and lift martial law.

Most of those taking part in the democracy movement believed that they enjoyed great support from within lower levels of government. They had good reason to feel that way. During some of the largest demonstrations, many members of the Communist Party—including some prominent cadres—had endorsed their actions. The length of time it took for the crackdown to come was another indication that the government was heavily split. It seemed obvious that only a very few men, with the all-important backing of Deng, were responsible for martial law. Surely the National People's Congress would have the courage to denounce what was wrong. It was a hope that tens of thousands of students would cling to desperately.

Throughout that long, hot Saturday, Beijingers packed into Tiananmen Square. As many as half a million people filled the plaza during the afternoon. Changan Boulevard seemed to have become a democracy promenade with as many thousands walking towards the city centre as away from it. Some, no doubt, had come out of curiosity—to see the students, the helicopters and the possible confrontation with the army. In doing so they were breaking martial law and ignoring their government's authority. Everyone was breaking martial law. The chanting was more defiant than ever, the speeches more passionate.

"The people will win!" shouted one man. "We will fight to the end. Now you will see the power of the people!"

"Even if there's only one man left," sobbed an emotional protestor, "we should keep fighting. We will keep our places in the square." He was half crying, half shouting through his megaphone to an enraptured crowd. "As patriotic youth we don't really know every-thing about the country. But we don't know what's happening be-cause the Party tells us the 'truth'. What do you think of that?" Tears streamed down his face. "The Party is controlled by a few people who do not really represent the real communists. The Party is not in the hands of the people but of a clique. . . ." He continued haltingly, then broke down completely and began to cry, mourning for a dying dream.

As darkness fell over Beijing that Saturday night, students prepared for the worst. Many believed that their lease on Tiananmen Square had expired; that the army would soon carry out eviction or-ders on behalf of the landlords. Medical staff and volunteers shuttled through the maze of tents, ensuring that everyone was equipped with moist cotton or cloth. Word spread that troops would spray tear gas at 2:00 A.M. Television crews on the Monument joked nervously and waited for the expected assault. Loudspeakers played the Interna-tionale and the Chinese national anthem amidst a scene reminiscent of the sinking of the Titanic. The students were frightened. Many were crying, or holding each other tightly. They knew a damp rag would provide little protection against tear gas or clubs, but they found some comfort in the knowledge that the masses had once again rallied behind them. An estimated one million people were guarding the streets leading into Beijing and Tiananmen Square. Unlike the previous evening, however, soldiers were seen holding AK-47 assault rifles. One Western journalist saw truckloads of troops with the weapons at the Liuli bridge, southwest of Tiananmen Square. The guns appeared to be more for show than anything else; the reporter noticed that the soldiers did not have ammunition clips in their rifles.

In a repeat performance of what had happened during the early hours of Saturday, tens of thousands of Beijingers swamped each and every PLA convoy. More fuel lines were cut, more tires were deflated and more soldiers were re-educated as to the nature of the democracy movement. Many citizens, realizing that the troops knew little about the situation in the capital, offered them copies of the *Beijing Daily* and other newspapers. Some soldiers refused to read them, but others were swayed by the demonstrators. These were not the crim-inals and hooligans the army had apparently been prepared to en-counter. How could a grandmother who was offering cups of tea be bent on the violent overthrow of the government? Or a middle-aged man, carrying his son on his shoulders? It did not make sense. Demoralized and disillusioned, several young recruits were said to have taken off their army jackets and melted into the crowd. By dawn, a number of convoys turned and retreated, either on orders or of their own volition. The crowds cheered triumphantly and waved to the departing troops, many of whom smiled and waved back. The iron fist of the army had been overpowered by open arms.

When word reached Tiananmen Square during the night that the army was being held back, there was jubilation. Tears and fears vanished and the loudspeakers started playing music. This time it was neither the Internationale nor the Chinese national anthem. Instead, the sound heard in Tiananmen Square at 3:00 A.M. on Sunday, 21 May, was Beethoven's "Ode to Joy."

Triumphant that they had again vanquished the army, students and their supporters took down a few of the barricades so that traffic could flow more or less normally. Strategic blockades on the outskirts were left in place. On streetcorners everywhere, people made impromptu speeches—many of which were vitriolic attacks on Premier Li Peng. Why, they asked, would he send the army to crush a peaceful movement? There had been no chaos, no violence as Li had claimed. And above all, why would he call in the army if, as he said on Friday, the number one priority was the health and welfare of the students? Hundreds of thousands filled the streets, a remarkable number considering that a million Beijingers had been up all night. Banners were everywhere. Trucks loaded with demonstrators roamed Changan in triumph.

Despite the jubilation, no one knew with any certainty what the army was really up to. Some believed that several high-ranking generals were vehemently opposed to martial law and would not allow troops under their command to march on Beijing. This was a source of great inspiration, and students eagerly passed the word along to their comrades. The government, meanwhile, had made no statement since Li Peng's speech at midnight Friday. It was being re-broadcast frequently on CCTV, but there had been no other announcements. Was it a sign of another leadership struggle? Would the military depose Li and reinstate Zhao? The whole gamut of possibilities swept through Beijing's sizzling grapevine. The Chinese capital became awash with rumours as never before. One minute, armed troops were on their way to Tiananmen Square via the subway system. The next moment there was word that sympathetic workers had stopped them by cutting power lines. The minute after that students were telling each other that several top generals had resigned from the army in disgust. In martial law Beijing, anything was possible.

Regardless of the military, there were indications on Sunday that the Public Security Bureau had strict orders to keep tabs on those defying the emergency regulations. A CBC crew discovered this when they headed to the western outskirts of the city, where a PLA convoy had been hemmed in by several buses and several thousand people.

Scores of troops remained in their trucks, sweltering under the hot sun, but the majority were in a nearby compound, sitting under a walkway. In the cool shade, a few of them polished their AK-47s. A man in his early forties, who had been helping with the blockade, walked towards the crew. He told a reporter that he wanted to talk about martial law, the democracy movement and the Chinese leadership. He said he was willing to appear on camera, despite the regulations. Together with the crew he walked to their nearby car, which was about one hundred metres from the compound. The camera had not even been placed on the tripod when two members of the army, apparently commanders, spotted them. The men started marching briskly towards the car. "Soldiers are coming!" shouted some bystanders. Dozens of onlookers immediately formed a protective barrier around the sides and rear of the vehicle, blocking the officers but leaving the car with an escape route. The crew, along with the man who had volunteered to be interviewed, jumped in the car and sped away. The man said he still wanted to talk, but he was clearly nervous about being spotted again. It was decided to drive into central Beijing and record the interview in one of the small hutongs. All the way there, he spoke fluidly about the anger he felt over martial law; about his intense hatred for Li Peng. When an appropriate site was found, the man donned sunglasses in the hope it would protect his identity. The camera was set up and the interview began. It started smoothly, but soon the man began to stammer. "You . . . you know my situation," he said haltingly. "Really, I'm afraid." At that point the crew noticed a man in his early sixties sitting on a nearby bicycle. He was staring at the younger Chinese intensely. This would have been quite normal in Beijing, but soon the older man began asking questions. "Who are you?" he demanded. "What work unit are you from? What nationality are these journalists?" The man was scared to death. Then a member of the television crew saw why. Sticking out of a pocket on the older man's blue Mao suit was a walkie-talkie. The interview ended abruptly, and the younger man was bundled back into the car and dropped off in another section of the city. Both he and the driver were convinced the man on the bicycle was an agent of the Public Security Bureau. The driver, though also frightened, was not as worried about repercussions. He believed that the man would never be able to identify the car. That was quite probable, since the driver had removed his licence plates the day before. He had done so after another man, presumably an undercover policeman, had photographed the plates when the vehicle took the crew to see Beijingers blocking troops west of CCTV.

Back at Tiananmen Square, the helicopters returned to drop copies of Li Peng's hard-line speech. Students reached skyward to grab the documents, which they shredded even before reading. It was a sign that the premier was still in command and that there were soldiers willing to carry out his bidding. The reaction was immediate and intense.

"All of the Chinese people should stand up, should fight this reactionary government," screamed a stern-looking woman with Mongol features. Her persona and fury seemed to define the Chinese word *xiong*, or fierce. Shouting herself into an emotional fever, she had attracted quite a crowd. So compelling were her angry gestures and hoarse voice that people applauded her every word, even though most could not understand them. She was speaking in English. "If the army wants to push down the movement, we should *fight* with them too. I hope if there is one person in the army, he should stand up. He should say 'don't listen to Deng Xiaoping'. Our students are not afraid to die. I am not afraid to die. The people here are not afraid to die."

The reckless defiance of that one woman was reflected in the actions of the millions ignoring martial law provisions, and that gave them courage. Behind every face on the streets of Beijing lay the knowledge that the decision of Deng Xiaoping and Li Peng was not supported by a significant number of moderates within the Party leadership. Many believed that the reason why unarmed civilians had been able to stop the soldiers lay less in the power of the people than in the lack of resolve of top army generals. As the sun spilled over Tiananmen Square on Sunday, 21 May, people waited and speculated.

"Martial law has actually helped students get more support from workers," one student said. "The government is now afraid to come here." Another young man broke in, "In two or three days, we think some changes will happen in our top leaders."

By early Sunday evening, fresh news was rocketing through the city: the army would clear the square that very night. Li Peng, it was said, had ordered streetsweepers to be ready to clean Tiananmen at dawn Monday.

New barricades started going up immediately. Students and volunteers dragged countless bicycle dividers and drove or pushed more than two hundred buses into the streets. The task was performed with a sense of urgency which contrasted sharply with the euphoria that had prevailed earlier in the day. A brief announcement on state television confirmed what the protestors and their supporters feared: there was indeed an ultimatum. More volunteers were mobilized. Anything not nailed down was added to roadblocks. Students sent out fresh propaganda teams to try to reason with the PLA. By the time the sun dipped below the Fragrant Hills west of Beijing, demonstrators said that they had eight separate lines of defence on every main road leading into the city.

In Tiananmen Square it was becoming a familiar routine. Fresh cotton was distributed and numerous pails of water were scattered around the plaza for students to moisten their 'gas masks'. Protestors anxiously told one another that everything would be all right; that the defences would hold. Several journalists, believing an attack was imminent, brought clear plastic shower caps from their hotels on the advice of a West German cameraman. He had said that the caps, if pulled down over the eyes, would provide enough protection from tear gas to allow crews to continue rolling. Nervously, they joked and waited.

Around the square, citizens of Beijing were showing little fear. Several thousand took part in a bicycle rally which repeatedly circled Tiananmen. There were young and middle-aged couples, some with children balanced on handlebars. A few elderly Beijingers were carried on the rear of transport tricycles. They sang the Internationale and waved to the demonstrators, who clearly found comfort in the display. The students were also relieved to again see the Flying Tigers, the freedom-loving motorcyclists who were becoming part of Beijing's landscape. Beeping their horns continually, the cavalry roared around the square and up and down Changan.

Despite this support, the student loudspeakers were less than reassuring. Soldiers were getting close, they announced. Troops were said to be at the railway station, a cavernous terminal a mere two kilometres southeast of Tiananmen Square. Some students were convinced that the army was much closer than that. They were worried about a tunnel system which connects Zhongnanhai with the Great Hall of the People and the Revolutionary Museum. The shafts, they said, were large enough to drive troop carriers through. It was possible, if not probable, that soldiers were already in the Great Hall and the museum. All the army was waiting for, thought some students, was the order to strike. Many in the square pointed nervously towards the museum roof, where shadowy silhouettes could be seen looming over the parapet.

At around 2:00 A.M. on Monday, 22 May, student loudspeakers warned that the situation was "very dangerous." About a dozen medical students dressed in white smocks paced nervously near a large tent which had been set up outside the Museum. The tent, which bore a large Red Cross symbol, had been erected during the day. It was sheltered on three sides by a hedge and by a tree on the fourth. The students had intentionally placed the tent outside the

144

square. They believed that people might be seriously injured that night; Tiananmen would be no place for a field hospital. Inside were several cardboard boxes stuffed with surgical dressings. Underneath the nearby tree, several students from outside Beijing slept fitfully on urine-soaked ground.

Suddenly, the young interns stopped pacing. They stood completely still, straining to hear the democracy loudspeakers. What they heard was not good news. Student leader Wuer Kaixi was saying that the situation was more than just dangerous. He was predicting mass arrests and recommending that students withdraw to Beijing's embassy district for refuge. The speaker urged that demonstrators prepare to leave at 3:10 A.M.

"There are so many people," said one medical student, "I don't think they will all get into the embassies." "I think I will go," said a young woman. She sounded very unsure of her decision; torn between seeking safety or facing danger for a cause she believed in. The loudspeakers continued, warning that soldiers were armed not only with tear gas and rubber bullets, but with other weapons as well. A tall youth wearing a white doctor's cap stared sadly towards the square. "They [the soldiers] want blood," he said. "It will be bloody."

No one made a move. There appeared to be some indecision among the student leaders, for now new voices were issuing forth from the loudspeakers. A huge cheer echoed off the museum walls.

"There are different opinions," said a medical student, "as to whether the students should withdraw or not. These people say they will not withdraw. . . . They say many people support them, many workers, and many soldiers will refuse to beat them. So they think it would be better to sit here, rather than rush to the embassies."

"I think we should stay," added another young man. "This time is a very important time for Chinese. We young people have a duty to our democracy. If I and my students withdraw, I think the future of China is very dim."

For some time, the student leaders played out their infighting over the democracy loudspeakers, Wuer Kaixi arguing adamantly to leave while others insisted that students should remain. In the end, the demonstrators decided to stay in the square, and Wuer lost influence as a leader of the protest. The students still believed that the soldiers could come, that the ultimatum was real, and that there might be bloodshed. But they also held on to the belief that the army could be either dissuaded or blockaded. The remaining hours before dawn were to be excruciatingly long and equally nerve-wracking. As they waited for the troops to come, two women in their early twenties, both medical students, sat down in front of the hedge by the red cross tent. They were dressed head to toe in white, and their uniforms

145

reflected the soft light from Tiananmen Square. Under the stars, they held each other close and sang "Silent Night." The soldiers did not come.

Although Li Peng had sworn to have the square clear by dawn, the military apparently had plans of its own. In a complete reversal of the warning broadcast three hours earlier, a television bulletin late Sunday night said that the PLA would not storm Tiananmen. The army had no intention of suppressing the students, said an announcer, and was only in Beijing to keep the peace. It was either a trick or a sign that the military was refusing to obey the premier's orders. Judging by the mood in the square that night, the students chose to believe that they were still in grave danger. For hours, they clung to their cause and to each other, fearing a violent attack. An hour before sunrise, when workers were supposed to sweep the square clean of democracy, an announcement came from the People's Liberation Army. Students were told that they could remain in Tiananmen Square, providing they maintained order.

The tension which had permeated the plaza during those long hours was washed away in a flash flood of jubilation. Again they had won. The students and their supporters celebrated their victory with cheering, chanting and a hearty rendition of the Internationale. When the buoyant laughter and exhilaration finally subsided, people started trying to fit the latest pieces of information into an increasingly complex jigsaw puzzle.

"Some generals do not agree with what is happening," speculated a youth. "There must be some struggle in our government offices." At first, it appeared he was wrong. Helicopters returned to Tiananmen Square, dropping more leaflets which urged people to oppose "lawless elements" and reminded the students that they were forbidden to shout provocative slogans. The pieces of paper also bore a list of twenty phrases people were permitted to chant, one of which was "Firmly support Comrade Li Peng's important speech." Most of the leaflets were torn to pieces.

But there were also signs that the student may have been correct. Word came that as many as one hundred top members of the military, including a former minister of defence, opposed the emergency measures. Copies of a letter they had supposedly sent to martial law command were distributed by students in Tiananmen Square. "The people's army belongs to the people," the generals wrote. "They cannot be used to suppress the people and they must never fire on the people. To stop the situation from getting worse, troops must not enter the city." A lack of will was also seen in the troops stalled on the outskirts of the city. CCTV interviewed a colonel commanding one

146

such unit that had been trapped in western Beijing for sixty hours. "Our superiors are letting us remain here while awaiting further orders," he said. "We have seen that the college students are quite reasonable. Like us, they try to avoid confrontations." The officer fretted over the condition of his men, who had been ordered into the capital without bedding, rain gear or rations. "Just now I made an inspection tour," he said, "and it was painful to see." A local steel plant provided the troops with food.

Such reports were taken as clues that the Li Peng faction was losing its power struggle. When martial law was initially declared, China Central Television did not mention the blockaded troops, focussing instead on Li's speech and the new regulations. Television anchors relaying the premier's hard line seemed distinctly uncomfortable and rarely looked into the camera. By Monday, 22 May, CCTV and other news outlets were giving coverage to those who openly challenged the wisdom of the emergency measures. In one story, a woman was shown riding her bicycle. "As the citizens of the capital," she said, "we are able to manage ourselves on our own. We are fully able to maintain order by ourselves." A man commented that people seemed friendlier than normal: "In the past, people were apt to quarrel when their bicycles ran into each other on the street. But now they are more likely to reach an understanding. They just wave their hands to each other and go." A shop assistant said supplies of food were adequate and there was no panic buying. Such reports contradicted Mayor Chen Xitong's contention that there were shortages. *China Daily* and other newspapers showed pictures of people pressing food towards the soldiers, and every media outlet gave Wan Li's speech in Canada big play.

The head of the National People's Congress was in North America on a ten-day goodwill visit. The trip had been planned long before the student uprising, and the seventy-three-year-old leader—number four in the Party hierarchy—was in Toronto when martial law was declared. Before an audience of five hundred Canadian Chinese, Wan appeared to be distancing himself from those who imposed the emergency measures. "We will firmly protect the patriotic enthusiasm of the young people in China," he declared to loud applause. "All these problems should be settled through democracy and the legal system. We should adopt a rational and orderly way to settle these problems." Wan did not specifically mention martial law, but in Beijing his remarks were interpreted as opposition to the measures; word spread that he had sent a strongly worded telegram to Beijing from Toronto expressing that opinion. According to other rumours, at least forty of the 158-member standing committee of the National People's Congress had signed a letter opposing martial law.

Even some messages which expressed support for Li Peng were interpreted by the students as endorsements of the democracy movement. Traditionally, a central government decision as monumental as the imposition of martial law would have demanded immediate backing from all thirty provinces and autonomous regions. Shows of unity were both essential and expected under such circumstances. But by Sunday, only nine provincial leaders had cabled messages to Beijing. The tally on Monday was fifteen; still only half the provinces had responded. While some provincial leaders called the premier's measures "significant and brilliant," students knew that these words had arrived late. The telegrams should have been sent only moments after Li Peng's speech. The delays, people argued, indicated that those provinces which had sent messages had done so with reticent acquiescence. Those which had failed to send them at all, therefore, opposed martial law completely.

By late Tuesday, 23 May, many were sure that Li Peng had been toppled, or was about to be. A swirling dust storm had blackened the sky at 2:30 P.M., followed by a violent downpour. For hours, a vengeful wind screamed down the length of Changan Boulevard. Entire parking-lotfulls of bicycles clanged to the ground like dominoes. Banners broke loose, spiralling into the dark air above Tiananmen Square. Open shutters slammed against apartment buildings, sending shards of glass tumbling to the ground below. It was even more threatening, more ominous than the tempest which had occurred the previous week—the menacing gale that had preceded the declaration of martial law. The wrathful sky augured change and could not be ignored.

Even if Li Peng chose to disregard the Mandate of Heaven, he could not deny what was taking place in the streets of Beijing. A million citizens were out, defying both martial law and the fury of the storm, to demand his resignation. Soaked to the skin and pummelled by a wailing funnel of dust and rain, they marched around Tiananmen and down Changan past Zhongnanhai. An effigy of Li Peng was hanged. "The more they threaten us, the more we feel united," said one resident. "We feel we are becoming stronger and stronger." In the square, rebel loudspeakers blared "Students, your final goal is not far away."

From all appearances, the gap was narrowing. Foreign Minister Qian Qichen told European Community ambassadors that Zhao Ziyang remained in office. Satellite service to foreign television networks was suddenly restored. Wan Li cut short his trip to Washington and was coming home, many thought, to rescind martial law. Most of the army convoys withdrew to bivouacs far from the city, one troop column in such a hurry that a soldier died after falling from a speeding truck. It appeared that the authorities were willing to listen to the popular will. On Wednesday, 24 May, when one senior Chinese journalist was told of rumours that Li was gone, he made several quick phone calls and then said emotionlessly "You may be right."

State-run media accounts of Tuesday's demonstration were another sign. A million voices had chanted "Down with Li Peng" and reporters had heard them. "The overwhelming majority of the slogans of the demonstrators were directed against the chief leader of the State council," read the *China Daily* account. Li was the head of the council, and while the newspaper did not mention him by name, its coverage was in clear violation of martial law provisions. The *People's Daily* found an innovative method to voice dissent by printing a front page article quoting Hungarian Premier Miklos Nemeth's declaration that "no political forces will be allowed to use troops to solve internal problems" in his country. The paper quoted Nemeth as saying that one of the most hated characteristics of Stalin's style was his use of the country's military forces to deal with its own people. Such a policy, Nemeth said, instilled in its citizens fear of the army that continues to the present.

As people waited for word of Li's dismissal, students tried to avoid giving the authorities any pretext for sending troops back into the city. They dismantled most of the roadblocks every morning after Monday, and re-erected them each evening. By Wednesday most had been taken down for good. Student leaders used the loudspeaker system to call on workers in gas, water and power installations to remain on the job. Municipal services, they said, must be maintained. Public transport was restored throughout most of the city, and slowly the buses that had been sent for the hunger strikers disappeared from the square. When three young men from Mao Zedong's home province of Hunan hurled paint-filled eggs and ink at his huge portrait on Tiananmen Gate during the demonstration on Tuesday, student leaders quickly caught them, interrogated them, and turned them over to the police. Within a few hours, authorities had replaced the desecrated painting with an identical copy.

Student leaders, though, were far more concerned about their fragile truce with the army. They were finding it increasingly difficult to control crowds intent on using violence against the military. Just before midnight Tuesday, when soldiers in the Fengtai district of southern Beijing tried to withdraw, local people thought that they were really advancing towards the square. Youths began pelting them with stones and bricks. The troops were exhausted after spending four nights confined in their trapped vehicles and responded in kind. Seventeen soldiers and three students were taken to hospital. A waiter described how his restaurant was destroyed "in a wink" under a barrage of flying rocks. Students pleaded with Beijingers to avoid conflict.

There were other ugly incidents. Pushy young men stood in the middle of streets waving long staves of wood, ordering drivers to stop and take them and others gathered at intersections towards the square. Many were overexcited students, but a few were mean-spirited thugs who used the democracy movement to intimidate. Many taxi drivers and other motorists quickly grew weary of being taken for a free ride.

In spite of such events, newspapers stressed that life was returning to normal. In some ways, the papers claimed, it was better than normal. The number of traffic accidents was down, as was crime. The *People's Daily* said that the situation in Beijing called to mind Hemingway's comment about "grace under pressure." The article recounted anecdotes of store clerks going out of their way to assist customers, of a lost camera being returned to its rightful owner, of a waiter who paid for a customer's meal because the man had lost his food coupons. Street vendors kept prices low, even when supplies were short. When asked why, one vendor told the reporter "At a time like this? You should be honest if you are a man."

Nonetheless, some students began to sense that their demonstration in Tiananmen Square could not go on forever. The durability and vitality of the democracy movement had been remarkable. But how long could they count on the people of Beijing to turn out in their millions? How long would the army be content to remain on the outskirts of the Chinese capital? Could those in Tiananmen Square bear to remain amidst the growing piles of soggy and rotting garbage? Crowds thinned and the number of hard-core protestors living in the plaza was dwindling daily. Still, Zhao Ziyang had not come to the rescue. People held varying opinions on what to do next.

"We will have more demonstrations," said a Beijing resident. "We will have more struggles. But a revolutionary should not be afraid of such things, should he?"

"This has gone to an extreme," countered one young man. "The government and we must find a way to settle this thing. If this lasts, it is not good for the people and our country."

7

Shei Tama Ai Ni?

W ednesday evening passed and Thursday, 25 May, came without the hoped-for announcement that martial law had been lifted, or that Li Peng had been dismissed. Instead, on the Thursday evening newscast, Li Peng sat comfortably in his armchair lecturing three new Third World ambassadors about the need to bring in the army. As to the failure of troops to clear out the square, Li said smugly that "anyone with common sense can see that this is not because the troops are unable to enter the downtown area, but because the government is the people's government and the People's Liberation Army is the people's own army. Because the people have not yet fully understood the meaning of martial law, the troops have exercised great restraint to avoid major clashes." That same day, the army sent a strongly worded message to its soldiers, telling them to obey orders "to the full." Saying that troops had been called to Beijing "with the strong wishes of the masses," the military command threatened to punish soldiers who disobeyed orders in "accordance with military law"—that is, they would be executed.

Yet another bad sign was the news about Wan Li. When he left Washington to return home, the head of the National People's Congress appeared to be in good spirits and full health, but the evening news reported that he had to leave the airliner in Shanghai for medical treatment. This spurious claim indicated to the protest movement that Wan Li was, at best, a politically impotent force; at worst, an ally of the hardliners. The government did not want his presence added to an already volatile mix in Beijing. As one Western correspondent commented, Wan Li had been shanghaied in Shanghai.

By Saturday, speculation that the chairman of the Congress would save the students ended. Wan had thrown his support behind the hardliners, arguing that martial law was necessary and making

151

veiled accusations about Party moderates. "All sorts of things," he said, "have indicated that a very small number of people are engaging in a political conspiracy, making use of student strikes and deliberately creating turmoil. . . ." Wan promised to convene a special session of the Congress on 20 June to discuss problems raised by students. "An enhanced sense of democracy and law and an environment featuring stability and order make it necessary to convene the meeting," he said. "Otherwise, China's expectations cannot be realized."

Wan's comments coincided with the publication in Chinese newspapers of a string of letters of support for Li Peng from other high-ranking figures. Notable only for their lack of imagination, virtually every one trotted out the same phrases the premier had used the week before. A few crowed about their victory over the moderates. Chen Yun, the eighty-four-year-old chairman of the Central Advisory Commission—a body created in 1982 to provide retired members of the Central Committee with continued influence—said that the Party must "resolutely expose schemes and intrigues of the very, very few people who intend to create turmoil, and resolutely fight against them." Peng Zhen, the crusty former head of the National People's Congress, said that students had been taken in by a "very small number of conspirators and bad elements who took advantage of the situation to create turmoil." Eighty-year-old Li Xiannian, the head of the Chinese People's Political Consultative Conference, said on Saturday, 27 May, that the campaign for democracy had been "taken over by a handful of people to create chaos. . . . An important cause of the current chaos rests with certain individuals within the leadership of the Communist Party." Even Deng Yingchao, the ninety-year-old widow of Zhou Enlai and Li Peng's adoptive mother, came out in support of the emergency measures. Yet another indication of the new mood was felt by foreign television networks. On Saturday, satellite transmissions were cut off again.

The effect of this cavalcade was to show that the hardliners had won the power struggle with Zhao. Everyone knew that the "very, very few people," the "very small number of conspirators" and the "certain individuals within the leadership of the Communist Party" were all references to the Zhao Ziyang faction. If the leadership was willing to punish Zhao severely for the unrest, how strongly would it come down on those who persisted in opposing the Party in the streets? On Friday, 26 May, the Beijing Military Command finally threw its support behind the government and expressed its determination to "fulfil the task. . . . to end the turmoil." Diplomats reported that soldiers were heading to Beijing from all over the country. By Saturday, some estimated that the number of soldiers encir-

152

cling the city had reached a quarter of a million.

At the same time, there was a staggering drop in the number of protesters in Tiananmen Square and throughout the rest of the city. Near the Marco Polo Bridge in southwest Beijing, where scores of armoured personnel carriers were standing by, only a few students kept watch. At Tiananmen, the number of people who camped at the square had dropped in a week from 300,000 to roughly five to ten thousand.

The exodus from Beijing was just as dramatic as the influx had been the previous week. The only free fares available under martial law were for trains going back to the provinces. Police throughout China were told to stop more students from heading to Beijing. Even those students who had legitimate business in the capital had to provide proof before they were allowed to go. The number of fresh youths arriving at the Beijing train station slowed to a trickle. Some students left simply because they came unprepared. One chemistry student from Sichuan university told *China Daily* "many of my fellow students came to Beijing with only a few clothes, and some have caught a cold or other diseases because they could not find proper accommodation and had to sleep in the open." For thousands of others, a sense of demoralization and frustration provided the motivation to leave. Even on the first day of martial law, many students wished the protests would end. "Last night I was worried," a young girl said on 20 May, "and I hoped the army would come and the movement would be stopped. We are too tired. Today, I think just the same. I hope tonight something will happen."

After the initial crisis with the army had passed, many people just drifted away, sickened by the noise, the filth, the stench and the boredom. Although an orchestra, a choral group and even a rock band came to the Monument to the Revolutionary Martyrs to serenade the campers that week, none of those diversions could mask the awful reality. The Xi'an student who had arrived at the train station just as Li Peng was calling in the army on 20 May decided a week later that it was time to go home: "I have been in Beijing for about eight days. That's too long, a little bit too long. I want to have a rest. It seems we haven't achieved anything. We hoped Zhao Ziyang would be the leader, and now it seems the position of Li Peng is so strong that we cannot shake it. We have lost." More than a quarter million students had made the trip to Beijing. By the end of the first week of martial law, only a few tens of thousands remained.

Some held out hope that they could still force the government to back down, but much of their enthusiastic confidence was gone. A Beijing student said at week's end "We think the government will treat us with a firm hand. Seven army units are in our country; six are for the government, only one is for the students. So things are getting worse. . . . We will lose our heart soon, we will lose our courage. So something must happen very quickly. The government must take action. I think it is wrong for them to pay no attention to our requests." Another student, this one from Henan University, spoke with great melancholy on Friday, 26 May. "I think the martial law, if it is really carried out, will bring great disaster to this country and to this generation."

At BeiDa, people had stopped making dazibao for the Triangle, and few people came to read those yellowing notices on the message boards. The crinkly glue-lacquered posters were a few centimetres thick in some places, but the site of such ferment only weeks before now looked like a neglected shrine to lost dreams. Most BeiDa students had given up going to the square. "Why bother?" Xiao Cong asked on Friday, 26 May. "It's boring. It's stupid." Four weeks earlier, she had proudly declared her willingness to fight for democracy, but now she said "I want class to start again. I sleep twenty hours a day in my dorm, and four of my roommates have gone home." She confided that although the class boycott was still on, one of her professors would secretly begin giving lectures again the next day.

By Saturday, Beijing was rife with rumours, none of them good for the democracy movement. Diplomats said that Zhao, fellow Politburo member Hu Qili and two other moderates were accused of forming an "anti-party clique" and were under house arrest. Planeloads of troops were being flown to the city. Some said that the army had been told to clear out the democracy camp within forty-eight hours. News reports that gave favourable coverage to the students had all but disappeared. Instead, stories about Tiananmen began to concentrate more and more on the undeniable filth. One report in the *Beijing Daily* quoted a Red Cross official as saying "the environment in the square is very bad and a serious epidemic could break out at any time." A case of hepatitis had already been reported. Hundreds of doctors came to the square each day to treat the ill, many of whom were suffering from throat infections and diarrhea. Faced with a shortage of medicine, the physicians started handing out disinfectant towels for students to use before eating. The Central Committee appealed to students to leave Tiananmen because it was "badly polluted." Television pictures showed municipal workers spraying disinfectant on huge piles of garbage, while others carted away refuse on trishaws. One Chinese newspaper recounted the story of a hospital that sent a car to the square loaded with toilet paper; the campers had been using rice-paper-thin popsicle wrappers. Although graphic and grim, such reports understated the true misery of those who endured life in Tiananmen Square.

Their selfless devotion to the cause became a source of wonder. By day and into the evening, tens of thousands flocked there to have their photographs taken, to bring their children, to wander among the squalid makeshift tents that made the site seem like some forgotten military camp. As one observer remarked sadly that Saturday, "it's just another tourist attraction now." One scruffy young American who managed to get through student marshals took the opportunity to become famous for fifteen seconds. Standing on the Monument to the Revolutionary Martyrs he claimed to be a member of the "People's Republic of Santa Cruz" and before a bank of foreign television cameras began to speak in English to the students. "In Greenpeace," he said, "we view the students and their struggle for freedom as an endangered species." The translator had trouble with the word 'endangered'. "You know," the youth explained, "like whales, dolphins. . . ."

Student leader Chai Ling lost heart completely and planned to go into hiding. She had become head of the democracy camp after Wuer Kaixi had recommended that the students quit the square after martial law had been imposed. Now, she, too, felt it was hopeless. At the apartment of an American friend, she recorded a taped message: "Students are asking us what our next step is. I want to tell them 'the next step is bloodshed. Only when the whole square is washed in blood will the people of the whole country wake up.' But how can I say such words to them? I can't tell my fellow students that we should be willing to use our lives and our blood to wake up the masses. They will do that if they are asked. But they are still children." Chai Ling changed her mind about leaving the square, and the twenty-three-year-old stuck with her children to the end. But she was correct—many students seemed to revel in the thought of a martyr's death. "Some students think they are real fighters for democracy," one student observed on 21 May. "They are willing to devote their life to realize that aim." A student from Hefei speculated on troops coming on 25 May: "We are worried, but we are not afraid. We will fight to the end." Yet at the same time he acknowledged that such a sacrifice might be worthless, that the students might not succeed. "We want Li Peng to resign from the government," he said. "It seems that is not likely." A Beijing student said about death "We are getting ready for it. If the government does that [uses force], it will arouse great anger. It would be worth it." A student from Sichuan said heroically on 26 May, "I will give my life for China." One student wondered what good it would do. "It's unfair. We even want to give our lives, but the government does not take us seriously." Another broke in, "I think if the government treats us in this way, I think it will arouse great anger among all the people." He was asked if that

155

made it worth dying for. "Yes it will be. I think it's the only way we can do that."

Students leaders tried once more to mobilize people, against the advice of Wuer Kaixi, Chai Ling and Wang Dan. They hoped that a million would march on Sunday, 28 May. Only thirty thousand turned out. To someone new to Beijing, it would have looked huge, but those who had been in the streets only a few days before knew that it signalled the death throes of the movement. The mood was sombre, the talk of defeat. A young man from the Shanghai Maritime Institute predicted that "Chinese society will be more dark. The reformers will be punished. This is what we call 'settling of accounts'. All the leaders of the students will be punished. . . . To systemize democracy and freedom is a very difficult thing. In today's situation, it's not very realistic. But we are beginning."

The growing sense of defeat kept the crowds away. It seemed futile to keep chanting on deaf ears. Many local leaders in factories and offices warned of serious consequences if workers took part in any other protests. One student in the square was not surprised by the lack of labour support. "They have their families and other things to consider," he said.

One student leader blamed the low turn-out for the 28 May protest on his three colleagues who had argued against the march, but even he was torn over whether students should leave the square. Sitting in the sweaty medical tent outside the Revolutionary Museum, the plump, bespectacled youth declared "They have finished their mission, but if they go back to their university, the movement will come down. It's finished. So it's difficult." When the questions got tougher, he became evasive.

"The government is stronger now," a reporter said. "What are you doing to do?"

"The student's movement is for democracy, and it's patriotic, it's not political. We know we won't get democracy in the short term."

"Do you fear organizers will be arrested if you leave the square?"

"If the government used that kind of power to end this movement, we would have to think about whether we want this kind of government."

"Do you think you'll be arrested?"

"This movement is the sun of democracy."

Later Sunday evening, students debated whether they should leave the square on Tuesday, 30 May. The majority of students voted to leave. But, in another strange twist of democratic theory, they decided to bow to the wishes of the minority. As long as one person wanted to remain, it was decided, they all would stay. Although thousands ignored this bizarre principle and slipped away in the night, the camp stayed put. By Monday night, Tiananmen Square had perhaps three thousand permanent residents, a large percentage of whom were from other cities. They vowed to remain until the National People's Congress held its session on 20 June.

An Australian journalist was greatly worried by the students' refusal to withdraw. The man had witnessed uprisings in Czechoslovakia, Poland, Hungary and France during his lengthy career and was convinced that the movement would be brutally crushed. Even during the first week of martial law he had felt that students would die if they did not leave the square. Although the reporter had covered thousands of stories spanning several decades, he described what was taking place in the Chinese capital as "the saddest thing I have ever seen in my life."

For many Beijingers, the lure of spring proved more attractive than Tiananmen Square. With the exception of two heavy storms, the weather in the Chinese capital was superb. The first watermelons of the year indicated a bumper crop for the city's favourite summertime fruit. People swam in the canals and rented rowboats to ply the many lakes in the city. In Ritan Park in East Beijing, old men and women practised their Chinese opera under a traditional pagoda. Passersby had varying opinions of the events in Tiananmen Square.

"I think the protests are a good thing," a young woman with her child declared. "People are thinking a lot more, thinking about democracy and a better China." That comment disturbed a middle-aged man who was walking by. He stopped and began arguing with her. "It's all instigated by a handful of extremists and the Voice of America," he said angrily. A frail old man who witnessed the exchange had little to say. "I'm eighty-seven. I just don't know about all this."

The old men in Zhongnanhai thought they did know, and they wanted the students out. They decided to play a waiting game, prodding the resolve of the students, threatening workers, keeping the propaganda fires raging. Government loudspeakers blared at the democracy campers throughout the night, demanding that they return home. Fifteen hundred soldiers were brought in to the Beijing train station southeast of Tiananmen Square. At night, they marched occasionally towards Changan Boulevard. The troops were watched closely and taunted by those who saw themselves as the guardians of the square—local citizens who stationed themselves by the hundreds at major intersections far from Tiananmen. Each night the troops would return without incident to the station, showing no indication of heading towards the democracy camp.

Troops were also stationed at ten key government installations, including CCTV, Radio Beijing, the *People's Daily* compound and the

157

Capital airport. At the television station, about two hundred soldiers lolled about in a courtyard and drilled in the parking lot. They did not appear to influence directly what went on the air, though their presence no doubt hammered home who was in charge. Complained one editor at Radio Beijing: "Everyone has been so frustrated with what's happening in China. There's been a loss of morale at our department. People have not been able to cover the story in a more candid and honest way." All the freedoms that reporters had enjoyed just two weeks earlier were gone. "Newspaper people are mostly government employees," the editor said. "When you are a government employee, you have to obey the law. Fighting for democracy does not mean you can ignore the law. . . . No matter whether you like martial law, you have to obey it. No government official ever came here to tell us what you can run and what you can't. It's quite obvious. You cannot write anything about the demonstration. That's liable to bring charges for instigating more riots."

On the square itself, the remaining students dug in their heels. They set up a few dozen tents donated from Hong Kong and reorganized the larger green military-style tents into regimented rows. Thousands of Beijingers still came to see the camp, especially at night, but it had lost much of its appeal. Donated food continued to arrive, but many entrepreneurs simply returned to the business of running their own restaurants. The hundreds of thousands who only a week before had walked off their jobs to demonstrate were back at work. Many of them, especially those who had lived through past campaigns, knew that the time for such reckless actions had passed.

The students could not fail to recognize the flagging support, and the apparent death knell it sounded. They needed something new, something powerful to rally the people of Beijing once more. With enough people behind them, perhaps the movement could yet be salvaged. They found that symbol in the Goddess of Democracy.

For three days and nights, students at the Central Academy of Fine Arts toiled in a compound at the rear of the institute. On a patch of earth turned white with splattered plaster, they fashioned the ultimate expression of defiance. She was built in four sections, using styrofoam, wood and a brilliant, snowy plaster of paris. Her sculptors constantly darted in and out of a nearby building, reappearing with fresh material. The nonstop activity continued until early Monday evening, 29 May, when it was declared that she was ready. The statue was assembled to ensure that the parts fitted, then taken apart again. The students planned originally to ferry the statue by truck, but the Public Security Bureau phoned the Academy and warned that anyone driving it would lose his or her licence. Several transport tricycles were quickly brought to the school and the sculpture was loaded.

Through the hutongs and streets, the Goddess inched towards her destiny. The crowd that gathered to watch her voyage was so dense that it appeared from a distance as if four white ships were gently plying the sea. Many thought that the artists had modelled the Goddess after the Statue of Liberty in New York harbour. A pair of American tourists standing outside the Beijing hotel were enthralled when she passed by. "Look, look!" shouted one of them. "It's, it's—" They went running towards the figure, clutching their cameras.

Two years earlier, students in Shanghai had paraded through the streets with a large portrait bearing Liberty's likeness. Politically, the new Beijing statue appeared to be an obvious symbol of the United States and its founding principles, but the artists had based her on a simple figurine of a Chinese peasant leaning on a wooden staff, grasping the wood above his head. In creating their gigantic copy, the students eliminated the bottom half of the rod and fashioned the top half into a torch of freedom. They changed the male figure to a woman by giving her collar-length hair blowing in the wind. She clutched the torch with both hands, as if fearful it would soon be taken away.

When the Goddess reached Tiananmen around 11:00 P.M., scores of photojournalists snapped off rolls of film from every angle; more than a dozen video sunguns bathed the square with light. It was like a surreal movie set, with directors and production coordinators shouting frantic instructions through megaphones. Organizers finally had to ask photographers to stop taking pictures for fear their flashes would blind those perched on scaffolding ready to reassemble the statue. Twelve hours later, at noon on Tuesday, 30 May, the Goddess was unveiled.

"We will dedicate this statue to the students' cause," a female student leader announced to ecstatic cheers of perhaps thirty thousand onlookers. "We dedicate this to the millions of students in China, to the people of Beijing, China and the world who support our movement. . . . We have won victory after victory because the power of the people cannot be defeated. This government does not have any humanity. They are using obscenities and cheating and lies to cover Beijing in a cloud of darkness. They want to kill the democratic movement in the cradle. But the judgement days are coming for these leaders."

The Goddess was a symbol that captured the best and worst about the democracy movement, its innocence and its insolence. Towering above the crowd she stared straight at the portrait of Mao Zedong, challenging the Chinese state. Like the students themselves, she seemed immovable, indestructible and permanent. For the five days she existed, the Goddess was a wondrous sight. But she was only a collection of plaster, foam and wood. The Tiananmen camp was made up of equally fragile materials.

The Chinese media exploded with apoplectic, but apparently impotent, outrage. The figure was an "insult to the site." The Tiananmen Square administration demanded the immediate removal of the "illegal statue." An unidentified architect was quoted on CCTV and Radio Beijing as saying that the Goddess would create a "very bad impression" for children who would be coming to the square for International Children's Day, 1 June. "The square is the place for commemorating only the heroes of the People's Republic," he said. Government loudspeakers in the square demanded that the statue be taken down, saying that no other city in the world would have tolerated it. Even some people who had been sympathetic to the students thought that they had gone too far. "I don't like it," one middle-aged cadre said. "They should not put American symbols on this part of China. It is not right." A senior Chinese journalist had a similar assessment. "That's a very stupid thing to do," he declared. "Tiananmen Square is a very sacred place, and if they want to voice their demands, yes—why, they can do it through pamphlets or seminars or organized meetings or whatever. Erecting that thing makes them not look serious enough. People will think that this is a bunch of students trying to get more press exposure or attract foreign notice. It seems to me that a lot of students are pushing for a confrontation, perhaps in the hope that troops will come—that some students will even die and become martyrs in the hopes that they can once again mobilize the population of Beijing. . . . If they are looking for confrontation, that will only cause losses to the cause for democracy."

Public Security agents had begun making selective arrests of people associated with the movement. Among their first targets were three leaders of an unofficial labour union called the Independent Association of Beijing Workers. It had been formed the day before martial law was imposed. On Monday, 29 May, association leader Tian Liming told a crowd at Tiananmen Square that it represented thirteen thousand workers in Beijing. Early the next day Tian and two other union leaders were nabbed by police and taken to Public Security headquarters. When news of the arrests became known, two thousand students marched to the headquarters and staged a sit-in to demand the release of the activists. When they learned that the three had already been let go, the students stayed put and demanded that eleven motorcyclists in custody, members of the Flying Tigers who had cruised Tiananmen shouting anti-government slogans, also be released. The bikers had been arrested while attempting to free one of their members accused of beating up a policemen.

Youngsters did not get to celebrate International Children's Day in Tiananmen Square. Instead, a single event was held far from the plaza. Newspapers pointed out that the democracy campers ignored a letter from some high school students who had asked them to leave the square because they had "dreamed to see the raising of the national flag, and to ask the uncles of the flag team to teach them the revolutionary traditions."

Foreign journalists kept up their coverage, ignoring martial law restrictions. Because the satellite link had been cut off, stories were being flown to Hong Kong and Tokyo for transmission. Police confiscated a few videotapes during the week, but there were no serious incidents. There was, however, a growing feeling that the government was keeping close tabs on Western reporters. During the hunger strike, students often asked journalists to sign autographs on their clothing. Most reporters considered it a harmless, if somewhat silly exercise, but under martial law things changed. An increasing number of Chinese men were showing up on the Monument to the Revolutionary Martyrs with expensive Japanese cameras. Many of them spent their time taking photographs of Western journalists. Often, they would ask for autographs in their notebooks, followed by another request. "Please," they would ask, "write down some thoughts on the movement. Make sure to add the name of your press agency." Some people warned that the men were agents of the Public Security Bureau who had gained access to the Monument by showing forged credentials. Several reporters autographed the books with names ranging from Moammar Gaddafi to Donald Duck.

Other situations were more serious. On several occasions, a CBC crew was in the middle of a crowd when someone tried to incite protestors to turn on them. One night outside the Great Hall of the People a man began yelling "Who are these damn foreigners? Let's knock them down and smash their camera!" He began shouting and thrashing, apparently trying to stir up others. He did not succeed, and an onlooker warned the crew that the man was likely an agent. Certainly, such incidents seemed out of place. For the most part, reporters and camera crews were welcomed openly, if not applauded, by demonstrators who knew that they were breaking the law to continue covering the student movement.

The government, which was infuriated by the foreign coverage of the students and their demonstrations, responded by trying to stage a rally of its own. On Wednesday, 31 May, reporters were invited to watch four thousand peasants and workers shout pro-government slogans while shuffling about Daxing county south of Beijing. The demonstration was held there for two reasons: the government feared that this orchestrated bit of propaganda might provoke an angry response from those who supported the students, and—were it staged in Beijing—it would have violated martial law. One Chinese who witnessed it just shook his head. "One person would be chanting a slogan really loudly, really enthusiastically leading the crowd," he said. "Then you would hear people in the crowd say it in a very low voice, half-heartedly." Privately, Chinese reporters said it was a farce. "After the cameras and the television people left," one said, "the demonstrators immediately dispersed. It was just a show for the cameras." It was not a good show either. On state television, the demonstration looked puny; the marchers, many wearing straw hats to protect them from the sun, appeared uncomfortable in their role as vox populi. It was said in the square that many had been lured by the offer of a ten yuan ($2.80 U.S.) participation fee. Perhaps as a result of this public relations fiasco, government officials reminded foreign journalists the next day to heed the martial law restrictions limiting their coverage.

Pro-democracy demonstrations, meanwhile, continued in many other cities. One Japanese tourist who travelled through southeastern China said that everywhere he went, he learned of local protests and the moves to contain them. To the north in Xi'an, authorities had run out of patience. Students there had been boycotting classes since 16 May and still enjoyed public sympathy. They had even set up their own broadcasting tent in the city centre. Loudspeakers relayed the latest events from Beijing, as well as information taken from BBC and Voice of America broadcasts. Many citizens continued to gather daily at the site, listening intently to the defiant students or reading dazibao which had been pasted to buildings. From the government's point of view, it had to end. And so it did. In one overnight sweep, authorities removed every visible trace of the democracy campaign in Xi'an. Residents who wandered downtown the next day discovered that the broadcasting tent, the posters, newspapers and leaflets had all vanished. Aware of the implications, crowds no longer formed at the once-popular location.

Back in Beijing, the Goddess—and the students—continued to lose their drawing power. People still came to the square to take pictures of the rebel statue, some offering support to the students, but the movement was ebbing. The plaster monument had done her job for several days; now a new catalyst was needed.

Student leaders knew that a demonstration at Zhongnanhai would be pointless, so they decided to target a facility where they might at least gain some ground. They chose the *Beijing Daily*, reasoning that an effective protest might prompt some journalists to again defy the government and print sympathetic stories. On Friday morning, 2 June, more than a thousand students and supporters marched or cycled to the newspaper's compound in eastern Beijing. It was a small number and the protestors knew that they would have to make their point dramatically. Initially, it was anything but dramatic. The group gathered outside the gate and pumped out the tired old slogans. *"Beijing Daily* tells lies," they chanted. *"Beijing Daily* is full of baloney!" Such words now were not likely to win them sympathy. Perhaps the students knew that, for their next move was far more powerful. They cleared a circle and laid down thousands of copies of the newspaper. Then, to a thunderous cheer which belied their small numbers, the students set the papers on fire. A huge cloud of smoke, then flames, rose above the heap. Burning bits of paper floated up and over the crowd. Students shouted and swatted angrily at the charred and hateful words of the state. The bonfire raged for some time, to a continuous accompaniment of chants and howls. But the inferno was confined to the street; the workers at the *Beijing Daily* would no longer fight for press freedom. As a wind scattered the blackened ash down the streets and hutongs, so, too, vanished any hopes that reporters would again join them.

There was still an ace the students could play, an ace which might once again bring a million people into the streets. A hunger strike. Not like before, but a new fast—with prominent and respected Beijingers. With the right people it could galvanize the movement. Four such people were already in place, willing to suffer in Tiananmen Square for the sake of democracy. One of them was Hou Dejian.

* * *

He was thirty-two years old, with a chiselled, intense face and an extraordinary past. The son of a Guomindang officer, the singer was one of the most famous rock stars in China. It was not just his celebrity status which made him a noteworthy candidate to volunteer for the hunger strike: Hou Dejian had been born and raised in Taiwan. His father, Hou Kaobong, had fled Nanjing when the Communists routed the city in 1949 and had settled in a small Taiwanese city to begin anew.

Life in Taiwan was not easy for the young Hou Dejian. The locals treated him as an outsider. "We were called 'Mainland Pigs' by the Taiwanese," he said. "They felt we were occupying their land; occupying their homes. . . . In my classroom, there were only five or six children from the mainland. The rest were Taiwanese. After school, there would be children waiting on the side of the road. We'd fight very often." Hou Dejian understood why the locals wanted to beat him. In some ways, he even sympathized with their feelings that the Nationalists were a force of occupation. "The officers in Taibei were in charge of everything," he said. "Land owned by the Taiwanese was divided among the Guomindang. The Nationalists wanted everyone to speak Mandarin instead of Taiwanese or any local dialect. Even though I was the son of a Guomindang, I didn't agree with it. I was very, very ashamed. I didn't think what the Guomindang had done was good."

He sought escape, even at that early age, in music. It was a diversion which would blossom when he moved to the capital city to attend high school. He played guitar in a band with a group of American soldiers at a club in Taibei. The young man found in their company an escape from the alienation he had grown up with. "I felt close with them," he said. "Sometimes I wished I was American. So free, so individual—I could love, I could hate, I could sing. . . ." But the joy he experienced during those evenings in the army nightclub brought Hou Dejian frustration. The more he saw of the freedom his three American friends enjoyed, the more he felt trapped by the conformity which Chinese society demanded. "I knew I could not be as free as they were. I was not American, and couldn't pretend to be."

Hou Dejian began to question everything—traditional Chinese values, the education system, the supreme authority of the Taibei government. It all seemed geared towards conformity, towards producing people who were like "small machines." Even the popular songs being written in Taiwan were little more than copies of tunes which had already proven successful in Japan or Hong Kong. Hou recalls one particular night when his frustrations boiled over. It happened during university, when he had gone to see a movie. As usual, people were expected to stand and sing patriotic songs before the film began.

"I was at a theatre which was packed with about 1,500 people. Suddenly, when Chiang Kaishek's picture was on the screen, I felt that he was like Hitler, or Mussolini. I just couldn't stand up. So I sat there, while everyone else stood up to sing. And after about three seconds, my head was hit very hard by someone behind me. When I turned around, I saw the person was the same age as me. I was really hurt in my heart; I thought we had been fooled by the Nationalists for such a long time. I said 'I pay respect to your attitudes, to your loyalty—you should pay respect to mine'."

The feelings which so pained Hou Dejian found expression in his music. The song which would make him a star was penned in thirty minutes on 16 December 1978—the day the United States announced that relations with Beijing would be established on 1 January 1979.

The news that Washington was going to recognize the leadership in Beijing over Taibei shocked Hou's classmates. Many were crying, saying that the U.S. had betrayed them. Hou was confused and saddened by his fellow students' response. With a pencil and paper, he sat down to write "Descendants of the Dragon."

"The song just talks about the Chinese," said Hou. "We are a very ancient and very historic people, but our quality of life is still very poor. Can anyone tell us why? Have we ever thought about these questions—deep in our heart? The major power to destroy the family, or the people, or the nation, is not from foreigners. It comes from ourselves. With that song, I wanted to make it clear that everybody should be thinking from the inside; that we should take a good long look at ourselves."

Hou recorded a rough demo of the song at a radio station that very day. By 19 December, he had received more than two thousand letters praising his work.

"It seems," recalled Hou, "that people were searching for some sort of words, a concept, an idea of what exactly is a Chinese. I provided them with an answer. We are descendants of the dragon. . . . They realized that the common culture we share is much more lovely than a political party, or socialism, or the Four Principles of any 'ism'. . . . It's the way we perceive ourselves. I was able to somehow express these feelings that people had."

The popular anthem rocketed Hou to stardom, so high that he "could not find the stairs to come down." His fans would constantly stop him on the street, asking about the future of China, the future of Taiwan. Hou Dejian felt bound to find the answers.

During an interview with journalists in Hong Kong in 1981, Hou said that he had nothing against the Chinese Communist Party. He spoke openly and candidly, saying that something had to change between Beijing and Taibei. "The Taiwan government was very unhappy with my ideas," he said. "The Guomindang realized I was an individual, that I would not behave the way they wanted me to." Hou Dejian's continuing quest for answers ultimately took him to the Chinese capital. "I had a very strong feeling about Beijing—that it was the centre, the most important centre, which might provide or solve the answer of all the Chinese, including overseas Chinese. Although Taibei is very well developed it did not contain the answers. Nor did Hong Kong. It had to be Beijing."

He planned a trip north "for inspiration," stepping off the plane at Beijing's Capital Airport in June of 1983. Hou felt it was "so stifling. There was no life. Everyone was dressed in uniforms, every face was so pale. They were just like the Guomindang had described to us in school. . . ." But the sight did not disappoint him. "No. That's what I

165

wanted to see. I didn't come to see the view, to see the houses, to see the palace. I wanted to see the people, and I wanted to be close to the people." He felt that he was learning something he had been missing all his life. He decided to stay in China.

Hou Dejian joined the *Dong Fang* (Oriental) Song and Dance troupe and later applied for a licence to set up a record company in China. "After that I got into the real social system of China. And it's very crowded and greedy and hungry. Hungry for power—for any kind of power. Wherever there is power to be had, there is greed and hunger. All kinds of hungry people, just like flies. And I was just like meat."

It was too much. He quit the troupe in December of 1984 and went to Guangzhou, only to find that his troubles were just beginning. As a result of a dispute with his former employers, he went through a lengthy period when he was effectively blacklisted from working in China. He said that the Minister of Culture issued statements which read "Hou Dejian is a bad element. No work unit must cooperate with him from now on." From 1985 until mid-1986 he went without work in China. He slept in hotels, at the apartments of friends, and—when his money ran out—in his car. It was a difficult period. Were it not for his Chinese wife, a singer from his original Beijing troupe, he would have left.

He did not. Hou eventually joined another work unit and began writing new songs and producing videos. Money from royalties on his works poured in, mostly from Hong Kong. By 1988 Hou Dejian was living a relatively palatial life in Beijing, travelling frequently to Guangzhou and Hong Kong. His home contained all the latest electronic toys, and he proudly drove a brand new red Mercedes.

He seemed to have everything, but it was his constant search for the Chinese identity, and for his own, which took Hou Dejian to Tiananmen Square the afternoon of Friday, 2 June. "What people are thinking now must be related to what people were thinking about six or seven hundred years ago. If you are not clear about this line of development, it will be very difficult to understand the Chinese."

* * *

Hou Dejian went, along with three others, to stage a seventy-two-hour hunger strike beginning at 4:00 P.M. on 2 June. His partners were Liu Xiaobo, a lecturer at Beijing Normal University, Gao Xin, a former editor and member of the Communist Party, and Zhou Duo—a senior official with one of China's most successful private companies, the Stone Corporation. What they hoped to accomplish was contained in a four-page manifesto, a doctrine which proposed concrete steps towards a more democratic China. While acknowledging that the student movement had mobilized Chinese as never before, it pointed out that many supporters "lack a civic consciousness with a sense of political responsibility." It called on people to go further than being merely sympathetic bystanders: "Shouldering responsibility in social and political affairs is the natural responsibility of every citizen." The document also stated that merely deposing Li Peng, or any leader, would not be enough to guarantee democratic freedoms: fundamental structural changes were needed to ensure that no single person in government could impose his will on the masses. The historical thread of the manifesto made it appear to be the work of Hou Dejian.

> For thousands of years, Chinese society has experienced a malicious cycle of overthrowing old emperors and then putting up new emperors. History proves that the fundamental problems of Chinese politics cannot be solved by the downfall of leaders who have lost people's support and the upsurge of leaders who have won people's support. What we want is not a perfect God but a sound democratic system. Therefore, we advocate: firstly, the formation of legal autonomous organizations by people from all social groups, in order to achieve a check and balance between political powers of the public and the government. The essence of democracy is check and balance. We would rather have ten devils who check each other than have an angel who holds absolute power. Secondly, by dismissing leaders who have made serious mistakes, we hope to establish a sound dismissal system gradually. It is not important who is in or out of office, but it is very important how to decide who should be in or out of office. Undemocratic procedure of appointment and dismissal can only lead to dictatorship.

The document also criticized the students for their "organizational confusion and lack of efficient and democratic procedures."

> Their theory is democratic but often their means are undemocratic; they lack cooperation, and therefore their power is offset and decision making is ineffective. Their financial management is in a mess, which gives rise to a huge waste of resources; they are more emotional rather than rational; they have more sense of privilege rather than equality, and so on. For the past hundred years, the Chinese people's struggle for democracy has mainly remained at the level of popularizing ideas and slogans. There has been more ideological enlightenment, but little practical operation; much talk of goals, but little discussion of means, procedures and processes. . . . Therefore we advocate that Chinese people should discard the naive notion of democracy in empty ideological slogans. . . . We have to change the strategy of the democratic movement from the enlightenment of democratic consciousness to the construction of operational procedures. . . .

167

The manifesto concluded by suggesting that the government "should learn a painful lesson from this mass movement for democracy, and try to get used to hearing people's voices. . . . seeing people express their own will with constitutional rights, and learn how to run the country by democratic means."

Tens of thousands were in Tiananmen when the hunger strike began. The main points were read over the loudspeakers, and Hou Dejian led the crowd in a haunting rendition of "Descendants of the Dragon."

There is a river in the far east,
It is called the Yangtze River.
There is a river in the far east,
It is called the Yellow River.
Although I have not seen the beauty of the Yangtze,
I often explore the river in my dreams.
Although I have not heard the roar of the Yellow River,
I hear it in my dreams.

There is a dragon in the ancient Far East,
It is called the Middle Kingdom.
There is a people in the ancient Far East,
They are the descendants of the dragon.
I grew up at the feet of the dragon,
I grew up to become a descendant of the dragon,
Black eyes, black hair, yellow face,
A descendant of the dragon forever.

In the quiet night of a hundred years ago,
In the dark night before the great change,
The sounds of guns and cannons broke the peace of the night.
The cannons are still rumbling after so many years.
Wipe your eyes, giant dragon,
See clearly forever.

The four men were to stage their fast on the upper level of the Monument to the Revolutionary Martyrs, and a green canvas tent had already been set up for the purpose. For the moment, however, those in the square could not get enough of Hou Dejian. They surged towards him, eager to sign their names on his white shirt or to have him autograph their own. By the time he finally retired to the tent, his shirt was almost totally covered in inky signatures.

The numbers in the square began to swell. By 8:00 that evening there were several hundred thousand in Tiananmen. Student marshals protected the hunger strikers fiercely, keeping reporters and admirers at bay. The volunteers were rough, pushing and shoving at those who wanted to be near. One young woman swatted at a reporter who wanted to get through to see Hou Dejian. "But I know him," explained the journalist. "I'm sure he wouldn't mind." The woman snapped back with angry sarcasm. *"Everybody* says they know Hou Dejian." After his story was checked, the reporter was ushered into Hou's tent.

There was a continuous dull roar from those who had gathered in the square and the canvas offered little protection. Whenever the wind whipped open the flap facing Tiananmen, all one could see was a kaleidoscope of faces which extended right to Changan Boulevard. Hou sat cross-legged on a mattress, his back to the crowd. He was planning to fast for only two days, as he was due to fly to Hong Kong for production work the following week. He knew it would be a long forty-eight hours. As one of China's more wealthy residents, Hou also knew he was risking a great deal by taking part in the hunger strike; he admitted that there might be repercussions.

"I hope not, but I think there will be," he said. "But I don't care." Hou clearly felt that he was doing something on behalf of all descendants of the dragon. With an unwavering resolve, he stated that he would remain for what he believed in. "This is the last chance for us to stand straightly and directly and ask for democracy," he declared. "If we don't do that, if we lose this chance, we will lose everything." Asked if he honestly believed that the movement would succeed, he replied "I doubt it."

A student of economic management from Beijing University also conceded that there was little chance of success. "We hope the government will take our advice," he said, "but right now we see it's impossible." With the exception of one trip home to wash and change clothes, he had been on the square since 16 May. His parents were worried and had tried to convince him to stay away from Tiananmen.

"They were very afraid of the situation," said the twenty-year-old. "They say it's very dangerous outside. But I explained the reasons to them. I think the older generation and our generation have different thoughts—maybe a generation gap. They always obey orders from the government. They are trained to be machines; they only work and do not think. We have our brains, we should think about our country's future."

Although dedicated to the cause, the smiling youth seemed drawn to the square as much by its festive sense of camaraderie as by democracy. The scene inside his tent seemed reminiscent of Woodstock; a group of smiling students were huddled together singing popular rock songs. Within its green walls they shared food, tea and ideals. It was the sort of atmosphere conducive to instant and powerful friendships. "I am learning a lot that I can't get in college classes," he said. "At college you can have a boyfriend or girlfriend, go to the cinema, play cards—that sort of thing. Not very interesting. But here you can feel that people are powerful."

Yet the young man was aware the power was fading. "If you think about it," he said, "we should go home. But other students are not satisfied. They want something more, but what they want is impossible." He acknowledged that the military might use force to clear Tiananmen but felt convinced that there would be no bloodshed. As a student of economics, he believed that China would not risk frightening off foreign investors. He also placed great faith in the strength of the foreign media, saying that the government would not crack down with the world's journalists in the capital. That sense of security was one of the factors which prompted him to stay in the square, even though he felt sure the students would not succeed: "I don't think this movement will accelerate the process of democracy in China. But I believe it will give people something to think about. . . . We are the pioneers; every country needs some pioneers."

About 10:00 P.M. on the evening of Friday, 2 June, a police jeep sped towards Tiananmen, weaving around bicycles and bystanders. There were many people on the streets; small knots of protestors guarded strategic intersections leading to the square. About six kilometres to the west of the student camp, the vehicle slammed directly into a group of cyclists at a place called Muxidi Bridge. Three people were killed, another seriously injured. Some believed that the driver had plowed into the victims intentionally. Word of the incident spread immediately, as did rage. Were it not for the timely arrival of student leaders at the scene, the driver might have been summarily executed by the crowd. For the next few hours, hundreds maintained a vigil at the spot and chanted their hatred for the military. Chinese authorities would later claim that the jeep was not on any sort of army mission. They said that the vehicle had been on loan to China Central Television and was merely returning to eastern Beijing. The driver, it was said, had been speeding and lost control. It was an accident. But that was not the rumour which spread through the streets and hutongs of Beijing Friday night. It had been deliberate, people were saying, and this was taken as a sign that the military was getting ready to march on Tiananmen. Thousands began moving towards the square, ready to protect the students. They would soon be needed.

Sometime after midnight, several thousand troops were spotted quick-marching down Changan from the east. They appeared to be anything but a potent force; reports suggested that they had already been walking for four hours. The men were young—few appeared to

170

be more than twenty years old; they looked almost like children who had been drafted and given crew-cuts that very day. They did not seem to be carrying weapons, though students would later say that they had seized machetes from some of the fresh-faced recruits. The majority of the young soldiers did not wear army jackets. They were dressed in green military pants and white undershirts; knapsacks, rain ponchos and water canteens dangled from their shoulders. A few had radio transmitters, but no one seemed to be in obvious command.

At roughly the same time, several buses filled with soldiers started rolling towards Tiananmen from the west. Unmarked cars containing officers were part of the convoy. As both of these forces moved in, more and more Beijingers abandoned their homes. Some rushed into the street, clad only in bathrobes or pajamas. They, along with the students, headed towards the soldiers. For a brief period, Tiananmen Square became a ghost town, with only a few hundred campers remaining in the plaza. The rest were on the streets. Students would later say that they had received advance notice of the military's plans from a sympathizer within the government.

Near the Beijing Hotel, city buses were used to blockade the advance of the young troops. The soldiers tried to get past the barrier by marching in the bicycle lane, but the growing crowd swarmed around, pelting them with shoes and shouting "Retreat, retreat!" Without apparent leadership, the young recruits quickly became confused, then humiliated. Groups of angry Beijingers surrounded them, lecturing them on the democracy movement. Some supporters leaned in with megaphones, shouting directly into their faces. Others began to taunt them, ripping off their knapsacks and pulling out the contents. Packages of noodles and steamed buns spilled onto the street. Many citizens, not just students, jeered and thrust the bags of food at the soldiers. On the western side of the hotel, which was under construction, a separate crowd had penned in hundreds of uniformed men. They, too, tried to re-educate their captives, explaining that soldiers were neither needed nor wanted in the Chinese capital. The men had little choice but to sit quietly as the embarrassing scene was played out. Add to that the presence of foreign camera crews and photojournalists, and it became the ultimate disgrace. The crowd cheered as bright television lights and flashguns blazed over the trapped men. Even when the lights were off, many soldiers continued to stare directly at the ground.

Across the street from the hotel, the bullying continued. The once-formidable line of soldiers had completely disintegrated into tiny clusters of frightened and ashamed young men. Crowds enveloped groups containing as few as two or three soldiers, alternating be-

171

tween mocking them and trying to win them over. Not every recruit had the same fate. One young man stood quietly, and apparently respectfully, as an elderly Beijinger spoke to him in soft tones about the democracy movement. The older man pulled out a cigarette and offered it to the youngster, who accepted it. They stood together for some time; one was reminded of a grandfather passing along choice wisdom to his grandson. Not far away, another soldier was being stripped of his army jacket.

Finally, the vast crowd felt that its mission had been accomplished. Young and old formed two long lines down the street, leaving a corridor between them. The soldiers, some crying, others hiding their faces in disgrace, made a hasty retreat. The multitudes applauded, chanted and occasionally jeered as the soldiers made their way back east. A few shouted "We love you!" to the fleeing troops.

To the west of Tiananmen, near the Beijing Telegraph Office, the PLA was suffering an equally humiliating blow. People had not only blockaded the buses and cars but slashed their tires as well. Inside, soldiers sat quietly as the throngs chanted at them. These troops, however, were armed. Protestors anxiously led journalists to the rear of the buses, where automatic weapons could be seen stacked behind the window. In the cars, ashen-faced commanders fumed as television cameras probed their windshields, filming the AK-47s which rested on top of dashboards.

The students and supporters considered it a great victory, but even that night, some were wondering how the state would react to this supreme loss of face. A government cadre, though pleased the soldiers had been stopped, was worried about the response it might provoke. As he spoke of his fears at 1:30 A.M. on the eastern edge of Tiananmen, a transport tricycle laden with uniforms and a few weapons was being wheeled triumphantly into the square. They were trophies—the spoils of war. "I think the government will be quite angry about the actions of the students and the citizens," he said. "Maybe after this, they will take another step."

Many journalists felt certain that the Chinese leadership would do exactly that. Some people speculated that the PLA had been sent in with the full knowledge that such ill-equipped troops would not be able to clear the square. They had been young, mostly unarmed and terribly disorganized. It was suggested that the recruits represented a final attempt to remove the students peacefully, but the prevailing analysis was more sinister: the government had ordered the soldiers to advance in the express hope that they would be humiliated and turned back. Such a scenario would justify using greater force later. The disgrace would also, with luck, stiffen the resolve of the People's Liberation Army.

On the morning of Saturday, 3 June, Radio Beijing's English service made no mention of the incident. Instead, its news broadcast invited tourists to come and visit China. An announcer quoted a government official as saying the situation in the Chinese capital was "stable."

In truth, it was becoming increasingly chaotic. Barricades went up at a frenzied pace. Bicycle lane dividers, trolley buses, trucks—anything and everything was dragged into the streets once more. The events of the past few hours had convinced students that the military would make a concerted, more violent effort to clear Tiananmen that evening. They, along with their supporters, became doubly determined to stop the People's Liberation Army. Before the sun rose on Saturday, there were new troop movements and new clashes. Details of the skirmishes reached the square in bits and pieces; half rumour, half fact.

Early in the afternoon, two Westerners—both employees of the Chinese government—witnessed a violent exchange at the southwestern corner of the Zhongnanhai compound.

The confrontation had been sparked when soldiers fired volleys of tear gas to disperse a growing crowd. Canadian Derek Sidenius said that almost everyone was outraged that the authorities had used gas on their own people. A Chinese in the area said that the troops were firing the gas maliciously, directly at bystanders. He saw one canister strike an elderly woman in the leg. The man said it tore through her clothing, slicing open a gash in her thigh. Sidenius, meanwhile, was pulled to the side of the road by a group of anxious Beijingers. They pointed to a Chinese who they said had been beaten. "The guy was leaning on his tricycle," said Sidenius, "and he had a very stunned expression. He had just been hit by an electric cattle prod."

Many in the crowd started hurling rocks at the soldiers; several responded by picking up the stones and throwing them right back. Numerous rounds of tear gas were fired and the troops charged forward. Demonstrators backed off, only to advance again. The cat-and-mouse game continued until the soldiers retreated after firing a final volley of tear gas.

After the troops left, the crowd vented its rage on the army vehicles which had brought them, parked near a big billboard which read "Welcome to Beijing." "They attacked the buses." said Sidenius. "They broke every window—just took bars and shattered every window. At one point they started rocking the buses."

Sidenius and his companion left the intersection and continued towards the square. "The moment we got past Zhongnanhai," he recalled, "it was like emerging from a violent tunnel—it was suddenly just the same peaceful street leading to Tiananmen. In the square, the

173

student loudseakers were playing 'Onward Christian Soldiers'." But the tranquil scene in Tiananmen could not erase what he had just witnessed. "Something had happened," said Sidenius, "to turn this from a peaceful movement into a violent one. Now they were destroying things in a wanton and deliberate fashion. It served no purpose. That was the critical turning point—something snapped in that crowd."

Not long afterwards, there was another clash at the rear of the Great Hall of the People. Hundreds of helmeted soldiers marched out of the building's west gate. Students and workers hastily erected barricades, using buses and jeeps to block their advance. Many protestors ripped tiles out of the sidewalk, flinging the jagged objects towards the troops. Several missed their mark and shattered the ornate light globes that adorn the area's streetlamps. Other people tore low-lying branches from trees and brandished them as clubs. The soldiers bore spiked whips, truncheons, tear gas and cattle prods. The clash was brief and bloody; several students and soldiers were injured. A jeep was overturned and military vehicles destroyed. Confrontations, big and small, seemed to be taking place everywhere. Outside Zhongnanhai, a banner read "The day the soldiers enter the city, the blood of the people will flow."

The next day, student leader Chai Ling would recall one particular incident which had occurred that afternoon. A young man was shouting, along with a group of protestors, at a line of armed police. "The people's police love the people and the people's police do not hit the people." According to Chai, an officer walked up to the student and said: *"Shei tama ai ni?"*—"Who the fuck loves you?"—and kicked him in the stomach.

8

The Massacre

A warm breeze drifted through Tiananmen Square that Saturday evening, nudging banners and flags to flutter lazily. Below those flags, nestled amidst the security of the Democracy Camp, were the faces which had grown so familiar during the past weeks. The student of economic management joked that he had yet to return home for a bath. His friends grinned as he glanced towards his armpit and laughed "the smell, you know, is not very good." A truck filled with waving and smiling demonstrators circled the plaza. In the heart of the camp, young men and women wearing lab coats wandered through the maze of shelters dispensing medical supplies and advice. There was little chanting. The occupation of Tiananmen Square was about to end.

But not without resistance. At 9:00 P.M., thousands of students pledged their willingness to die for the cause of greater freedom and democracy. They stood, among the makeshift tents which had become permanent fixtures of the square, and raised their right hands. Chai Ling recalled their oath:

> I swear, for the democratic movement and the prosperity of the country, for our motherland not to be overturned by a few conspirators, for our one billion people not to be killed in the white terror, that I am willing to defend Tiananmen, defend the republic, with my young life. Our heads can be broken, our blood can be shed, but we will not lose the People's square. We will fight to the end with the last person.

Many students began to prepare. Once again, they dipped face cloths and shreds of banners in buckets of water, then tied them over their mouths with surgical masks. Others, however, thought that soldiers would go beyond using tear gas. At 10:00, said Chai Ling, "many angry students, workers and civilians came to our head-

175

quarters and said that we should take weapons. But the students from the headquarters told everybody that we represented a peaceful movement and its highest principle was sacrifice. . . . We knew that this was a war between love and hatred, not between force and force. If our students were to take sticks and bottles to fight with soldiers driving tanks and carrying guns, it would be the saddest moment of our democratic movement." Many students stood by that principle, but others gathered anything which could be used as a weapon: rocks, clubs and sharpened pieces of bamboo. A few students prepared Molotov cocktails. One youth posed proudly for television cameras with two such firebombs strapped to his waist. They expected members of the People's Liberation Army to attack with truncheons, cattle prods—perhaps even rubber bullets. No one expected live ammunition.

Most of the students simply sat near the Monument to the Revolutionary Martyrs or inside their tents, waiting. The soft sound of guitar music issued forth from a few of the canvas shelters, where classmates huddled together and sang. Their voices sounded different that night; the youthful enthusiasm, the sense of invincibility which had characterized the democracy camp for the previous three weeks was gone. In its place was a grave, almost suicidal sense of commitment. Young men and women reassured comrades who were frightened and borrowed courage from those who were not. As patriots, they were bound to remain in the square.

"I think there are two possibilities," said the economics student. "One is that the citizens will prevent the troops from coming in. And if the troops do come into Tiananmen Square, they will send us back to our schools. Maybe they will just push us, or surround us. . . . They won't do much harm to the students." The young man's parents, however, were very concerned.

"This evening my father came because I haven't gone home for a long time. He wants me to take care of myself and, if possible, go home and have a bath and change my clothes." His father wanted him home for more reasons than that. A broadcast at 7:00 P.M. on China Central Television warned people not to go out on the streets, saying that "nobody can use any pretext to. . . . obstruct troops imposing martial law from fulfilling their task." Another bulletin cautioned that "organizers and troublemakers will be responsible for all results." It was another sign, if any were needed, that the military would carry out its orders.

"My mother did not sleep well last night," said the student. "She waited up until two in the morning. I can understand she's worried about me." His father shared that anxiety and had difficulty accepting the youngster's decision to remain.

"He understands, but he does not respect it. He thinks sometimes I am foolish." The student was, however, far more rational than some of his comrades. They had pledged, and seemed ready, to give up their lives for the cause. The twenty-year-old said he was not frightened of the troops, but he quickly added "I am not willing to die. I think if the soldiers use tear gas, then we will run away. If they beat us, then we will run away. And if they come and push us, I think that we will not fight against them. If they want us to go somewhere, then we will go somewhere." He would not entertain the possibility that soldiers might use guns.

"I don't think that will happen. . . . To worry is not useful right now. So we will just stay here and wait—nothing more. We should not think about anything more." As for his parents' concerns, the young man said he wanted only to spend one more night in the square. His father had left after his unwashed son promised to return home for a bath Sunday morning.

Student loudspeakers affixed to the Monument blared the Chinese national anthem and the Internationale nonstop. Hundreds of students and workers—even parents with children perched on their shoulders—gathered near the Goddess of Democracy, which looked as bright as ever. She had graced the north end of Tiananmen Square for five days, a remarkable symbol of both defiance and hope. Nearby was another symbol of equal audacity which had been christened that evening—the "Democracy University." It was a large green tent, a centre which had been established to disseminate the very kind of thought that the government was so bent on vanquishing. Loudspeakers strung up outside the 'university' trumpeted the names of several intellectuals who openly backed the student movement.

Dozens of other loudspeakers in and around the square were not controlled by those who supported democracy. They were the voice of the Chinese government, and what they thundered was far more ominous.

Now the situation is getting fairly grave. A small number of thugs spread rumours and incited the people to surround, insult, beat and kidnap soldiers. They have also seized weapons. In addition, they surrounded Zhongnanhai and the Great Hall of the People. These thugs are still trying to get support from people of all circles; they may make more serious turmoil at any moment. In order to keep the social order of the capital and protect most of the civilians, the People's Government of Beijing and the Martial Law headquarters cannot ignore this. For these reasons, all the civilians should heighten their vigilance. From now on, please do not go to the streets. Do not go to Tiananmen Square. All workers and staff members should stay at their place of work and all residents should remain at their homes to ensure your safety and avoid unnecessary losses.

As the announcement boomed over the area, a group of young men prepared to march onto Changan Boulevard—the street of Eternal Peace. The smiling youths, wearing identical white headbands, brandished sharpened bamboo stakes.

There was no doubt that the army would try to come. The only question was whether the students and their supporters could hold the troops back. Most of the city's ten million residents would obey the state's threat out of fear, loyalty or indifference, but hundreds of thousands took the stern government warning as a direct challenge. They left their homes and streamed into the streets, ready to protect the students. The exact numbers will never be known, but cyclists, pedestrians and scattered crowds swarmed the entire length of the main avenue which cuts through central Beijing—a distance of at least fifteen kilometres. Crude barricades were already in place at many intersections, but people thought that more would be needed. They worked at a furious pace, pushing or dragging buses, trucks and garbage cans to strategic points. Hundreds of volunteers teamed up to lug the heavy concrete and steel guard rails which normally separate bicycle lanes. Some of these blockades were placed directly across streets, others in crazy zig-zags that even bicyclists had trouble getting past. The thrust of the activity was on the main road which leads to Tiananmen Square, but barricades were also going up in other parts of the city.

Forty years earlier, Beijingers had gathered to cheer triumphantly the arrival of the People's Liberation Army—the patriotic force which had forced the despised Nationalists to flee to Taiwan. On this Saturday in 1989, citizens were doing everything within their power to keep that same army out. Everywhere, the work was done with a united sense of urgency.

By 9:30 P.M., word reached the square that citizens had blocked a PLA convoy at Muxidi. Another column was said to be barricaded in the east. Small groups of students, some armed with makeshift weapons, headed in both directions. The vast majority remained in the square, but those who marched off towards the army meant business. Some were armed with iron bars and wrenches. Three young men who strode the short distance west to Zhongnanhai carried long poles, which they whacked on the ground with each step they took. One was reminded of riot police beating clubs against shields in unison. The crowd on Changan parted to allow the warriors through. On the other side of Tiananmen, near the Beijing Hotel, a similar group was heading east. This one was composed of about half a dozen students and workers, all of whom were carrying sharpened sticks. A stout, grey-haired woman rushed towards them, handed over two wooden clubs, and wished them good luck. From somewhere, the faint wail of sirens could be heard.

Tens of thousands of people were out on bicycles, riding up and down Changan. Random shouts of "Down with Li Peng" and "Long Live the People!" mingled with the continuous ringing of bells. The six traffic lanes were filled with these cyclists; bottlenecks formed every few blocks as they tried to get past blockades. Many had to lift their bicycles up and over the debris which blocked their path. A commandeered city bus, bursting with flag-waving demonstrators, weaved back and forth down the road, navigating the serpentine barricades. Demonstrators leaned out its windows and doors, cheering and hooting as the vehicle moved eastward. Several of the protestors held red banners, which they waved victoriously as the bus rolled through downtown Beijing. An open truck, packed with young men and women, also wheeled past. "One, Two, Stop the Army!" they chanted. Two Canadian journalists riding eastward on the same street were treated as heroes by passing cyclists. "Please, tell the world!" many said, along with "Thank You!" One man greeted them like old friends, saying they shared "*tongxin*"—the same heart—as the Chinese people. The reporters were in a pedicab, and its middle-aged driver drove like he was on a mission of national importance. His legs pumped up and down furiously; his shirt became thick with sweat. He told the journalists that he was not concerned about money; what was more important was that they send reports back home. He believed, as did many other Chinese, that the world's media were powerful allies in the struggle.

At the Jianguomenwai overpass in eastern Beijing, the struggle was on. It was about 11:30 P.M. and tens of thousands of people jammed the traffic interchange, blocking a line of more than fifty PLA trucks. The tail end of the convoy was below the overpass; the canvas-covered trucks snaked from there up and around a steep exit ramp and onto the bridge itself. The lead vehicles in the fleet were barricaded by city buses and the mass of Beijingers. The rest of the trucks were completely surrounded by people, most of whom did not appear to be students. The crowd seemed shocked, puzzled and angered that the People's Liberation Army was in the Chinese capital. Their fear built when word passed through the crowd that the soldiers were from Shenyang in northeast China and had been on the road for five days. People told journalists that the troops had been isolated from news coverage and had only been instructed that there was a rebellion in Beijing. Men and women, young and old, anxiously told the soldiers their own version of events—that the students represented a patriotic and peaceful movement which had considerable support from the general population. Some people leaned right inside the backs of the trucks, half-lecturing, half-pleading with the army not to believe what they had been told by their superiors. A few soldiers said that there was no cause for alarm; they were merely in the city to "restore order." They appeared to be prepared for much more than that. Many of the young men cradled AK-47 machine guns; others bore long, sturdy whips of perhaps two metres in length. Mounted on the ends of these whips were pieces of metal cut in the shape of a starfish. The pointed spikes looked very sharp and very lethal.

One thirty-three-year-old woman who was helping to blockade the soldiers said that there was no chaos in the capital and no need for the troops. "I think as normal Beijing citizens," she said, "we have a normal daily life. We can go to work, we can go shopping—everything is okay. We don't need them to come here." Asked if she was concerned the troops would try to clear the square, the woman replied "Yes, we are afraid these things will happen. So we came here and will stay here."

"The people prepare," broke in one man. "The people prepare." Although the scene was calm, those in the crowd offered varying opinions as to whether violence could break out. "Impossible," stated one man. "It's possible," countered another.

"We don't have any weapons," continued the woman. "But we have some thoughts. We want to persuade them to stop here."

For a while, it looked as though they would be successful. But there was one thing the people blockading troops in eastern Beijing at 11:30 P.M., 3 June, did not know: in the west, the killing had already started.

When Australian journalist Geoff Goddard arrived at the Muxidi bridge shortly after 9:00 P.M., several thousand people were already there. Two buses and a truck, along with bicycle lane dividers, had been set across the road. They were blocking an army convoy which included jeeps, trucks and armoured personnel carriers. The formidable line of vehicles had earlier pushed through barricades farther west to reach Muxidi but was now paralyzed by the blockade. Initially, the troops did not try to pass. Armed soldiers did, however, march to the front line of the convoy. Citizens tried to reason with the troops, and, when that failed, began to shout insults. Finally, people began hurling rocks at the men. It escalated for some time, perhaps as long as two hours, before troops opened fire. According to the government, "martial law troops entered the city proper at 10:00 P.M. However, they were still obstructed at major crossroads of the city. Even so, they restrained themselves from taking any retaliatory measures despite savage provocations which included beatings, loot-

Military helicopter flies low over the square after martial law declared, 20 May. *(S. Simmie)*

Protestors fraternize with soldiers, 20 May. *(J. Annells)*

Martial law troops stalled at Liuli Bridge, 20 May. *(J. Annells)*

Putting the finishing touches on the "Goddess of Democracy" statue at the Central Academy of Fine Arts, 29 May. *(S. Simmie)*

The "Goddess of Democracy" at her unveiling, Tiananmen Square, 30 May. *(S. Simmie)*

Protestor lectures soldiers after troops fail in their first attempt to take the square, early morning, 3 June. *(S. Simmie)*

Twenty-four hours before the massacre, protestors still erect new tents. *(S. Simmie)*

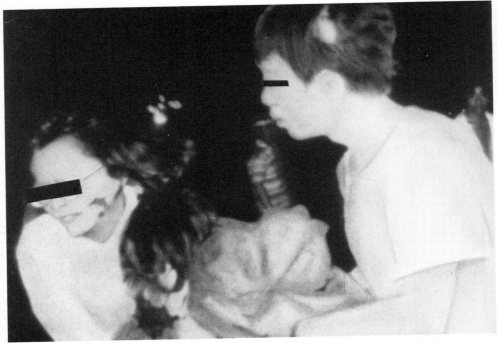

Wounded young woman carried from square early morning June 4, 1989 *(C. Banknight)*

People clamber aboard military transports stopped by protestors, east Beijing, 3 June. *(S. Simmie)*

A lone bicycle silhouetted against the flames. *(J. Annells)*

Youths hurl rocks at troops outside Zhongnanhai, 3 June 1989 *(D. Sidenius)*

"Blood Road" — Changan Boulevard looking east towards 6 km of destruction on the way to Tiananmen Square, 4 June. *(J. Annells)*

Chinese characters written in blood on the side of a bus, Muxidi, 4 June. *(J. Annells)*

Burning army supply truck on the Jianguomenwai flyover, 6 June. *(J. Annells)*

The military consolidates its hold on the city. Tanks assemble at Jianguomenwai, near the diplomatic compound, 7 June. *(S. Troyer)*

Curious onlookers inspect burnt out vehicles, 5 June. *(J. Annells)*

The aftermath: crumpled barricades and empty streets, looking east towards Qianmen Gate, 5 June. *(J. Annells)*

ing and arson." As Goddard witnessed, there was some restraint, but when the shooting started, troops went on a rampage. Many civilians, including bystanders who were not hurling rocks, were shot dead. British journalist Jonathan Annells, who visited the scene in the early hours of Sunday morning, found one bus raked by bullet holes. The marks where shells had pierced the metal walls were large; the bullets had gone in one side of the vehicle and out the other.

"The bullets appeared to have gone through the bus from the eastern side of the barricade," he said, "as if someone had gone through the barricade and then turned around and fired back. There was a lot of blood running down the side of the bus—some of it had been drawn into characters. There were large pools of blood in the bus. It seemed apparent that a lot of people had been killed there, or at least severely injured.

"On the road there were thick pools of blood at least six feet long. I don't know when the shooting occurred, but the blood was thick enough still to be wet. On one end it was smeared where a body had been dragged away and heels had gone through. There was an awful lot of blood, and a lot of chipped masonry. Chinese handed me four live rounds, one spent one, and I was shown a lot more as an indication of what had happened."

In shock and grief, people ferried the wounded, the dead and the dying and began taking them to hospitals. The closest facility was the Fuxing Hospital, a short distance away. A doctor there would later tell foreign journalists that thirty-eight corpses and more than a hundred wounded had passed through its doors by dawn, adding that there were "many bodies" yet to be taken to its morgue.

The army pushed through the barricade and continued its advance. Cries of "Bastards!" and "Fascists!" were shouted as the column moved forward. Rocks and insults were hurled with equal defiance. The convoy did not get far before it ran into another barricade, this one on the Fuxingmen overpass. The traffic interchange is about one hundred metres east of Radio Beijing; on the eastern side of that building are high-rise apartment buildings which house many of its employees. Several people, awakened by gunfire, peered outside from the safety of their homes. One worker who made the mistake of peeking out his kitchen window was shot dead. A Radio Beijing employee would later say that two of his colleagues had been killed in their apartments by gunfire.

The barricade on Fuxingmen was similar to the one at Muxidi, except that the buses had been set ablaze. Helmeted soldiers advanced on foot, firing their weapons to scatter the crowd. Below the overpass, witnesses said, Beijingers screamed their defiance. As word of the killings spread, more and more people—mostly young men—

181

began to arm themselves with rocks, sticks and metal bars. The government claimed that "near Fuxingmen overpass, some rebels opened fire from an armored car they had commandeered. Ringleaders of the illegal 'Autonomous Worker's Union' proclaimed through loudspeakers that they had captured a military station and military codes. In addition, many vehicles carrying grain, bedding and clothes for the soldiers were hijacked and looted."

During a propaganda blitz mounted after 4 June, the government would show videotape of citizens stoning troops and destroying vehicles. It has yet to offer proof that anyone fired on the soldiers. And while many military vehicles were destroyed during the army's push towards Tiananmen, the majority of the vandalism appears to have occurred after troops reached Tiananmen Square.

The convoy made it through Fuxingmen overpass and continued rolling. Some versions suggest that a patrol of riot police armed with metal truncheons and tear gas served as an advance guard, clearing protestors and bystanders. Photographs taken by Western journalists, however, show that tanks and armoured personnel carriers crushed several people in their paths; some victims were literally pulverized. The weight of the vehicles was so great that steel bicycle tubing was flattened to the thickness of cardboard. Chinese witnesses would later tell of specific, and horrifying, incidents. One story which quickly swept through Beijing was that a tank driver, frustrated at being blockaded by people, gunned his engine and ran over an eight-year-old girl, pulping her. The crowd went into an uncontrollable rage, pounced on top of the tank and forced open its turret. The driver was pulled from the vehicle, beaten and burned. Other witnesses told of elderly men and women who stood bravely in front of tanks, only to be crushed by them.

Such appalling events seem to have occurred with greater and greater frequency as the army got closer to Tiananmen Square. As people learned of the deaths, they became doubly determined to stop the troops. And as the troops continued to meet resistance, they apparently became more and more merciless. Several Chinese described the members of the People's Liberation Army as "things"— inhuman killing machines. One young man who had witnessed clashes earlier in the day said "they hate people. . . . Their eyes are red when they beat the people."

As the convoy pushed on, it left in its wake a trail of dead. Near the Minzu Hotel, Chinese bystanders said that a member of the PLA shot and killed an old woman. Her two sons, according to witnesses, charged the soldier and beat him to a bloodied pulp. His body was hanged from the nearby Fuxingmen bridge. The violence had turned into a vicious but unbalanced cycle.

To the east, the carnage was just beginning—and the People's Liberation Army was on the losing side. At about 11:45 P.M., an armoured personnel carrier raced from the eastern side of the Jianguomenwai flyover towards the blockade. The APC travelled at about eighty kilometres an hour. One Canadian diplomat watching from his balcony said "every time they had people in front, they didn't slow down. They just gunned their engines." People scattered, but not fast enough. The APC crashed into an army truck, and kept going towards Tiananmen. One man got in the way; the treads of the vehicle burst open his head. His shattered corpse lay face down where he died for three days, even though the PLA had ample time to remove it. He was left, it seemed, as a reminder that the army was willing and able to crush those who opposed it.

Closer to the square, the carrier ran into fierce resistance. The vehicle was pelted with stones, bricks and pieces of steel as it approached Tiananmen but managed to either evade or simply run over the numerous barricades along its route. When it reached the north end of the square, it was attacked by people with Molotov cocktails. Large bottles filled with gasoline and kerosene were hurled on top of the carrier; the dark green paint which coated the APC burst into flames. The blazing vehicle kept moving until it reached a blocked intersection at Xidan, roughly two kilometres west of the square. It came to a stop there and continued to burn. Australian journalist Peter Ellingsen watched as a furious mob shouted at the driver. He told ABC News "the crowd was howling, screaming for him to get out, but waiting, knowing he would have to. . . ." After ten minutes, the hatch opened. According to Ellingsen, the driver was "torn limb from limb."

At roughly the same time, another armoured personnel carrier was fighting its way over extra blockades which had been dragged across Changan on the north side of the square. Long guard rails made of concrete and steel blocked the street, along with an iron fence. Some protestors hurled sticks and steel pipes like javelins, trying to jam the carrier's tread mechanism. It began to slow, lurching forward in jerky movements. When it tried to climb over another barrier, the vehicle got caught. A huge roar went up and the crowd moved in. The carrier rocked back and forth, then pitched forward and began to move. A shower of sparks flew from where a pipe was caught in the treads. The APC got perhaps five metres before it ground to a halt. The mob pounced on it, smashing steel pipes against the pillbox-style windows. Shattered glass sprayed into the air. A man in shorts and an undershirt jumped on top of the vehicle and began pounding it viciously. Others joined him. Before long, more than ten people wielding sticks and iron bars were hammering the vehicle. Molotov cocktails were readied and the assailants jumped down. A couple of the firebombs hit the rear of the APC's roof and caught fire. The man in shorts took a blanket soaked in gasoline and laid it on top. A thick cloud of orange smoke began to rise. The crowd surrounded the rear door of the carrier, pounding on it and chanting for its occupants to get out. Many were waving sticks and steel bars. The door finally opened; a flurry of rocks was thrown in its direction. The driver jumped out. One witness said he was killed, but students apparently intervened and managed to save the other crew members from being beaten to death. The injured soldiers were carried to a bus, then to an ambulance.

To the west, the relentless onslaught continued. Sticks and stones were no match for bullets. Reporter Arthur Kent watched as the soldiers moved towards Tiananmen. He said "the students would typically slow them down with a stone-throwing flurry, which did not last long in the face of direct gunfire. Those who resisted too long came under fire, first over their heads. If they stayed too long, the soldiers would take aim with their assault rifles. One boy was hit in the head and died on the spot." Derek Sidenius, who days later visited the scene, saw bullet holes at chest height at many locations on the street.

After exacting a heavy toll, a volley of tracer bullets heralded the arrival of the PLA convoy at Tiananmen. It had shot and crushed its way the entire length of Changan Boulevard. At 2:00 A.M. a menacing column of tanks and armed soldiers were lined from the northeastern corner of the Great Hall of the People as far back as the eye could see. Billows of smoke and flames poured forth from the avenue. Much of it came from buses and military vehicles that had been torched, but several trees were also burning. The government would say that those fires had been set by students. The students countered that troops had used flame-throwers on the trees to prevent people from hiding. On the north side of the square, not far from Mao's portrait, the armoured personnel carrier was still blazing. One young man posed by it for an American photographer and defiantly gave the "victory" sign.

The scene was black and frightening, lifted straight from the pages of Dante's *Inferno*. It was a moonless night and the square seemed much darker than usual; the glow from the flames flickered and danced off the front of Tiananmen Gate. Swirls of amber smoke rose past the impassive gaze of Mao. One person lobbed a Molotov cocktail at the massive red wall his portrait adorns. The bomb burst into a short-lived fire to shouts of "Good, Good!" Rounds of heavy gunfire were coming from the troops, but they did not, at least initially, appear to be hitting people in the square.

One student, however, told journalists that thirty people on the north side of Tiananmen had already been killed. Student and government loudspeakers droned continuously as the gunfire continued to chatter. Most people were now heeding the state's call to leave, while others continued to swarm in on bicycle and on foot. Hundreds, if not thousands of students were on the street, running back and forth towards the front lines. There was a constant clanging of metal as people gathered pieces of steel from the ground or dropped them as they fled. Bicycle bells and sirens added to the cacophony. For the first time since the student occupation had begun three weeks earlier, Tiananmen was filled with the sound of absolute chaos.

The gunfire sounded almost surreal, like firecrackers popping. Many students believed that the sounds were, in fact, from firecrackers or blanks. They rushed towards the tanks, only to be sent scattering by another volley. *"Bu yao pa"*—"don't be scared," they shouted. When they were perhaps fifty or a hundred metres away from the tanks they would stop running and reassure each other with nervous laughter. "Don't run, don't panic," they said. Then they would turn around and approach the firing line again. A sustained burst of gunfire broke out and a ricochet zinged off the ground. The shells could be heard slicing through the air. "Real bullets," screamed one young man, "REAL bullets!"

"No problem," said another, "don't be scared." The first man, in a rage prompted by frustration and disbelief, began to shriek "Fascists! Real fucking fascists!" There was another volley, someone nearby let out a blood-curdling scream, and a heavy metal bar clanged to the ground. "They really are shooting people!" shouted a man. "This is no joke!" A moment later, a youth walked up to a journalist, said "Hello" in English, giggled and ran away.

Below that madness, in a pedestrian underpass, many students were huddled on the floor—some lying down in a seeming attempt to sleep.

It was difficult to get close enough to the front lines to know whether students and workers were trying to attack the soldiers or just to blockade them. From all appearances, the gunfire was holding the bulk of the crowd at bay. One young man who spotted a group of Canadian journalists rushed up and said "I think you should take a lot of pictures. This is a very good chance." When asked if he was scared, he replied "Yes, of course I'm frightened. I'm a student." The reporters had not yet seen anyone killed and felt somewhat reassured by the large numbers of people around them. "They're not going to fire into a crowd like this," commented one. Just then, another volley ripped through the air. A young man, apparently a student, ran towards them and said "It's dangerous—you should leave!" He pulled back his shirt to reveal a wound where a bullet had grazed his shoulder.

The gunfire, which had come until then only in sporadic bursts, started to sound continuously. Frenzied shouts were heard. Two students pushed through the crowd, holding up a young woman who had been seriously wounded in the head. More bullets hit the ground and ricocheted, followed by more screams. A trishaw wheeled through, bearing the body of a young man. His face was entirely covered in blood; it appeared he had been shot in the neck. The reporters retreated to the eastern side of the square. Gunfire, loudspeakers and ambulance sirens sounded endlessly. It was about 2:15 A.M.

One of the Canadian journalists went into the nearby Beijing Hotel. While she was trying to place a call at a pay telephone, a plainclothes security agent walked up with wire cutters and snipped the cord connecting the handset. He did the same to the other wall-mounted phones. Police rounded up Westerners and Chinese who were in the lobby and demanded film, cassette tapes and videocassettes.

The reporter remained inside for about an hour. During that time, a row of soldiers marched abreast past the north end of Tiananmen Square. Observers on the roof of the Beijing Hotel said that the soldiers fired directly at the crowd as they marched. Thousands of terrified Beijingers rushed to the building for refuge but were turned away at the door by security staff. When the journalist went back outside, the troops were in a kneeling position not far to the west of the hotel. Crowds of people, some standing on barricades, chanted their defiance at the men. The soldiers raised their weapons and started shooting. Sparks flew as bullets ricocheted off barriers. Several protestors dropped dead.

Behind this firing line, troops were surrounding the square. Thousands of armed soldiers poured out of the gate of the Forbidden City on the north side of Tiananmen. Witnesses say that another large group of armed troops moved in through the southeast corner of the square. Between three and four thousand students were still in Tiananmen, most of them huddled around the Monument to the Revolutionary Martyrs. CBS correspondent Richard Roth was filing reports back to New York over a portable phone as the troops began to move in. His voice, which was being tape-recorded in a CBS studio, sounded frantic. "We've got to get out of here. They're just— They're after Derek now, they're ripping away his camera and they're coming for us." The sound of gunfire and scuffling was heard. "We're trying to move back and move away. . . ." More scuffling, more gunfire, then Roth's shivering cry "Oh no! Oh no, OH NO—" Touch tones bleeped crazily, as if the phone were being wrenched from his grip. Then came a huge volley of gunfire and the line went dead. It sounded as if

Roth and his colleagues had been shot. They had not, but they were held in custody by soldiers for nineteen hours. The only foreigner believed to have been seriously injured by gunfire was Francisco Hsu of Taiwan. A bullet struck him in the back of the neck and exited through his front teeth. He later recovered in hospital. It was a night, it seemed, when Chinese soldiers only trained their guns on fellow Chinese.

Student leader Chai Ling gathered together her comrades. "I told them an old story," she would tearfully recall. "There was a group of ants, 1.1 billion of them. One day there was a huge fire at the foot of their anthill. The ants knew that their family could only be saved if they went down the hill, so they held on to each other and rolled down the hill together. Some of the ants were killed, but many more were saved." Her voice, recorded in secret on Sunday afternoon after the killings, was filled with sadness. "We knew the purification of the Republic could only be achieved by our sacrifice," she said, crying. "The students held each other's hands tightly and began to sing the Internationale."

At 4:00 A.M., the lights in Tiananmen Square went out. Government loudspeakers declared "Martial law command has decided to clear the square *now*." CBC reporter Tom Kennedy said "that basically signalled the final attack of the military. . . . Tanks came in from both ends—many, many tanks came in from both ends, firing indiscriminately on people at the side of the street." Lights continued to burn in several offices of the Great Hall of the People.

Rock star Hou Dejian and his fellow hunger strikers implored senior army officers to allow the students to retreat peacefully. According to the Chinese government, the following announcement was broadcast at 4:30 A.M.:

> . . . Martial law headquarters accepts the request of the students to be allowed to withdraw. All the people in the square should leave at once after hearing this broadcast. If anyone refuses to abide by the decree and stays in the square, troops will enforce [martial law] by any possible means. The square will be under control of the martial law troops after it is cleared. It is hoped that all students and other people who are patriotic and unwilling to see disorder in the country will actively cooperate with the troops in the clearing operation.

"After hearing this," read the government account, "the students joined hands and started to leave the square in an orderly manner. At about 5:00 A.M. troops vacated a wide corridor in the southeast part of the square to allow the students to withdraw unhindered. A few students who refused to leave were forced to leave by policemen."

Chai Ling recalled a somewhat different sequence of events. She said that before student leaders had announced their decision to leave, "soldiers wearing steel helmets and carrying guns broke their promise and moved onto the Monument. They shot at the loud-speakers. This is the *People's* Monument, the *People's Heroes* Monument—they shot at it." Chai Ling and several Western witnesses say that when the lights came back on at 4:40 A.M., armed troops were positioned on all four sides of the square. Government loudspeakers called on the students to "leave the area immediately." Armoured personnel carriers drove in and began crushing the bamboo and canvas tents. Some accounts suggest that many students, including perhaps two hundred from Nankai University in Nanjing, were still inside their shelters when the APCs rolled in. Those students, it was said, had voted to remain in the square. Other witnesses said the only thing shredded by the vehicles was bamboo, bedding and clothing. Chai Ling maintained that many students had stayed in their tents, harbouring the belief that they would merely be led away by the army. "But when they were still in their tents," she sobbed, "the tanks drove over their bodies and crushed them into meat. It was said that when we were leaving the square, the soldiers used gasoline and set fire to the tents, the clothes, and the bodies of students. Then they cleaned up every trace."

Both the government and Chai Ling do agree that a path was cleared for the students to leave the square. They joined hands, sang the Internationale, and passed through a corridor of heavily armed soldiers at the southeast corner of the square. The troops did not use their guns, but observers said that soldiers hit some students with truncheons as they abandoned their stronghold. What would happen next was much, much worse. As the students marched away from the square, they ran directly into a convoy of approaching tanks. A Spanish television crew which was with the students said that the vehicles began to shoot. Chai Ling said a tank drove towards the marchers "and ran over their bodies. We could not even find the entire bodies of about ten students." A Chinese doctor in the square told American journalist Margaret Herbst that, as the protestors marched out, "soldiers fired on the last to leave." Herbst spoke to the doctor at the Capital Hospital, which was being flooded with casualties.

"There was blood everywhere," said Herbst. "not just in the emergency room—but everywhere. Doctors took me down a corridor that was filled with injured people lying on blood-soaked mattresses. The mattresses were on the floor because all the operating rooms were already full. These were for the cases which were less serious, but they included people who had been shot in the head.

"I was just numb. Twenty people were lying in this corridor. I talked to ambulance drivers, and they said one of those shot in the head was a colleague who had gone to pick up the injured. Eight people were in the morgue at four thirty, and a number of them were pedicab drivers who had been shot while trying to bring wounded back." Herbst would make two more trips to the hospital that morning. The visits would become increasingly horrifying.

At roughly the same time as students were marching away from Tiananmen, people in the Beijing Hotel heard one final volley of gunfire coming from the square. An armoured vehicle moved in and toppled the symbol of the movement, the Goddess of Democracy. The first part of the statue to hit the ground was the torch. It shattered.

Other convoys of tanks and armoured personnel carriers were closing in on the square. Herbst was back outside by this time, where she saw soldiers gun down bystanders. "They shot at anything that moved," she said. "I was walking along the streets, and blood was everywhere—human pulp, remains. I started to run, then just dove for cover on the street, dragging myself through a thick pool of blood to get away."

Another American who saw the indiscriminate shooting was shielded from the gunfire by a man who literally jumped on top of him to cover his head. He believes that the Chinese was risking his life in an effort to make sure that someone would be able to tell the outside world.

After running from the convoy, Herbst returned to the hospital. Doctors told her that twenty-three people were dead. She went back a few hours later and was told the number had doubled.

"The doctors were crying, and took me to the morgue. They didn't have enough drawers for the bodies, so they had to stack them. All of the victims were young men, all of them were bare-chested, and none of them had any shoes. Many had writing on their chests and were wearing headbands. They were just piled up in there, half-way to the ceiling."

The exhausted and shocked students, meanwhile, continued their slow march back to their universities in northwest Beijing. As they walked, they viewed with disbelief the devastation which had been wrought. "We saw mothers looking for their children, wives looking for their husbands and teachers looking for their students," wept Chai Ling. "Changan was covered in blood. We could see there had been fighting, but we could not see any bodies. We learned that soldiers in the front had shot at people, while soldiers at the rear carried their bodies to buses. Some people put in those buses were still alive, but later suffocated to death. The fascists had covered their crimes completely. We wanted to demonstrate with our lives, to go back to the square, but civilians came out to stop us. They said soldiers had set up machine guns at Tiananmen, and told us that 'You should not sacrifice any more'."

The killing had not stopped. To the southeast of the square, in the Chongwenmen district, people awoke—if they had slept at all—to explosions and gunfire. Witnesses later said that a barricade of buses in the area had managed to hold back a convoy for the entire night. The soldiers had finally decided to bypass it by splitting up and marching through back alleys. Civilians set an armoured personnel carrier on fire and began chasing some of the troops. One soldier, it was said, unslung his rifle and fired on a crowd of bystanders, killing an elderly woman and a young girl. Mob justice prevailed; the man was beaten, doused with gasoline, and set ablaze. His charred body was hung from a nearby footbridge. The Chinese government would later declare this soldier to be "a revolutionary martyr."

To the west, at Muxidi, crowds were just beginning to vent their rage. Jonathan Annells pedalled his bicycle to the bridge at 6:00 A.M. On his way, he saw barricades of burned-out buses at almost every major intersection. When he reached the bridge, people had gathered once again in large numbers at the spot where the violence had begun just a few hours before. Annells stayed at the scene for almost three hours and witnessed a remarkable display of courage, defiance, restraint and confusion.

"On the west side of the bus there was a long convoy, several hundred metres long, of mixed command vehicles, armoured personnel carriers, liberation trucks, motorbikes, jeeps. . . . The front of the convoy was completely surrounded by people in small knots and groups, who—with no regard for their safety—were tearing what they could away from the vehicles which still had soldiers inside. They were tearing off wing windows. They were battering the bonnets with their hands. More people were around the back, quite beyond themselves in hysteria, tears streaming down their cheeks, screaming at the soldiers who were sitting—still with their guns—but not in any threatening gesture. Some were screaming 'Japanese devils', some were screaming 'We're Chinese, you're Chinese, you're the People's Army—how can you do this?' They called them 'fascists'. The soldiers looked very, very nervous. They seemed very moved by what they saw; some were even tearful. They couldn't find it in themselves to fire on people like that.

"One man in particular—the image brings a strange tingle over me every time I talk about it—was standing there with a broom. On the end of it he had his daughter's dress, which was ragged, torn, and soaked in blood. He was holding this up right under the nose of these soldiers, and crying 'Look what you've done—you've killed my

190

daughter!' One could see from the size of the dress that she could not have been enough of a threat to need to be shot. The soldiers were quite frightened. They really didn't know what was going on. They made no attempt to open fire, or threaten people."

Some Chinese told Annells that he should leave, that what was taking place was none of his business. Most, however, seemed to welcome his presence. As he moved off to the side of the bridge, someone shouted "The tanks are coming again!" A convoy of thirty tanks smashed through the barricade of buses at high speed. Men who appeared to be commanders stood in their turrets, and people began to stone them. The officers disappeared inside the rumbling tanks and closed the hatches. In the middle of the convoy was a single truck filled with soldiers. The tarpaulin was not up on the sides of the vehicle, and the men had no protection from the flying stones. Annells said that one of the rocks shattered the windshield, and the driver missed the clearing which the tanks had made in the barricade. The truck crashed, then stalled. The tanks continued rolling, apparently unaware of what had happened to the truck. People then began to approach the vehicle, throwing stones as they moved in. When the crowd reached the rear of the truck, people simply grabbed the soldiers and hauled them out. They disarmed the men and frogmarched them back to the rest of their convoy. Guns were seized, and many in the crowd tried to smash them on the ground. Some of the weapons were returned to the soldiers, but only when they had been marched a safe distance to the west of the barricade. Citizens then stripped the truck of its contents and set it on fire. The crowd was now armed with smoke grenades, flares and tear gas canisters.

"I was given one," said Annells, "which I stuck in my pocket. Someone asked me if I knew how to make them activate. I'm not sure I did, but they found out soon enough themselves and started throwing tear gas at the soldiers."

Armoured personnel carriers which had been bringing up the rear of the convoy were now blocked by the blazing truck. As the people turned on them, the APCs started firing their own tear gas from externally mounted launchers. There was only a slight breeze and soon a dense pall of yellow smoke enveloped the vehicles. The cloud drifted slowly westward, towards the rest of the convoy.

"Eventually the lids came off the APCs and these half-blind, half-choked, half-dead soldiers came out, sort of surrendered and abandoned the vehicles. They couldn't stand it any more, and they just walked towards people who were chucking rocks at them. It was the lesser of two evils—they were probably going to be asphyxiated, or choke, or vomit themselves to death if they'd stayed. They couldn't go back to the convoy, because that would force them to continue into

191

the tear gas. So they came out the side—south—walked into the barrage of rocks and, almost oblivious to it, they lay down on the river bank, choking, eyes streaming. They took no notice of the people—some of whom stood over them with pick-axe handles, screaming at them, ready to smash their heads in. These soldiers were generally saved, either by women or older men who argued with the other protestors. They eventually dragged the soldiers off to a courtyard where the soldiers could wash the stuff from their eyes.

"I saw one or two instances of violence. The soldiers would be led away, someone holding onto each arm, to a safe area where a lot of them were sitting. But young men would run up as they came near and hurl rocks at their heads from perhaps two, three or four feet away. Most of those people had head injuries by the time they reached the safe areas. Blood was streaming down. Understandably, some people were trying to attack them, but people were trying to protect them as well, because they—presumably—were not directly responsible for the killings, and had in a sense surrendered."

Annells watched as more and more carriers were abandoned by their crews. A series of small explosions scattered some people, who mistook the sounds for gunfire. As it turned out, the sound had come from ammunition which was inside a burning carrier. The crowd became bolder. Almost methodically, it stripped APCs of bedding, provisions and weapons before moving on to the next one. Drivers and soldiers abandoned their vehicles as the crowd moved along. Some, however, remained in their carriers.

"As they moved down the line later," said Annells, "they were setting fire to them with the crews still inside. There was one man in particular who had a piece of rag on the end of an iron traffic divider, and he would ignite the canvas cover on the gun on top of the APC, then try to pile stuff on top of it to make it catch fire. Occasionally, the lids would pop open, and a soldier would clear it away, and then the lid would close again. But the man would just put it back."

Annells was puzzled by the soldiers' apparent willingness to be overrun by the protestors. At least a dozen vehicles were set ablaze, and the military had done nothing to stop it. He speculated that they were perhaps unaware of what had happened during the night, or were simply reluctant to begin killing all over again. No one, other than the men who had disappeared with the tank convoy, seemed to be in control.

"There appeared to be a kind of command vacuum. That column was not ready to open fire and fight its way through, as had happened the night before."

Television pictures of the morning's events at Muxidi, taken by a surveillance camera, would be played repeatedly on Chinese television during the weeks after 4 June. In its reports, the government would trumpet the footage as proof that soldiers had been provoked into using violence, as dramatic justification for the carnage. What the state would never tell its people was that the incident had taken place hours after troops had shot and killed hundreds while taking Changan Boulevard.

Annells left the area sometime after 8:30 A.M. and began riding back to his hotel, located not far from the university district. When he neared the Capital Gymnasium, he saw "the beaten and bedraggled students returning from the square. They were marching back, very quietly. Some of the injured were on the backs of trishaws; others were walking wounded. A number of students held up blood-soaked and ripped clothing. There were a lot of onlookers, and they were mostly silent. There was the odd bit of applause or cheering as they came past, but it was pretty much stunned silence."

As the students slowly returned to their campuses, state-run radio proclaimed that the men of the People's Liberation Army had "crushed a counter-revolutionary rebellion." An announcer on the English service of Radio Beijing, however, had something very different to say. He interrupted normal programming and managed to blurt out the following message: "The soldiers were riding on armoured vehicles and used machine guns against thousands of local residents demonstrating who tried to block their way. When the army convoys made a breakthrough, soldiers continued to spray their bullets indiscriminately at crowds in the street. Eyewitnesses say some armoured vehicles even passed foot soldiers who hesitated in front of the resisting civilians." The announcer said that hundreds had been killed in what he described as a "gross violation of human rights." He called on all "friends of China" to condemn the government for its action. The broadcast ended abruptly.

Back at Tiananmen Square, a thick pall of smoke rose from the plaza. Soldiers had bulldozed all of the tents, bedding and banners into a heap and set fire to it shortly after 7:00 A.M. The huge dark column fueled speculation that the military was burning the bodies of students.

Outside the Beijing Hotel, the curious and the defiant continued to gather. People ventured onto the street to hurl insults at soldiers, who responded with bullets. Margaret Herbst was there and recalled, "couples were out holding hands, people were riding bicycles, some people carried babies—and there's this line of soldiers just a few hundred yards away. I couldn't believe it. This one guy had commandeered a Red Cross vehicle. He was bare-chested—he had writing on his chest and a headband. It looked like he was going to get in the van and drive it on a suicide raid down to the square. He was en route when people stopped the man and pulled him out. Then they sent the van careening towards the troops. That got the soldiers mad. The front lines of the troops had been crouched down, and they stood up and started chasing and firing on us. It was incredibly crowded with people, and some didn't want to abandon their bicycles. You couldn't run anywhere. We just got on the ground, and the troops were getting closer, running after anyone and firing. People were falling—at least fifty people died right there. I was on the ground, going nowhere. When I first tried to run away, I lost my shoes, and as I lay there I suddenly remembered that no one in the morgue wore any shoes either, and I said to myself 'I'm going to die'. When the firing eased up again, I got up and ran."

A few minutes later, she returned to the street and watched people picking up the dead. As they tried to recover the bodies, new volleys were fired. The stunning brutality prompted many people to run for their lives. But the shootings also provoked such blind rage that many suppressed their fears and ventured into the line of fire.

When contacted by the Canadian Broadcasting Corporation early Sunday morning, the Red Cross said that 2,600 people had been killed during the night. An inconceivable sixty thousand more were reported wounded. The organization would later deny those figures, which were also given to other news outlets. By late afternoon, journalists were having difficulty trying to get an accurate count of the dead. A few hospitals which had earlier released figures were saying nothing. There were reports that some facilities had been infiltrated by agents of the Public Security Bureau. Unknown men wearing white lab coats were said to be wandering the halls of several hospitals, looking carefully at—but not examining—student victims. Hospitals started turning away visitors, with the exception of immediate family members. As a soft rain started to fall on Sunday afternoon, scattered crowds gathered at the gates of many hospitals. Outside the Sino-Japanese clinic, there was a group of more than a thousand people. Some had come to donate blood; others, to identify victims.

Several witnesses saw anguished Beijingers parading the dead through the city. A truck carrying the body of a student was seen winding through streets and alleys, with the victim's classmates screaming that it was the work of the PLA. A middle-aged man, overcome with grief, carried the bloodied body of his daughter right up to a convoy of troops. He cradled the limp body and wept as soldiers looked on.

In the days following the massacre, helicopters circled overhead and rounds of gunfire reverberated through the streets, those Chinese who ventured outdoors could see the evidence for themselves: drying pools of blood, spent shells, bicycles crushed by tanks. On the streets and hutongs of the capital, Chinese who had not seen the madness heard the truth from those who had. Groups of people gathered in the streets and alleys, pressing around eyewitnesses for details. In a normally bustling market near Jianguomenwai, a number of young and middle-aged men exchanged tales of horror. With each new example of atrocities, they became more enraged. "The top leaders are fascists," said one man. "They say the students are hooligans. I'll tell you, the *real* hooligans live in Zhongnanhai." Another paid the government the ultimate insult. "What they have done to their own people," he said, "is far worse than anything that happened during the Sino-Japanese war." Until 4 June, that vicious conflict was the yardstick by which many Chinese measured inhumanity. Several of the men expressed hope that the military would stage a coup; that tanks would roll right into the government compound and seize power. One man used his hand to imitate a pistol. He pointed and pretended to shoot repeatedly, saying "Li Peng, Li Peng, Li Peng. . . ."

One Chinese woman who had witnessed the slaughter of civilians near the Beijing hotel on Sunday said the mass killings would compel people to oust the government—regardless of the cost. "Even though I have seen people die," she said, "I have great hope. The Chinese people will not stand for this."

The army had issued a frightening statement which was broadcast by state-run radio and television. The assault on Tiananmen Square, it said, "was just an initial victory. It's only the beginning of a long battle against the dregs of society." On Monday, 5 June, one of those 'dregs' would display a selfless courage which captivated the world.

It happened during broad daylight on Changan Avenue near the Beijing Hotel. A column of tanks pulled out of Tiananmen Square and began heading east. A lone man rushed into the street and stood directly in front of the advancing convoy, almost daring it to run him over. The lead tank swerved, trying to get past, but the man jumped into its path. The tank again switched directions; the protestor managed to block it. Finally, the vehicle ground to a halt. The man clambered on top and began pounding on the heavy steel. A burst of gunfire rang out, apparently warning shots, but he stood his ground. The turret popped open and a soldier stuck his head out. *Asiaweek* quoted the protestor as crying "Why are you here? You have done nothing but create misery. My city is in chaos because of you." The conversation ended and the man climbed back down to the street. He stood, for a moment, at the side of the armoured vehicle. The indecision lasted only until the tank began to move. The man rushed back out in front, but within seconds other bystanders ran into the street and dragged him from harm's way. The image of that one man, standing unarmed before a mountain of lethal machinery, seemed to define the very nature of the struggle. Less than an hour later, after the tanks returned to the square, a few shots rang out again. The crowd, perhaps five thousand people, ran for cover again, and a few minutes later a trishaw raced by carrying a young man who had been shot above his left eye. He was dead.

At intersections throughout the city, groups of Beijingers, often several thousand strong, continued to gather in shock and grief. Memorials to dead students and civilians were hastily set up. Wreaths hung from charred buses. In northwest Beijing, a blood-soaked jacket was draped over a stick planted in a mound of earth. Student loudspeakers at Beijing University no longer called on young men and women to fight for democracy. They played funeral music. A black banner adorned the gate of the Second Foreign Languages Institute. It read: "Where will we find the souls of our heroes?"

The Sleeping Volcano

"There is no truth to the so-called 'Tiananmen bloodbath'." With those words, the propaganda department of the Communist Party's Beijing branch tried to convince the people of China, and the world, that it had never happened. The horrific images seen on television screens and newspapers in almost every other country were a lie. Pictures of soldiers kneeling on the eastern edge of Tiananmen Square, firing continuous volleys of gunfire at bystanders, were simply not true. Yes, admitted the party, there had been civilian deaths, but those came only after vicious mobs had beaten, blinded and burned patriotic members of the People's Liberation Army. In a detailed account published on 19 June, the government stated that "By 5:30 A.M., the clearing operation of the Square, which lasted half an hour, was complete. During the whole process. . . . no one died. This shows that rumours of 'rivers of blood' running in Tiananmen Square were completely unfounded." Some Chinese accepted the lie. Those who did not were too frightened to challenge it.

The banners, the tents, the hopes were all gone. There would be no civil war, no avenging army, and no democracy. Rumours that Deng was dead or dying were put to rest when he appeared—frail but healthy—on television on 9 June. A smiling Deng congratulated army commanders on a job well done. There would be "stability and order"—words the Chinese government of 1989 uses to define repression. Even as reports were circling the globe that the PLA factions were about to fight one another, a relative of a high-ranking military figure confided that it was all over. "Do not expect civil war," he said. "Expect mass arrests." By 14 June, machine-gun-toting PLA soldiers and their military commanders had pledged their loyalty to the Party and the State—and the jails were filling.

Officially, the bloody end to the 1989 movement was declared to have been necessary to quell a "counter-revolutionary rebellion." The *People's Daily* would tell the nation that "most of the students were unaware that from the very beginning their good intentions were shaped to the ends of a handful of conspirators whose goal is to negate the leadership of the Communist Party." Weeks after the massacre, officials were still revising the death toll, and by August they were able to deliver only an approximate count. The government said that dozens of troops and about two hundred civilians, including thirty-six students, had died. Three thousand soldiers had been injured, as were three thousand civilians. More than one thousand military trucks, sixty armoured personnel carriers, thirty police cars and 120 buses were damaged or burned. Official estimates of destruction ran to more than $350 million U.S. Most of the civilian casualties, Mayor Chen Xitong said, were "rioters who deserved the punishment." But he also admitted that innocent people had been killed or injured—doctors and others who were shot while rushing to treat the wounded.

The dead soldiers have been given special praise for their sacrifice. "The Chinese people will always cherish the memory of their contribution to defending the republic, the constitution and the people," reads the official history of the events. "The great losses the martial law soldiers suffered are eloquent testimony," it continues, "to their restraint and tolerance. Does this not reflect that the army is an army of the people and defends the people at the cost of its own life?"

Foreigners put the number of casualties much higher, up to three thousand people dead and twenty thousand wounded. Regardless of the scale of the tragedy, the Chinese officials are partially correct. It was a rebellion, but a justifiable rebellion, one that need not have occurred had troops not moved in on Tiananmen Square the night of 3 June. It was a rebellion, because the Chinese leadership made it a rebellion. They wanted to restore not just order, but *their* order, and they were prepared to pay a tremendous price to do so.

The people of China have continued to pay. The witch hunt for 'counter-revolutionaries' has been almost as shocking as the taking of the square. cctv showed mugshots of twenty-one student leaders wanted for inciting the rebellion. About half had been rounded up by mid-summer; Wang Dan was one of them. Others escaped to the West, including Wuer Kaixi and possibly, according to reports in two Taiwan newspapers, Chai Ling. Some of those who made it out, such as intellectual Yan Jiaqi, formed organizations dedicated to overthrowing the government. For that the government called them "thieves who sold out the country," "traitors on the run," "despicable buffoons" and agents of Taiwan. By August, foreign diplomats said that seven thousand people had been arrested in Beijing alone, though the government would admit to only five thousand throughout China. Many of those apprehended were questioned and released after a few weeks. Some said that they had been beaten, others that they had received courteous treatment from their interrogators. A few dozen suspects, none them students, were singled out for execution. In Shanghai, three men were shot for setting fire to a train that had killed six people when it plowed into a group of protestors blocking the tracks on 6 June; the court rejected claims that two of the men were mentally handicapped. One of the people sentenced to death in Beijing was Lou Hongjun. According to the official *Beijing Daily*, Lou received the death penalty for leaping "on an army supply truck being blocked from entering the city. He began to throw down wildly the army uniforms, condensed food and other supplies inside and shouted crazily to the people surrounding the truck, inciting them to attack and loot. He grabbed a vegetable knife in his own hand and began to hack and chop." His appeal was turned down, and he received a bullet in the back of the head.

Lou's fate was an example of the government inspired 'white terror', a sense that everyone is a potential enemy, and everyone a potential victim. A woman in Xi'an was praised for turning in her brother, a student leader. A woman in Dalian told how pleased she was to denounce "rumour monger" Xiao Bin, a forty-two-year-old rubber factory salesman who had told an American television crew that twenty thousand people had died in the crackdown. Xiao's picture was flashed across the country after CCTV intercepted a satellite signal being beamed from Hong Kong. He received a ten-year sentence. The three men who had defaced Mao's portrait on Tiananmen Gate were given sentences ranging from sixteen years to life. A telephone hotline was set up for people to denounce others. Some people even turned themselves in to authorities, following the example of 151 "leaders of illegal organizations or turmoil makers" in Nanjing. The *Zhejiang Daily* reported that "they all confessed their illegal behaviour. . . . and promised a frank and full account of their activities so as to win lenient treatment. Some of them also exposed illegal activities of other people."

Those students who remembered that the government had promised in April not to "settle accounts" now knew that anyone was a target. Their movement, according to the state, was counterrevolutionary. In late June, Li Peng said that most of the millions who took part in the demonstrations would be given lenient treatment "even if they had extremist opinions." They would, of course, have to change those opinions. Political study sessions were stepped up throughout the country. "Everyone was told to toe the party line," one intellectual said, "so everyone acquiesced." Students were required to write their thoughts on the troubles before they could graduate. Those who still did not correctly understand the nature of the rebellion were told to write their essays again. Some students simply copied verbatim speeches that had been made by important political figures. They passed. There are now new entrance requirements for students at BeiDa: each freshman must spend a year of military training. The entire nation was told to seek "unity of thinking" by studying the speech Deng Xiaoping made five days after the massacre. Deng had accused the conspirators of attempting to establish a Western-style bourgeois republic. The media engaged in a near-deification of Deng, advising people to read his speeches the way a minister advises his congregation to read scripture. Two new books of Deng's thoughts appeared, as did a biography and a film of his early revolutionary days.

The Politburo launched a purge of the Communist Party, with Zhao Ziyang heading the list of targets. On 24 June, he was stripped of everything but his party membership. Li Peng delivered the verdict:

> At the critical juncture involving the destiny of the party and the state . . . Zhao Ziyang made the mistake of supporting the turmoils and splitting the party. . . . Especially after taking charge of the work of the Central Committee, he took a passive approach to the adherence to the four cardinal principles and opposition to bourgeois liberalization, and gravely neglected party building, cultural and ethical development and ideological and political work, causing serious losses to the cause of the party.

Hu Qili, the Party propaganda chief who had told journalists that they could report the "actual state of affairs," was also ejected from power, as was Yang Mingfu, who had earlier declared the student movement patriotic in an attempt to placate the hunger strikers.

Zhao quickly became a whipping boy for China's political and economic ills. On corruption, Li quoted Zhao as saying that "corruption was unavoidable" under the economic reforms and therefore had to be tolerated. On intellectual freedom, Zhao's "no interference, no intervention" policy was blamed for ushering in an invasion of bourgeois liberalism, which had poisoned the minds of young people. Zhao was blamed for inflation and profiteering, economic deficits— anything that could be linked, however tenuously, to the unrest. Supporters of Zhao were to be rooted out. The Commission for Discipline Inspection proclaimed that "those party members who deviated from the correct political stand and violated party discipline during the turmoils and the counter-revolutionary rebellion should be strictly punished. . . . including expelling them from the party."

Zhao was replaced as Party general secretary by Jiang Zemin, the sixty-two-year-old former mayor of Shanghai who had ordered the dismissal of Qin Benli from the *New Economic Herald* in April. Jiang is a multilingual technocrat who, like Li, had studied in the Soviet Union, had escaped persecution during the Cultural Revolution and was related to top leaders of the old guard. The son-in-law of former President Li Xiannian, Jiang had a reputation for aggressively pursuing foreign dollars to build Shanghai's economy. He set his task as Party leader to "genuinely win the trust of the people" and affirm China's commitment to open door and reform.

The United States was the subject of much self-righteous condemnation by China's leaders. They demanded that the U.S. return dissident Fang Lizhi, who had sought and been given asylum at its Beijing embassy with his wife on 5 June. Arrest warrants were issued for the couple, who were denounced as counter-revolutionaries—"the scum of the Chinese nation." America was accused of "gross interference in China's internal affairs" for harbouring Fang, as were other nations that offered asylum to dissidents who had escaped to the West. Fang's presence at the embassy actually made it easier for China to blame the turmoil on some foreign-inspired conspiracy. Two official newspapers would claim that "without encouragement and support by international reactionary forces, this counter-revolutionary rebellion could never have reached such a serious scale." Radio Beijing said that these forces were based in the U.S., Canada, Hong Kong and Taiwan. The U.S. was accused, with some justification, of flaunting the banner of democracy, freedom and human rights to destabilize and subvert all socialist countries. "Every day, South Korea suppresses a student movement, but America does not interfere and in fact stations troops there," the *People's Daily* commented. Yet while China furiously condemned such meddling, the Middle Kingdom ignored international denunciation of its actions. Several foreign journalists were expelled, the Voice of America was frequently jammed, and foreign magazines and newspapers were banned from sale. The police captured thirteen 'spies' from Taiwan whom they said were stirring up trouble. One Radio Beijing analysis said that students had been duped by foreign values. They "took in large amounts of Western ideas and culture, but they could not digest them. Bourgeois liberalism overflowed and this was exacerbated by their blind adulation of bourgeois democracy."

Not even the Communist Party of China could put all of the blame on scapegoats. In a soul-searching editorial to mark the sixty-eighth anniversary of the founding of the Party on 1 July, the *People's Daily* wrote "the arrival of this disturbance has alerted us to the fact that enemies inside and outside the country are opposing us with mad force. But at the same time, it has made us understand the dis-

201

turbance has a lot to do with slackness in the Party."

"There are errors in our work," National People's Congress head Wan Li commented, "and things that anger the public, such as unequal economic growth and income distribution, slackness in the party, producing corruption." The government promised to address these problems. Newspapers stopped reporting on arrests of students and began highlighting corruption cases. High-ranking officials were given lengthy prison sentences for such offenses as making illegal profits on refrigerator sales, selling bootleg liquor or building houses for themselves with public funds. Some people were even executed for their economic crimes. Party members were encouraged to engage in "plain living and hard struggle" to enhance the organization's image. The huge corporation linked to Deng's son, Deng Pufang, was broken up, its operations under investigation. The government banned top officials from driving imported cars and exchanging banquets and gifts paid for with state funds. The practice of foreign 'inspection tours'—a euphemism for tourist junkets—was also to be discontinued. The government ordered the closure of special shops for top leaders and said that they would have to pay the market price. In an effort to eliminate nepotism, it also limited what type of work the children of political figures could do.

Intellectuals were told that their work is still valued. Young people studying abroad were told that they would not be punished for their "extremist words" abroad. The *People's Daily* suggested that "the party and government should open up more channels for the people, students in particular, to voice their views on politics and democracy in a positive and reasonable way. . . ." But such statements were made against the backdrop of mass arrests, purges, political study meetings, everpresent armed soldiers and executions. Popular Maoist terms such as "reactionary," "class struggle" and "spiritual pollution" regained prominence in China's political lexicon.

"People watched the arrests shown on the TV with heavy hearts and nerves tingling," one intellectual wrote in July 1989, "then people got scared. I slept badly for a whole week, I could no longer put up with the anxiety. With the cliches of the fifties flooding back, I have the eerie sensation that time in this land does not tick forward, but ticks backward. The majority of the elderly intellectuals I know, I among them, are presently torn between two emotions: sympathy for the young fighters whose war cries have voiced the long-cherished yearnings of the nation, and resentment over the youths' foolhardiness, whose over-eagerness to push through these reforms has jeopardized the little fleeting freedoms we enjoyed. In these conflicting emotions lie the real tragedy and frustration of the intellectuals of this land. Everyone is being urged to eradicate decadent Western influence, but this pressure comes from the very persons who have been sending their own children abroad to be polluted in these cursed Western countries. All logic and rationality come up to a stone wall before the mentality of these rulers. This is beyond me."

Foreign outrage was dismissed as politically motivated slander. Several countries put relations with China on hold. The United States suspended its military sales to Beijing, and other Western nations made similar token gestures of protest. The Soviet Union, its new friendship with China only weeks old, made no official comment on the massacre. Romania, still a Stalinist nation, supported China's iron heel tactics. Many nations extended the visas of the eighty thousand Chinese students studying abroad, a move that could permanently deprive China of badly needed academics and scientists. China responded by tightening visa controls on future students, saying that in the past the government had "neglected the personal quality and political attitudes of the candidates."

People in many nations called for economic sanctions. But as the summer wore on, some movement towards restoration of trade relations could be seen. Cutting China off from access to more loans would jeopardize its ability to repay massive current debts, and most countries recognized the bargaining power of Chinese officials who warned foreign governments that sanctions would only hurt themselves. Nevertheless, the crackdown slowed the growth of foreign investment in China. To calm these investors, some special economic zones began to offer "political risk insurance," that would be paid in the event of revolution, riots or crises.

China's tourism industry, worth billions of dollars each year, has been hit hard. In spite of bargains and a propaganda campaign directed at the world's travel agents, people registered their distaste by going elsewhere. The traffic from Hong Kong, which accounts for the bulk of the tourist trade, dropped off substantially—despite the fact that the neighbouring Guangdong province to the north was largely untouched by the unrest.

The crackdown terrified people in the British colony of Hong Kong, which is scheduled to revert to Chinese rule in 1997. One million of the colony's nearly six million people marched in protest against martial law on 21 May, and hundreds of thousands more after the massacre. Many became more desperate than ever to leave before the Communist takeover, fearing that Beijing would not keep its promise to allow Hong Kong to retain, until at least the year 2047, its capitalist system.

The problem for China's leaders now is that virtually everyone doubts their sincerity. As one taxi driver told a Reuters reporter in late June "In the Cultural Revolution people told you what to say, you said it and you believed it. Now they tell you what to say, you say it, but you don't always believe it. So China has hope." The Mandate of Heaven had slipped from the grasp of China's leaders, and, many Chinese believe, they must atone for their part in the Tiananmen massacre.

China's tragedy will continue after 1989 because the nation is still ruled by the myth of the Four Cardinal Principles, sometimes called "the four stick-to's," that Deng enunciated in 1979. The myth assumes that the Communist Party speaks for everyone and builds a socialist nation according to Marxism-Leninism and Mao Zedong Thought. But because in real life such unanimity is illusory, the Party has the right to purge, arrest, denounce, even execute those bold enough to disagree. For most of the 1980s, the government refrained from exercising that right. It could afford to do so partly because the economy was expanding and people were happier, partly because the Cultural Revolution had so suppressed basic freedoms that the flowering of expression could be channelled into non-threatening avenues such as literature and art, and partly because the legacy of Chinese communism had created a people who do not individually challenge authority. Until the spring of 1989, token political reform had been enough to pacify the masses. The Hundred Flowers Campaign, the Anti-Rightist Movement, the Cultural Revolution, the 1979 Democracy Wall, even the short-lived student movement of 1986–87 had taught them the dangers of speaking out.

The death of Hu Yaobang was one of those accidents of history that offered an opportunity to display dissent. No one could have predicted that it would grow so large, involve so many people. Or could they? Even Deng Xiaoping commented after the massacre that "such a riot was bound to take place sooner or later under the exigencies of. . . . China's domestic political climate." The growth of corruption, inflation and other ills had built resentment. The problem China's leaders faced was that they had been unable to find an effective safety valve to deal with the pressure cooker of dissent. Even during that first demonstration, the axe was poised—and everyone knew it. But circumstances conspired to stay that axe. How could the government crush a movement that honoured a great revolutionary and paid tribute to the heroic students of 4 May 1919? Given the opportunity to complain, the people seized the only safe way possible— en masse. The protests quickly went beyond the control of the students, beyond the control of anyone. In such anarchy, the Deng-Li faction found the formula to reassert its control. The strength of the opposition to martial law indicated how pressing was the need for more political reform.

On 25 June, police arrested Liu Xiaobo, the teacher at Beijing Normal University who had joined Hou Dejian on that final hunger strike. The media called Liu a "black hand"—an anti-Party activist—for saying such things as "In China, Marxism is not a creed, but a rule for the rulers to exercise their dictatorship. We need a multi-party democracy system to replace one-party dictatorship, private ownership and a market economy to replace the planned economy, diversity of opinion and freedom of thought to replace unified opinion, and modern world culture to replace Chinese traditional culture." The arrest is as much a tragedy for the Communist Party as it is for Liu, because after forty years of rule China's rulers are still so insecure as to feel compelled to crush those who dare to speak their mind. Some of the 'conspirators', those students and intellectuals who led the democracy movement, might have desired a "Western-style bourgeois republic" as Deng Xiaoping claimed. But the Communist Party has forty-seven million members, one for every twenty-three Chinese citizens. Its influence pervades every aspect of Chinese society. What was threatened was not Communist rule, but Deng Xiaoping's version of it, his four stick-to's that have kept China in a political straitjacket. Students were not seeking the creation of a bourgeois republic; they were not even an anti-Party movement. They were demanding a system that allowed people the freedom to give voice to their visions without fear of persecution. Those visions included Liu's bourgeois republic, but they also included a Gorbachev-style model of socialism, and a host of others. Rather than tapping that intellectual energy, the government once again chose to stifle it.

Few believe that the lid can be kept on for long. Tens of thousands of Party members marched during the democracy movement; millions agreed with its aims. They, too, were weary of the four stick-to's, equally anxious to give communism a new face. As it has done so many times in the past, China's leadership bullied, cowed, terrified, imprisoned and slaughtered those it chose to call enemies. Such tactics are doomed to fail. As one intellectual put it, "They can imprison our bodies, but they can't imprison our minds." A student would comment, "China is a sleeping volcano, and may break out again, if the basic problems aren't resolved."

China is now at the low ebb of a familiar tide. Bai Shuxiang, Xi Ruisen and Yang Xianyi have endured such tides in the past, as have millions of others.

Wen Huaisha, the traditional Chinese philosopher who accidentally set in motion the Hu Feng purge of the 1950s, saw this latest upheaval of 1989 coming, and he welcomed it. "In China, when you are trying to make some progress, you must make a lot of sacrifices, you must shed your blood. Democracy is not a favour to be conferred on anyone. You must fight for it. If there were only a trace of individuality in China—a place infested by ignorance, backwardness and dirtiness—there would still be a bright future awaiting us. We are now trying to travel a road in only a few dozen years that western Europe took five hundred years to travel. From the Dark Ages to sexual liberation. Don't be too pessimistic. Happiness does not lie in the gaining of it, but rather in the pursuit of it."

Index